Automotive Heads and Tales

Memoirs of a U.S. Auto Analyst

Arvid Jouppi
with Slim Litwin

Edited and Revised by
David C. Strubler, Ph.D.

A historical book of Arvid Jouppi's personal stories and insights into the automotive industry and its leaders through the greater part of the last century. Co-written by Slim Litwin, presented and revised by David Strubler, the book is a timely apologetic for the struggling U.S. auto industry.

Rochester Media • Rochester, Michigan

Cover design by David Jouppi and Joshua Jouppi

Table of Contents

Arvid Jouppi

DEDICATION

Arvid Jouppi, the author, passed away in 1995. As history unfolded, Arvid has proven to be generally accurate in his predictions for the auto industry, with some exceptions. His passion for the American automobile industry was evident to all who knew him which we hope is obvious in this book.

Perhaps even more apparent to those who knew Arvid Jouppi was his honest concern for the people around him. He had a belief that God was involved in the life of each individual with whom he came in contact. He cared for each member of his immediate and extended family, each kid in his eighth-grade Sunday school class, as well as for the personal welfare of the business men with whom he associated. The Arvid Jouppi family dedicates this book to his memory.

PROLOGUE

Welcome. I am Arvid F. Jouppi, automotive and financial analyst. Logically enough, I have written about what I know best: the automobile industry, Wall Street, Washington, D.C., and the interaction among the three over most of the past century. This book is intended to be a combination of 'automobilia,' stories of related Wall Street research activity, and reports on associated involvements by the governments of the United States, Canada, Japan and several other nations.

I don't deliberately hide, but my exposure is limited mainly to people with more than a passing interest in the three areas which are topical in this book. Obviously, I am not as well known to the overall general public as are some of my contemporaries; people like Lee Iacocca, John DeLorean, Roger Smith, Philip Caldwell, Owen Bieber, Henry Ford II, Eiji Toyoda or Dolly Parton. However, as the Holy Bible says, "Blessed are the meek: for they shall inherit the earth." As soon as my inheritance comes in, I stand ready with a number of changes.

The backbone or binding agent of my book is a cursory history of the automotive industry, bolstered by other segments of the chosen troika, and flavored liberally with stories about the giants of the past who inhabited these arenas, and about the giants of today who are legends in their own time.

A principal reason for writing this book is that I now know and have known many of the great names in the three diverse, but often converging, areas of endeavor. I know some of them intimately. I know others casually. I know almost none socially. I am a workhorse among racehorses but, at times, we did graze together in the same meadows and braved common elements.

I have hundreds of anecdotes stored in my memory about these racehorses that now need to be verbalized, else they may never become known to those who could be interested. Many of the anecdotes about well-known people need to be rescued from oblivion. Another important reason is that great accomplishments of persons not as well known might go into limbo along with, sadly, even their names.

Dr. Dolf Dilardi was a great road racing driver of the 1950s. He was my friend in the 1960s, and especially so at delightful dinner meetings at Sardi's in New York City. Dolf was a world class driver. His colleagues and competitors began a session one evening asking each other why they risked their health, and even their lives, driving at such high but necessary speeds. Dolf concluded, "If you have to ask why you drive, you should not." Finally, I want to show how a harmony and rapport has developed in the United States and Canada among the money, the people, and the ideas surrounding the auto-related activities. The harmony is developing as a result of some unique threats to the very existence of the automotive industry.

Walter P. Chrysler, one of the automotive giants, managed to appropriate the New York state automobile license number "C-25" on a permanent basis. It was assigned to the Chrysler Corporation to symbolically mark the year of its birth. That license plate, in the 1960s, came to belong to a member of the board of directors, John A. Coleman, Chrysler Corporation's most influential Walt Street-er. He proudly drove company vehicles bearing this plate through the streets of New York. He was a big man on Wall Street, and became a special friend and confidante of Lynn A. Townsend, then Chairman of Chrysler Corporation, because of his Wall Street background. In 1978, when Pope John Paul I visited the United States, he was driven about the city of New York in a Chrysler vehicle carrying the license plate C-25. At one point in a crowd scene, John Coleman, who had been accompanying the Pontiff, whispered into his ear that he wanted to arrange delivery of a gift for him, a Chrysler Imperial. The Irish whisper was picked up by the microphones of the media, and soon the world knew about the kind offer.

The automobile industry, Wall Street and the government have not always been the greatest of friends. In fact, their kinship can be best described as a love/hate relationship. There has often occurred bickering, even within each of the factions, which lends added interest to this entire arena. Lee Iacocca, in one of his ultimate moments of self-gratification, was able to put onto an NBC documentary, in 1984, a terse description of the man who made him president. He called Henry Ford II a "bastard." This was the same Lee Iacocca who told me as he opened his office door to let me out on my last visit, "I was not a great engineer at Lehigh University. Fortunately, Charlie Beacham and Bob McNamara encouraged me to go to Princeton and to pursue both marketing and engineering. Without them my career would not have led to the presidency of Ford Motor Company."

A few months later, Dennis Wholley, on a national television network while interviewing Mr. Ford, asked him, among other things, how he felt about Lee Iacocca. Henry Ford II declined to comment except to say that no one likes to be called a "bastard" in public. This was as close as Mr. Ford ever publicly came to violating his philosophy of life, "Never complain - never explain." The interviewer quickly moved on to other facets of Mr. Ford's career.

My long professional involvement has been in finance, with engineering remaining not far behind. Both finance and engineering permeate the entire automotive spectrum, from planning, styling, design and supply, to manufacturing and distribution. Conversely, the automotive field has its own way of pervading our society and economy and, by now, its effect has become world-wide. Indeed, the future is now wide open with opportunity to elevate the life and standards of more than five billion individuals, which is more than twice the total on earth when the automobile came into being in1886. Additional billions are waiting to be born into the automotive world and partake in a relatively good life, or at least to explore the possibilities of a better life.

This book is my legacy to the generations which will follow. I here attempt to harmonize the automobile industry, finances, and government as if they were a musical triad. I include counterpoints and stories about the most unusual individuals who have or still inhabit the chairs of authority in the three areas which this book comprises.

This book is not my autobiography but rather a biography. In the main, it is what I have seen with my eyes and heard with my ears. It is a little bit about me, and a lot about these times and the future.

I only hope that you will find the reading almost as interesting and enjoyable as I have found the writing.

CHAPTER ONE

THE AUTOMOTIVE FUTURE - 2000 A.D.

Editor's note: ...As the future appeared to the author in 1986.

We should all be concerned about
the future because we will have to
spend the rest of our lives there.
- Charles F. Kettering

By the year 2000 A.D. the world will have to face the task of supporting more than 6 billion people, who will then be driving some 600 million vehicles. This is not an idle threat but a projection from today's 4.8 billion people and 470 million cars and trucks at the current rate of increase...

The world will be faced with two basic problems. It will be difficult to feed that many people, and it is equally as difficult to build that many vehicles. However, one solution may help the other. The automobile must become a social assignment: a partner with agriculture and other basic industries to help produce and deliver the goods to the consumer. The world's automotive manufacturers must stand ready to produce many vehicles for the good of mankind.

Phrases and moments from movies often leave lasting impressions. I recall Greer Ciarson in one particular movie scene. She was in the gallery of the House of Representatives in Washington, D.C. making a plea that became a motivator for many of my own activities in the automotive industry. She was pleading for funds to fight world hunger. She said dramatically, "I, myself, cannot sleep comfortably, night after night, knowing that there are millions of children in this world crying and unable to sleep because of hunger." The car and truck came to mean to me, and to millions of others, better food, clothing, shelter and communication.

Mainland China is the harbinger of the emerging nations in the 2000s. It has over a billion people, one-fifth of the world's population, yet only some four million vehicles. It possesses enough resources to be one of the wealthiest countries on earth, yet the resources cannot be easily harvested. Roads and pipelines cannot be built to exploit the vast deposits of minerals and fossil fuels. Steel cannot be mined to build machinery in order to build more machinery. At this point the population of China, of the third world, and of other emerging countries, is growing too rapidly for a natural, orderly evolution into industrialization. That should have been accomplished decades ago.

China formerly could depend on "coolie labor" where thousands of people, each doing a tiny bit of the total could get the job done. This can still hold true for farming and serves well to feed the individuals actually doing the work. However, there are many times more people living off the farms in settlements and cities who also get hungry. The food must be grown and delivered to them and as rapidly as possible.

The need for automotive power in China is so great that people are inventing trucks, adapting them from bicycles, from mopeds, from motorcycles, and even from garden equipment. In fact, it is not unusual to see a cart being pulled by a gasoline engine powered garden tractor traveling the highways between the cities.

China is certainly not now in the Stone Age but is having great difficulty in the closing days of the industrial era. Interested investors from industrialized nations researching China become quickly disenchanted when a quick profit, or even a promised return on the investment, is not probable.

Wall Street's Walter B. Delafield was the father of the research boutique. Unlike today's connotation, a Wall Street research boutique was a specialty shop which brought together specialists in many investment areas. The specialists traded their advice for commission business from traders who came to the boutiques. Walter's first boutique was Alliance I, and specialists soon pushed him aside and took that firm over. He quickly formed a new firm, one with his own name, Delafield Childs, Inc. However, in 1974 there was a market slowdown and institutional investors were already moving away from relatively slow and tedious manual Wall Street research to computer aided studies within their own institutions.

It was at that time, in 1974, that I persuaded Walter Delafield to accede to my visit to Mainland China for the purpose of establishing a research base, and to gather information for possible future trade relationships between China and the United States.

My every effort to obtain a visa from China failed. I wanted, especially, to somehow get the automobile into the long-term goals of the Chinese people. That remains an objective even today. The need is now greater than ever. Since that journey did not materialize, I granted myself the great opportunity of circling the earth on an auto-related self-assignment. Today, China is only one of the countries caught momentarily on the horns of this vehicular dilemma. The same holds true for many nations in Africa, India, Eastern Europe and the Middle East. In Poland, for example, individuals may labor during their entire productive lives with the sole ambition of some day buying their one and only automobile, a tiny Fiat. And even if one could afford it sooner, there are no cars to be had. The entire world is being caught up in automobiles, and the entire world is crying out for an economic change.

Great names have passed through the years of my automotive research. I have never met Lech Walesa, the leader of Solidarity, the Polish labor movement. However, I have used his example to justify U.A.W. philosophies with hard-line, anti-union U.S. automobile executives. In our competitive society there has been a natural antagonism between automotive management and the union. To the hardliners I bring forth Lech to point out the fears of Soviet aggression, Afghanistan being a prime example. It was he who stood up to the Soviets even while under their domination.

Years earlier, in the United States, Waiter P. Reuther drew the labor force into an operational unity. Without this accord, we would not have been as successful as we were in World War II. Walter created a community and loyalty among workers, both within local unions and across to other companies. The unions, in the classic Reuther model, represented humanity. He was adept at portraying the management as representing merely greedy profit.

The humanity and profit viewpoints are, of course, valid and practical by both the unions and management. In my view, management has been far more successful in elevating humanity than have been the unions in elevating profit to its proper place.

Earlier in 1947, an antagonist had fired through a window of Walter's main home, then on Appoline Street in Detroit, Michigan. Walter and his wife, May, thereafter feared for his life.   Walter Reuther was our neighbor in Rochester, Michigan. He lived on Paint Creek near the Goodison Cider Mill. This location was chosen because there was no spot in the surrounding area from which a sniper could fire into the Reuther home. Walter's gardeners carried .38 caliber automatics. The entire property was fenced and even passage down Paint Creek was restricted, from shore to shore, by a concrete fence, which included horizontally inserted culverts, large enough to let fish and small wild life pass through but not human beings. This home was Walter`s retreat, where he composed his speeches and sometimes "scabbed" as a laborer. He was a highly skilled carpenter and even built the staircase in his home. Many chided Walter for doing that work rather than hiring a card-carrying member of the appropriate union.

It was our daughter, not I, who was on occasion invited to the Reuther home. Walter loved to take part in games at his own children's parties. At these times, with his dancing and clowning, he became a child. GM's vice-president Louis Seaton, his frequent adversary at the bargaining table, never saw that side of Walter Reuther.

As an aside, Walter introduced a special breed of dog to the Rochester area; it was the German Shepherd. Another neighbor, Murat Boyle, editor of the Engineering Journal of the Engineering Society of Detroit, became a breeder. The dogs could, on the one hand, be gentle enough to play with children and, at the same time, serve as guard dogs for the Reuther secluded home. Soon that breed of dog became very common in Rochester. German Shepherds were often being used as guide dogs in the "Leader Dogs for the Blind" program.

The automotive industry in all of the industrialized nations and especially in the United States has long been accused of selfishness, greed, and the pursuit of profit at all costs. Some aspects of these indictments are true, and some are not. The decade of the 1980's was an era when a full one-third of the world's population went to bed hungry. However, it is also the era when new feelings began developing in the industrialized countries, a concern about world hunger, world welfare and the world well-being.

This is the age of concentrated application of technology toward the solution of a social problem. Outright gifts are only a short-term answer, eventually causing more problems than they solve. Furthermore, as Harlow H. Curtice, ex-GM president, once said, "We should teach people to develop themselves. It is not the responsibility of countries or companies to develop people." People should be given the means, the tools of bettering themselves, and improving their standard of living.

Fears persist in many nations that the elevation of the poor into a higher status can lead to dissatisfaction and eventual revolution. That may be the case, since it has a basis in history, but that revolution is far less imminent than the revolution of hungry and desperate people. Progress has its dangers but also its rewards. This progress must now begin with the dissemination of technology. Therein lays the role for the automotive industry. It is not a benevolent association, and yet one capable of helping others while, at the same time, helping itself and those associated with it.

In my opinion, the world leader in farm machinery development, production, and distribution is Deere and Company. In 1965 a young junior officer led a Deere team to Wall Street. The team was seeking capital for Deere to increase its outreach, especially into Europe. The young team leader was Clifford Peterson, who later rose to the position of executive vice-president of the company before his retirement. Clifford spoke at an early dinner group of Wall Street analysts, at the Lawyers Club in the financial district of New York City. The message that came through is that farm machinery would need to find its place in improving the food production of all countries, especially the disadvantaged nations. He then startled analysts by declaring, "If we do not feed the hungry in the most remote areas, we run the risk of them coming at us, even with knives and clubs, if that is all they have."

Then and often afterwards those words reminded me of the farmers in northern Lower Michigan. Even early in the century, they had more than ample supplies of food for themselves but were having difficulty getting foodstuffs to the nearby cities. The Ford Model-T had arrived in the 1930's, and the food distribution system began to improve.

Charles F. (Boss) Kettering, former GM vice-president, is perhaps best remembered as the inventor of the automotive engine self-starter. This device eliminated the crank, countless broken arms and millions of profane words spoken in anger. The self-starter was very much akin to the bumblebee, which, by all laws of physics and aerodynamics, cannot fly. The starter overloaded the circuit with power and Kettering's engineers said it would not work. It did, it does, and it will.

Kettering, the inventor, was also an eloquent speaker, homespun philosopher and charismatic communicator. On one occasion I took six educators, college deans and professors to Kettering's office to meet GM's then "living legend". I asked for only 15 minutes of his time. The "Boss" continued to weave a spell for 2 1/2 hours. The educators were reluctant to leave and Kettering was enjoying them immensely. He was also able to dramatize engineering to the benefit of all.

One of the stories he told the educators was about the early light bulbs used in automotive headlamps. These were burning out in less than an hour's use through loss of vacuum. This angered and frustrated Kettering since his engineers seemed unable to solve the problem. Thus, whenever he would stop at a filling station, he would pull burned out, automotive light bulbs from the trash bins and take them back to work. Whenever one of his electrical wizards was out of the office, he would place a bulb on his desk, with no message whatsoever. The problem was soon solved.

Kettering expressed the value of the automotive industry in a presentation before a national television and radio audience in 1955 at the annual meeting of the Fisher Body Craftsman's Guild.   The discourse followed the standard, established GM party lines. However, once the red light on the broadcast camera went off, and he was sure of that, he let down his hair, brightened his blue eyes and said, "We are now going to speak as true General Motors' people."

He went into a discussion on how the automotive industry created its own world. Through the gasoline tax it created the highway system, useful both in peacetime and as a system of national defense. The automobile created the petroleum industry, which soon managed to become as large as its parent. Gasoline stations, four on every corner of the country, obviously couldn't exist without the automobile. It created the giant steel and rubber industries, and it even bolstered the fashion business.

"Boss" Kettering would not stop. He said that a person with an automobile is worth more to himself, to his community, to the company for whom he works and to his country. Mobility and carrying capacity permit more efficient use of time, decrease the burden of distances, and even give life a more defined purpose. Kettering said, "Even our spiritual life is enhanced by the automobile, by making it easier for families to gather for worship. It is managing to improve the entire fabric of American life, the food, clothing, shelter and, of course, transportation."

Kettering also discussed how he saw the automotive industry forming the basis for the farm machinery industry and for an entirely new commercial endeavor -- the road building machinery arena. This, of course, later became Terex, Caterpillar and LeTourneau. He also emphasized the fact that while all of the GM people in the room were enjoying a good life and a good income, each could feel gratified because the product that they were putting on the market held a double benefit for others. Primarily, it improved the person who bought it by enhancing pleasure and leisure. Secondly, it made possible improved income." Trucks are a story unto themselves," Kettering said. "These are found everyplace doing everything for everyone." He told how the truck and automobile mushroomed so greatly in the United States that the most logical alternative, the mass transportation system, was all but ignored and oven today is used only sporadically and inefficiently. Kettering in his close said, "We, the automobile manufacturers, are making ourselves rich and making everyone else happy, an enviable situation."

Today this bright and optimistic overall outlook can be related to the world in general. What was good for the U.S. today and yesterday will be even better for the world of tomorrow.

Corporations, General Motors among them, resist drastic innovation, especially in the product. GM came into great disfavor in the late 1950s when the automotive industry was going through one of its many periods of public dissatisfaction that said, "You could do it better." There was general criticism that none of the Big Three, GM, Ford or Chrysler, produced a car that people could own economically and operate efficiently. In Wall Street there were outbursts of accusation that the automotive industry did not properly respond to public need.

General Motors, during this period, seemed to emphasize profitability. Critics, however, felt that profitability and the objectives of fulfilling the automotive franchise could not move across the economic landscape hand in hand. I did not agree with that outlook and many times took part in heated debates behind the locked doors of research meetings.

Dennis Enright was a superb railroad analyst. He was also extremely critical of the automotive industry, as had been Pierre Bretey, another analyst with the old Hayden, Stone Company. In Wall Street as in the business world railroaders and motor truck people found themselves at odds with each other.

Dennis happened to be standing at the wire receiver when news flashed that there would be an imposed oil embargo. The Arabs had ordered a stoppage of all oil shipments. That was in the fall of 1973. Dennis leaped up and shouted gleefully to me, across the research area, "Arvid, Detroit is dead!"

Actually Detroit was forced into the greatest change that any industry had to face in our history. Better than almost any other, the automotive industry responded to the energy crisis. In the late 1980s it had developed vehicles for both an "energy short" and "energy normal" flow situation. Either way, Detroit became ready for the future, high gasoline prices or low.

The leadership of the automobile industry is always in a state of development. General Motors, Ford Motor Company, Chrysler Corporation and even American Motors, with its Renault support base on the continent, continually groom future managers. These are people now with tiny one-window offices who are striving to ascend to a position which would permit them to mold the next century of motor transportation not unlike Roger B. Smith, who was racing around the 14th floor of the General Motors Building in 1952 helping Harlow Curtice to put together a presentation for the U.S. Senate.

There will always be people in industry who are striving to answer the question of Charles F. Kettering: "What are you going to do when you can't do what you are now doing?"

CHAPTER TWO

VEHICLES OF THE FUTURE

Editor's note: ...As the future appeared to the author in 1986.

*The individual serves the industrial
system not by supplying it with savings
and the resulting capital; he serves it
by consuming its products.*
- John Kenneth Galbraith

Efficiency improvements for the vehicles of today and tomorrow can be derived through several avenues. First of all, the cars and trucks need to be lighter but not necessarily smaller. Lightness is generally achieved through material substitution. The trend, which began in the late 70's and early 80's, was for iron and steel to be used less and less with non-ferrous materials used even more. An additional benefit of this material substitution is increased corrosion protection. Today's trend toward lighter vehicle weight will continue into the future. Plastics will continue to play a key role in the area of vehicle weight reduction. Lightweight, corrosion-free plastics are even today being formed into complex, one-piece components. Plastic wheels are already on the horizon, as are plastic engines. Reinforced plastic panels are structural, strong, useful, decorative, and weigh very little.

Lightweight materials are finding their way into many functional facets of vehicle construction. Drive-train components, such as propeller shafts, will be made of graphite fiber and other composites. Fiberglass reinforced plastic leaf springs are already a reality today. Aluminum will be used for frames, axles, wheels and sheet metal components. An additional consideration is that as vehicles become smaller, safety experts must consider materials and structures that will absorb energy somewhat better than steel. The mass will, of course, be reduced to help.

Vehicle aerodynamics and aerodynamic devices will also play a major role in the cars and trucks of the future. Now about half of the fuel being consumed by a vehicle traveling at highway speeds is used primarily to overcome aerodynamic drag. Most of the vehicle designs of yesterday never saw a wind tunnel. Today, however, all available wind tunnels have "standing room only" business. A designer would not even dare propose a new or revised shape without having a scale model prototype tested in the wind. Follow-up development work produces optimum characteristics. Since automotive aerodynamic perfection is not practical, there are several different avenues which the manufacturers of today have taken. Ford cars all took like "jellybeans," a very efficient shape. General Motors' cars lean more toward a wedge shape, also very efficient.

The Indianapolis 500 mile race, a study in aerodynamics, provides truly the greatest and most dramatic spectacle in all of sports history. During a particularly interesting and productive Wall Street period, Mario Andretti, the race driver, was also one of my investment partners. He and I became well acquainted. Mario was then the world champion driver and had risen to supreme heights as the 1969 Indy winner. Indy racing went a long way toward improving automobiles by providing the ultimate laboratory for testing. Racing proved out not only engine and drive-train components, but aerodynamic design as well. The Indy Speedway was an expensive proving ground for Detroit. Mario remained a world-class driver into the late 1980's but by 1986 had not again won the Indy 500, although he is a perennial contender.

Aerodynamics always plays a role in vehicle stability, especially at higher speeds. As cars get tighter and move more easily through the air, they are also getting more difficult to control. Soon, all vehicles will include anti-skid braking which will be of some help. However, light cars, in some instances, tend to fly; computer controlled aerodynamic devices will one day stabilize the vehicle under all operating conditions. All future vehicles will obviously include on-board computers, capable of hundreds of thousands of commands per second in all vehicle operations including engine and transmission control.

In 1985, Goodyear Tire and Rubber Company celebrated the hundredth anniversary of the invention of the automobile at Akron, Ohio. To discuss the automobile with the automotive analysts who were present, they brought in the great road racing driver and communicator, Jackie Stewart. Jackie, whose voice is known wherever motor sport is followed, had some interesting things to say in the informal talks. Two ideas stand out in my memory.

Front-engine, front-wheel drive configurations are entirely feasible and practical on vehicles equipped with engines of up to two liters in displacement. He had thoughts, however, that higher-powered front engines needed rear wheel drive. He did not discuss the encroachment of the drive tunnel in that type of chassis design on the roominess in the passenger compartment. Jackie, by his profession, was concerned mainly with handling and performance.

Jackie, secondly, felt that ultimately there would be cars with front-engine front-drive, front-engine rear-wheel drive, mid-engine rear drive, four-wheel drive cars and even four-wheel steering. The four-wheel steering system is not new. It was introduced on Japanese show cars in 1983. The rear-engine rear-drive vehicles were effectively and perhaps permanently killed by Ralph Nader, the consumer watchdog, who unequivocally and unilaterally declared them unsafe at any speed.

A direct path to greater truck efficiency is also through the principles of aerodynamics. Today about half of the fuel consumed by a highway tractor doing its job at highway speeds is used to overcome aerodynamic resistance. The coefficient of drag for a standard tractor-trailer combination is about .610. In contrast, the best small van is .378. The actual resistance is obtained by multiplying the drag coefficient by its frontal area. That figure for a tractor and trailer is quite substantial. There is room for much improvement, especially since each .01 reduction in drag can result in 0.1 mile per gallon improvement in the fuel consumption rate.

The trucks of the future must also include functional aerodynamics. Involved will be speed sensitive, retractable air flow modifiers which would extend close to the road and trailer at highway speeds but retract at lower speeds when their usefulness would be minimal and increased maneuverability desirable.   Amazingly, the van, or loaf of bread, configuration is inherently efficient aerodynamically. Conversely, the pickup is aerodynamically impractical and a North American phenomenon. The future may see more vans and fewer, if any, pickups.

Despite the fact that other functional engine types already exist, the internal combustion reciprocating engine will remain "king" well into the twenty-first century. There are several reasons for this notion.

Petroleum, or something akin to it like methanol or ethanol, is an abundant and well-established fuel source. Thus, it will remain as the primary power derivative for the next few decades until all of the world's oil fields are nothing more than holes in the ground. It will be difficult for alternative fuels to displace today's fuels in the next twenty years.   Each alternative has a problem. Pricing uncertainty plagues natural gas. Biomass fuels cost three times as much as gasoline. Coal, either crushed or converted to petroleum, is twice as expensive and causes black-lung disease. Shale oil requires massive refining investment. Other fuels require drastic and very expensive basic engine changes.

However, should vehicle mobility be a prime consideration, with cost or price purely, natural gas and coal stand out above the rest, primarily because of their abundance. The supply of natural gas can extend well into the twenty-second century. Furthermore, it is usable in today's engines with absolutely no modifications and with only about a ten percent loss in power and performance over gasoline. Shortcomings include more difficult refueling and very difficult on-vehicle storage. The fuel needs to be stored at extremely high pressures to provide a practical volume and vehicle range. This requires high-pressure cylinders which would be charged at refueling stations. A normal refill process would require about eight to ten hours although a much shorter time is possible with more expensive and sophisticated refill equipment which could be utilized. Although natural gas, even under high pressure but in qualified containers, is relatively safer than gasoline, some prejudice remains; and vehicles carrying high pressure gas, including passenger vehicles, are not allowed to use vehicular tunnels in some areas of this country.

The other very abundant fuel resource is coal and, fortunately, the United States is its major source of supply. The availability of coal should extend well into the twenty-third century. Its current major utilization is as a fuel by power generating plants to produce electricity. Powdered coal can be used directly in internal combustion engines without first being converted to liquid fuel. Actually, on a cost for BTU basis as compared to gasoline, powdered coal is cheaper. However, that is where the advantage ends. An experimental turbine-powered vehicle burning this fuel has been developed by GM. Problems remain with the processing of the coal, on-board storage, pollution control, engine durability and the distribution of the powdered coal itself.

Also, the vehicle passengers cough a lot and are forced to take frequent baths or showers.

George H. Love was a coal man. At one point he was chairman of the Consolidated Coal Company. In 1960, Con-Coal found, in Chrysler Corporation, an opportunity for diversifying. Soon Love became chairman of the troubled Chrysler empire. It was in 1960 that the investment community first moved strongly into Chrysler, just as had the bankers into General Motors in 1910. The banking figure in 1910 was James W. Storrow, who came in briefly as president of GM after its 1908 beginnings and when it quickly ran into a rough financial road.

Because of George Love, Chrysler became, for a time, an organization of mystery. Since he was basically a coal man, and since there was no word to the contrary from the fifth floor of the corporate headquarters, those on the fourth and lower floors presumed that the age of powdered coal was around the corner. The rumor mill had it that a six-foot diameter slurry pipeline was being built to connect the coalfields to Lake Erie ports. The slurry would deliver coal to be burned by Chrysler-built cars.

Many are of the opinion, current worldwide public opposition notwithstanding, that the eventual ultimate power source of the future has to be nuclear fusion or fission. For the most part, this would never happen until all of the world's oil wells are dry, the coal mines just empty holes in the ground and the natural gas all burned away. This will not occur until about the 25th century.

Nuclear power is an irresistible force mainly because there is no viable alternative. However, nuclear power installations are large, complicated, very expensive and potentially dangerous on a worldwide scale. They are currently best suited for generating steam which, in turn, drives turbines. Thus, nuclear power is best used for electricity generating stations or for driving large vehicles-such as surface ships or submarines. Cars and trucks will have to wait until absolutely fail-safe nuclear power can be condensed into the size of a gasoline engine. The most feasible possibility lies in electric vehicles whose batteries are being recharged by electricity generated by nuclear power.

Other experts consider hydrogen as the ultimate fuel of the future for automobiles and trucks. At this point in history hydrogen holds much promise but also seemingly insurmountable obstacles. Water, mostly abundant seawater, will be used to produce hydrogen gas through a sophisticated process of high technology electrolysis. The process will break water down into hydrogen and oxygen in large quantities. However, the system requires large amounts of electricity and would have to depend on nuclear power to become economically feasible.

Hydrogen is extremely explosive. It also has to be stored at cold temperatures and high pressures. However, since this is also a project far in the distant future, technology will undoubtedly develop ways of minimizing or totally eliminating the negative aspects. On the positive side, hydrogen can be used in the current design of internal combustion engines. It burns very cleanly, so there are no pollution problems. Water is very abundant in this world, and eventually the burned hydrogen will again combine with oxygen to form more water.

Coal continues to hold short-term promise, not in its powdered form but rather as the automotive liquid fuel of the future. Because of the current costs, the direct liquefaction techniques have not attracted sufficient interest, both from the standpoint of investors and of research as well. However, as petroleum supplies dwindle, coal remains the number one alternative.

By the year 2000 A.D., alternative fuels are expected to account for less than ten percent of U.S. liquid fuel consumption. But, as demand increases for petroleum, there will also be added pressure on its price. The possibility always exists for yet another oil crisis. U.S. domestic petroleum production will never match the demand. In fact, we cannot even keep the dependence on foreign oil from increasing.

The reciprocating engine, using huge quantities of petroleum, is king because it is not made of exotic materials but only those common to the earth's surface or slightly beneath it.

Furthermore, the internal combustion engine is flexible and adaptable. The maintained engine will start at 20 degrees F. below and at 120 degrees F. above zero, and will operate well at the entire range of temperatures in between. It may slowly idle one minute and be required to propel a car at 55 miles per hour the next minute. It must start with the turn of a key and stop instantly without whimpering. However, the engine's efficiency today is about twenty percent. There obviously exists room for great improvement. Manufacturers are experimenting with adiabatic engine technology, using ceramic materials in the fabrication of diesel engine parts. Plastic engines, on an experimental basis, are also a reality.

Increased efficiency will also come from a more scientific understanding of the burning of the fuel charge. The stratified charge engine is a move in that direction. Also, the trend today is toward some form of fuel injection which, together with optimized combustion chamber design and higher compression ratios, extracts more power from identical amounts of fuel.

Tomorrow's engines will have internal friction reduced to a minimum with such features as roller cam followers, more extensive use of low-friction bearings and the use of slippery surfaces wherever wear currently occurs, as in the cylinder bore, piston rings, bearing surfaces and camshaft lobes. Some accessories, such as the generator, water pump, fan and power steering will be gear driven, becoming an integral part of the engine.

Most noticeable, however, will be the elimination of the rat's nest of wiring and hoses found in today's engine compartment. These will be clean and neat, with many of the vacuum lines replaced by cast-in passages and with much of the added on equipment built into the engine assembly.

The most formidable contender for the reciprocating engine, should there ever be a serious one, is the gas turbine design. It is not a new concept, having already been road tested in actual vehicles several decades ago, and then shelved for various reasons. All three major automotive manufacturers had operational turbine engine vehicles. However, as the description of an elephant differed coming from three blindfolded persons, one of whom was holding the tail, another the trunk, and the third a tusk, so did the versions of the turbine-powered vehicles.

Chrysler built three different gas-turbine passenger cars that traveled all around the country. The turbine engine is relatively quiet and can operate without modifications on almost any conductible liquid fuel. Thus, when the Chrysler cars were being shown down East, this fact was dramatized by having the vehicles refueled with whale oil. On another occasion in New York, the cars performed very satisfactorily using only Arpege perfume as fuel. The combustion process did not destroy the fragrance; and, for a while, these were probably the sweetest smelling vehicles in the world.

GM's entry into the turbine market, after several ordinary prototype predecessors, turned out to be the Turbo-Titan II. It was a very futuristic 280 horsepower aerodynamic tractor which pulled a 40-foot trailer. The engine was a third generation design, non-polluting, as economical to operate as a diesel engine and with a cool exhaust because it was being regenerated. The clean exhaust feature was often demonstrated by having a lady wave a silk handkerchief in its stream. On one specific occasion at the GM Technical Center, the vehicle was being driven from the outside through a hallway into an auditorium for display. The hallway ceilings were quite low. The exhaust was not as cool as advertised. When the exhaust stacks came into proximity with some fire sprinklers, the hallway was instantaneously turned into a truck-and-people wash.

Ford Motor Company went in still another direction. Their design was a huge tractor and double-bottom trailer combination, 96 feet in length, with a gross combination weight of 170,000 pounds. Powered by a 600 horsepower turbine engine, the whole rig could easily cruise at 70 miles per hour, the legal speed limit in 1965.

A turbine engine uses no oil unless there is a leak and easily meets every pollution standard without any additional equipment, such as catalytic converters. However, where the elapsed time required for a vehicle with a reciprocating engine to reach a certain speed, such as 60 miles per hour, can be measured in seconds, the turbine engine mar take a minute or two. The driving public is not blessed with patience.

I was allowed to drive one of the Chrysler turbine cars from New York to Boston. It was a very satisfactory and smooth vehicle once highway speeds were attained. The turbine engine even sounds fast because it makes noises not unlike those of smaller jet planes. I am convinced that had the turbine engine been invented before the reciprocating version, we all would now be happily driving turbines.

Pierre Bretey was a writer of books, a professor at New York University and a leader in building the professional financial society and its body of ethics. He was also a financial analyst and coined a phrase which quickly spread through Wall Street. It was "gasoline by wire" and was his way of looking forward to the electric vehicle. Pierre was one of the founders of the Financial Analyst Federation, which has become the most influential international organization of professional Wall Street research men and women. He also edited the Financial Analyst Federation Journal for a number of years, and continued as emeritus into the 1960's.

Pierre literally went back to the era of the horse. As with so many who grew up with that noble animal he was rather antagonistic toward the automobile and its makers. One of his major complaints was that it was permitted to set wage and benefit packages which only the automobile industry could pay. The union patterns, which were set there, were unaffordable by others, not even by the railroads. He was vehemently opposed to what he called "featherbedding", or union inflated manpower requirements, on the railroads. He also saw some of the same kinds of abuses in the auto industry and decried them. Pierre saw transportation as a single entity which comprised rail, automobiles, trucks, airplanes, canals and pipelines. It was he who noted that transportation was really a good use of energy. He felt that the most reasonable energy source was coal which could be converted into electricity and moved by wire, ultimately to the end uses which included even electric cars and trucks.

The electric vehicle remains an enigma. It has been in existence since very late in the nineteenth century. In fact, the first gasoline-powered truck, the 1898 Winton, was converted from an electric van. Electric automotive power has had tremendous potential for almost a hundred years, yet has never blossomed. Amazingly enough, the same weak link that blocked its evolution then is still the problem today. It is the storage battery. The vehicle has never progressed out of the 50 mile operating range. In 1985 Bedford of England began exporting commercial vehicles to the United States, with a gross weight of about 6,000 pounds, 2,000 pounds of that being vehicle, 2,000 pounds payload and 2,000 pounds battery. The batteries have a useful life of about four years and cost more than $4,000 to replace. Furthermore, eight hours of operation requires about eight hours of battery charging. The vehicles have an absolute top speed of 50 miles per hour.

However today, with 90 percent of all scientists who ever existed in the history of the world alive and well, the storage battery problem should be solved before the turn of the century since we now have greater incentive than ever. Perhaps storage will not be accomplished through the use of batteries. Most likely electricity will be stored by virtue of a system unknown to us today.

Electrical companies are looking forward to the electric vehicle with somewhat selfish interest. Power draw is very low during night hours, and this is when most car or truck batteries would be recharged. Furthermore, a medium-size commercial van uses about as much electricity annually as does a normal household with teenagers. Electric vehicles will be refueled in several ways. The main method will be a charging station in the owner's garage or driveway. However, it will need to be something more substantial and sophisticated than an outlet and the well-known extension cord. Public facilities, such as motels, hotels, parking lots, garages and entertainment complexes, will provide special areas with charging meters which will accept either cash or a credit card allowing the charging costs to be added to the customer's household power bill by computer.

Electric vehicles will force some user compromises. Gasoline and diesel powered vehicles of today use large amounts of horsepower to drive such accessories as air conditioners, power steering, cigarette lighters and rear window de-icers. With most of the electrical energy being jealously saved for motive power, electric vehicles will not include high amperage draw conveniences. There also will not be an inherent source of central heat, as with liquid cooled engines. The electric cars will have to be heated or air conditioned with small gasoline or diesel burners which would also provide windshield defrosting capabilities. Electric vehicles in unknown numbers will definitely be a part of our lives around the turn of the century. Power by wire pipeline may become the only viable alternative or even the only choice for some of us.

The 50 mile range of electric vehicles is generally not satisfactory. However, on an average, the majority of vehicles do not travel that far daily. If the range could be extended to 100 miles, about ninety-five percent of consumer requirements would have been met, except for occasional trips. In the decades ahead, trips longer than that may have to be undertaken through a public transportation system.

In the mid-1980's, there were approximately 100 million trucks and buses registered on earth. About forty-two percent of these were registered in North America. That is a truck for every sixth person in the United States and Canada. Asia, with a population of 2.6 billion, has 22 million trucks or one truck for each group of 120 people. Mainland China has only 900 thousand commercial vehicles or one truck for 1,140 people. Africa, with a population of 470 million, and some 4 million trucks and buses, is another area where the need and demand for these vehicles grows as the world economy improves. To a lesser degree, the same is true of South America. Even Europe, with thirty-two persons for each truck, is an area of need for commercial vehicles.

In 1985, the ten most populous countries on earth were China at 1.1 billion, India at 670 million, USSR at 270 million, USA at 230 million, Indonesia at 153 million, Brazil at 130 million, Japan at 118 million, Pakistan at 82 million, Nigeria at 78 million and Mexico at 67 million. Of the ten, only three, USSR, USA and Japan, can be considered industrialized nations. Two, Brazil and Mexico are emerging nations. The other five are classified as developing nations, all ready to accept varying degrees of progress and in great need of trucks to advance that progress.

The trucks of the future may not be too drastically different from what they are today. Trucks are an evolutionary concept. They are what they are because that is what is needed. The functional needs will not change to any great degree in the industrialized nations but may even regress somewhat for the emerging and developing countries to a more basic nature. Trucks are fundamentally implements for doing work.

In the late 1960's, GM was implementing a program to introduce an all new line of light duty trucks for 1972. This was later postponed to 1973. Frank J. Winchell was then the director of Chevrolet Planning, and went on later to become GM vice president. At one of the financial meetings, Frank got up on his soapbox and announced, "GM does not need a new truck. A truck is like a hole in the ground, designed to contain things. You can make the hole bigger or smaller, deeper or shallower, but how does one make it better?"

Obviously, Frank Winchell's analogy was not entirely accurate. At worst, a truck is a hole in the ground, on wheels. Anything on wheels can be improved. Admittedly, today's trucks are far from being perfect, even for today's functions. Tomorrow's trucks for the world will need to show great progress in such areas as efficiency, fuel economy, quality, reliability, serviceability and a reasonable degree of innovation.

Tomorrow's trucks will also need to exhibit great strides in quality improvement. The quest for quality has become, by the mid 1980's, the supreme organizational goal for truck manufacturers of all nations, becoming a competitive effort in search of "world class" levels. Quality in trucks must first originate in product design through effective engineering and be later implemented in the manufacturing process. That is the course for the future charted by the entire world industry. Along with quality, the trucks of tomorrow must incorporate high levels of durability and reliability. The criteria can only come about through a monitored design process and consumer feedback with standards established by long-term experience. Improved testing procedures, more closely in line with actual customer vehicle usage, will further extend the useful and rewarding vehicle life in the twenty-first century.

Increased computer utilization will improve the reporting, analysis and projection of data in all aspects of truck quality, reliability and durability. However, vehicle quality and anticipated life must also be measured against the original vehicle costs. The trucks of the late twentieth and early twenty—first century will also include extensive and far reaching innovation, but all well within the established boundaries of evolutionary change. Truck engineers of today all have their favorite wish lists which they would bring to fruition if they should become chief engineers or high ranking officers. It is, therefore, inevitable that some, if not all, of these innovations will see the light of day when their time comes.

One item, high on the wish list of many engineers and very suitable for limited applications, is electromotive drive. A low pollution, internal combustion engine will drive a generator of sufficient capacity to handle electric motors at each wheel or a single larger motor driving the rear axle. A smaller version of this concept can also be used in combination with the current structure of the battery-driven all-electric vehicle to extend its range.

True electromotive drive will provide power to all wheels and will include "on demand" electric power steering and electric brake boost. The pure system eliminates transmissions, transfer cases, propeller shafts and differentials. It also produces a substantial degree of braking when the electric motors convert to generators when required. Electromotive drive will also permit the installation of electric motors at the trailer wheels to provide large increases in traction effort in certain operations, such as material delivery to off-road building sites. The generator could even be utilized to supply electricity to run power tools, which would be of great benefit to farmers, ranchers and construction workers.

Another item high on the engineering wish list is all-wheel steering for improved maneuvering. This is a natural with electric drive at each wheel. The wheels will all turn in the same direction to allow a vehicle to "crab" into a parking space, or provide a computer controlled degree of under-steer at varying load conditions. With the wheels also turning in opposite directions on demand, the vehicles will have incredible turning diameters.

Four-wheel steering will find favor with van users in delivery service in a congested city environment or on the narrow streets of Europe where a minimal turn circle is a necessity. Some special truck applications use the system today but only at slow speeds.

The wish list further includes a computer controlled central hydraulic system. Hydraulic suspension at each wheel will be controlled by the on-board computer which will react to road inputs. The system will modify vehicle ride and handling characteristics by controlling damping rates, roll rates and ride rates, as demanded by road conditions and vehicle loading, with some safe degree of driver override.

Added to this list will be a load measuring system at each wheel, not only to control vehicle trim and height but also, through an electronic display, to assist the operator in optimally placing the payload. This will avoid overload at either of the suspension locations. A road-surface versus vehicle-capability monitoring system will provide anti-skid braking which will result in optimum stopping distances under all possible road conditions. Similarly, acceleration will be improved on slippery surfaces by allowing power application only to the non-slipping wheels. This feature will be even more effective when coupled with electromotive-drive.

The very best handling characteristics, empty to loaded will also increase the measure of safety, especially in vehicles which are subject to wide variations in loading. An interesting approach to handling control will be the utilization of the vehicle's central hydraulic system to match the handling parameters with the road surface and loading conditions. Highway tractors, in addition to aerodynamic improvements, will also undergo appearance changes for reasons of economics. Today one of the most popular is the cab-over-engine tilt tractor. It was born of necessity when state length laws for tractor-trailer combinations were more stringent than they are today. The cab, however, offers excellent visibility, is roomy, and is a favorite of the truckers. There are also cab-over-engine sleeper cabs which include a sleeping compartment. There also now exists conventional cab models, with the engine located under the hood ahead of the cab. These are more economical, less roomy and are less popular with the drivers. The conventional cab models can also be equipped, externally, with a sleeper box.

The future highway tractor manufacturers will only be able to afford a single cab which will be the cab-over-engine type, altered when necessary by adding a hood or an integral sleeper compartment. Going into the twenty-first century, all vehicles will be equipped with on-board computers with almost limitless potential. This will make diagnostic, prognostic and navigational systems possible. This will be a very interesting accomplishment. Diagnostics in the reciprocating engine area will extend to the monitoring of compression balance, power balance, cranking torque, engine timing, turbocharger performance cooling system performance and other functions

The electrical system will also be included in the diagnostics; battery charge, starter performance, alternator performance, starter wiring condition and even lamp status will be able to be monitored. The opportunities are almost endless; and other proposed areas include monitoring of the air conditioning system, including Freon charge and compressor performance, air system leakage, the brake system, tire pressures and routine maintenance items. The on-board computer equipment will even be used for self-testing, abuse protection through warning or shut-down, service interval tracking, and predictive servicing. The truck of tomorrow will also include a prognostics system which will allow for storage and retrieval of operational data. This will be extremely useful for vehicle and fleet control purposes since it will aid in management of cost, vehicle use and downtime.

One of the more intriguing electronic developments will be a map and navigational system. Programmed by a digital data cassette and coupled to a convenient navigational satellite, this system will display a state map which can be converted to a metropolitan version. A dot on the screen will show the current location of the vehicle. The dot moves with the vehicle, and directional headings will be available at all times.

Finally, when General Motors purchased Hughes Aircraft early in 1985, Roger Smith, the GM chairman, went on record saying that one of the principal reasons for the purchase was to utilize aviation technology in the automotive field. This would include anti-collision devices and, specifically, radar or some form of sonar. These will be positive action systems only to the point of safety and will be used mainly to warn the driver of impending danger.

Charles L. McCuen, the GM vice-president in charge of Research Laboratories in the 1950's, spent very little time on considerations of truck transportation. I knew Charles as a quiet, mild-mannered, soft-spoken, slow-moving, thinker-type scientist. There is another side to this research executive. He loved speed and in 1953 he stood solidly behind the first Pontiac Firebird. It was a show car, ahead of its time, and many of its features eventually found their way into the Chevrolet Corvette. In fact, more of his innovations went into the Corvette than into the production Pontiac Firebird.

The GM Proving Ground high-speed oval was banked to accommodate speeds up to 100 miles per hour, without any side drift. Unfortunately, Charley's desire to go fast got the better of him. He was actually a frustrated test driver. On one early morning he took a portion of the oval at over 105 miles per hour. For a long time he was absent from his workstation at the GM Technical Center, where my office was also located. When he finally returned, he walked courageously with a cane.

About that time, General Motors began having an official inferiority complex. Its engineers had mostly come from the General Motors Institute in Flint, Michigan. There were then efforts started to recruit outsiders from the Ivy League schools and from leading engineering schools of the West. General Motors already had a modicum of representation from the Big Ten.

Albert Bradley, then Chairman of General Motors, and Harlow H. Curtice, President, thought that this was the right time to bring in a big name scientist to oversee the Research Laboratories. They chose the former chairman of the Atomic Energy Commission, Dr. Lawrence R. Hafstad. It was Dr. Hafstad who was the bridge from Detroit iron to what became the Saturn of the late 1980's. He left some quaint advice, which he often repeated to GM scientists whenever they worked relentlessly on a project without apparent success: "Stop a while. Imagine that you are swimming upstream in a difficult stream. Momentarily hang on to a rock and hold what you have and then, when you've caught your breath, move again upstream." That is how we must deal with vehicle design into the twenty-first century.

CHAPTER THREE

DESIGN OF THE FUTURE

When Nature her great masterpiece
designed, and framed her last, best
work, the human mind, her eye intent
on all the wondrous plan, she formed
of various stuff the various man.
                    - Robert Burns

As the vehicles of the twenty-first century will be considerably different from those of today so will be the methods of getting there. The design process is also gradually succumbing to the technological revolution and this is perhaps the one area where the North American vehicle producers are now ahead of both the Europeans and Japanese. It is an ongoing quiet revolution but very deep and comprehensive.

The engineering functions of creating, designing, drafting, building, testing and releasing a vehicle to the customer are all now aided, to varying degrees, by some form of computer application. The computer involvement is growing daily along with other technological advances.

The old accoutrements of design, such as layout tables, T-squares, triangles, pencils, and elbow pads are all going by way of the dinosaurs. They are being gradually but inexorably replaced by computer terminals which are currently three times as efficient but take up only one-tenth the space of the old drawing boards.

An outstanding feature of some of the design computers is their three dimensional capability. The part being drawn can be electronically rotated in any direction to show any view, any detail and always in the correct perspective.

Once a component is designed and stored in the memory bank of the computer, the contours can be retrieved and transmitted to physical activity equipment, such as milling machines and wood shapers, which transfer electronic signals into wood shapes for preliminary patterns in tool and die work.

Computers are also being utilized in design analysis. Mathematical models of parts or assemblies are created and stressed electronically to define points of weakness long before the actual hardware can be built.

Much of engineering testing is being done by computer without benefit of vehicles or hardware. Some computers are interfaced with a graphic system which is capable of displaying an animated dynamic visual response to selected inputs such as road surface conditions.

The physical laboratory testing is also succumbing to computerization and actual road input forces can be recorded and then duplicated on physical test stands. Furthermore, the tests can be monitored as to progress and durations by computer, then studied and analyzed without physical inspection.

The Computer Aided Design and Manufacturing (CADAM) system, in addition to analysis and machine interaction, can also be used for robot programming, automated inspection and interaction with the factories of tomorrow.

The days of the stereotyped design engineer with a slide rule sticking out of his pocket and a blueprint under his arm are gone. The engineer used to haul his completed design down to the supplier or manufacturing plant and personally argue the wisdom of his decisions with people who resisted change and who usually had more experience in how things should be built. Beginning today and into tomorrow, the computer aided design permits chosen suppliers, manufacturing plants, and assembly plants to be privy to the progress of a design right from its inception. Their advice and advance knowledge will inevitably result in greater product quality and cost savings.

Nor are oceans any barrier to the intercontinental design of common world products. International teleconferencing systems are even today being utilized to permit design meetings between engineers in different countries or even on different continents. These conferences, both audio and video, are the very next best thing to actually meeting face to face.

Transatlantic cable connections also permit transmission of drafting information across the ocean, from one engineering department to another at a speed-of-light basis. Today some 400 drawings a day can be electronically revised or upgraded to maintain identical files at both establishments even though they may be oceans apart.

The designing, drafting and testing processes of today are becoming ever faster, more accurate and more computerized. These are the basic systems that will eventually be giving birth to the vehicles of the twenty-first century. However, there is also the human aspect. The engineers of today are really the bottleneck. They are being forced to learn and simultaneously implement the computer-aided design processes. Many despise computerization and are thereby falling by the wayside.

The engineers of tomorrow will have been born into computers and will cut their teeth on these systems. They will use this developing knowledge as a stepping-stone into the twenty-first century, where the technological revolution may know no bounds.

The Japanese, amazingly enough for all their successes in the U.S. market place in the late 1980's, lag considerably behind the United States in applied technology. Their success is due principally to the personal philosophy and dedication of their employees. It's a completely different outlook and environment, a good example of what East is East and West is West is all about.

In the past several years, numerous engineering task forces from the United States have been visiting Japan to study the Japanese design techniques. The consensus is that this does not hold just unilateral potential. Benefits can be derived by both parties concerned since each has strengths and weaknesses. However, engineering is not where we need the greatest change since the U.S. seems to be ahead in applied electronics. Manufacturing improvement, according to Japan, is where most of our opportunities exist.

As is typical of Japanese industrial organizations, very much effort and meeting time at all levels of engineering management is devoted to consensus decision making with very significant "bottom-up" stress and involvement. This process includes extensive planning and communication between all departments and management levels in order to achieve understanding and agreement prior to significant action. The U.S. engineering process is now considerably less democratic.

Also, as is prevalent in Japanese industry, the engineers work hard; they work long hours; and they feel a strong bond to their company and especially to their work group.

The Japanese have specific and autonomous product validation groups which are concerned only with the quality, durability and reliability of the product. This obviously reduces the risk level for the design engineer who, in this country, is responsible, even if indirectly, for the levels of those qualities as well.

Japanese engineering organizations also have excellent, direct and early liaison with part suppliers. This greatly minimizes false starts for the design engineer who does not have to practically start anew when the purchasing department changes suppliers, in the middle of a program, on the basis of costs.

Furthermore, the Japanese carry large research and development organizations which contribute extensively to product innovation and product technology. This is readily apparent in the vehicles now being imported into the U.S. However, there are also areas where Japan could improve their effectiveness as compared to the U.S.

The engineering task forces traveling to Japan in the mid 1980's have discovered that their computer-aided design is just beginning and requires expanded application. The use of computers for engineering support systems and design analysis is also far behind our domestic applications.

Studies indicate further that the Japanese vehicle manufacturers spend relatively more money on product engineering, as a percent of sales, than do U.S. manufacturers who are not the epitome of efficiency.

As an example, Isuzu's annual truck engineering budget represents 3.3 percent of sales in dollar value while GM's truck engineering organization represents only 2.3 percent. There are indications that Toyota and Nissan engineering budgets are in the neighborhood of four to five percent of sales, almost twice the U.S. average.

Japanese manpower realignment for the start of new projects is more difficult since most organizations are aligned according to the product as opposed to more flexible organizations in the U.S. Most Japanese product line engineering budgets have remained constant over the years in spite of varying project demands. This is a less efficient use of manpower, but it does promote experience and knowledge gained through failures. There is less of an accent on youth and more respect for the wisdom of older age. Japan also uses graduate engineers for functions that, in America, are performed by technicians. Japanese industrial firms in high-technology oriented fields are heavily staffed with graduate engineers.

Most Japanese engineers are hired right after college graduation at age 22 to an entry-level position. After a three-month orientation- program, they are assigned to a specific department. There exists no formal method for organizing an individual's career path or growth. It is the responsibility of the departmental manager to train a newly hired employee. As a result, Japanese engineers tend to become specialists rather than generalists, as in the U.S. That may not be all bad.

Stability is emphasized at all working levels, and there are virtually no transfers prior to three years of service. Only after an individual has achieved managerial status, which usually happens after about ten years of service, are the opportunities for transfers then significantly increased.

Discreet inquiries by the task force discovered that Japanese engineering personnel receive about half the pay of U.S. personnel with equivalent responsibilities. In addition to a base wage, Japanese engineers receive a bonus paid twice a year, which could be almost an additional fifty percent of their salary. Most of the bonus amount is customary but about 10 percent of it depends on performance.

Japan and the United States are the major vehicle producers in the world. The engineering departments of each have strong and weak points but, in the final accounting, it appears that U.S. engineering will lead the world into the twenty-first century and beyond as it has in the preceding decades.

Charles A. Chayne, GM vice-president in charge of the Engineering Staff function, was an engineering purist. He would often draw together engineers from many of the GM Divisions into one room to share ideas, to discuss how they might reduce their product costs and, at the same time, improve quality. This is the obsession of the true automotive engineer.

I sat in on a number of those meetings. Charley unabashedly discussed strong points of competitive automobiles. He loved cars and collected them. One day he gave me a short lecture on the difference between a classic car and an antique. He finished by saying that there are many antiques but only a very few classics. An antique is merely something old. However, a classic represents enduring and timeless excellence in the opinion of experts. I suspect that Charley Chayne was responsible for some of today's existing automotive classics.

He was always lavish in his praise for excellent machinery. One day he told me that the best machine for its purpose, to his knowledge, was a garden tractor, a Gravely, which he used for tilling the soil at his home in Bloomfield Hills, Michigan. As with so many automotive engineers, he was a man who worked with his hands to sharpen his mind.

Many years later on Wall Street the president of Gravely Garden Tractors came to my office. Among many things we also discussed his tractor and I mentioned that Charley Chayne had described the Gravely as the best-engineered machine for what it was intended to do. The president looked at me and asked, "Of all machines?"

Reassured that his Gravely tractor had indeed been nominated by Charles Chayne as the best engineered "of all machines", the Gravely president's eyes lit up, and he acted as if this was the greatest endorsement that his leadership of Gravely had ever been given. Perhaps it was.

CHAPTER FOUR

MANUFACTURING OF THE FUTURE

The bourgeoisie, by the rapid
improvement of all instruments
of production, by the immensely
facilitated means of communication,
draws all, even the most barbarian,
nations into civilization.
- Karl Marx

Whereas the United States is now at the leading edge of technology when it comes to engineering the product, we are, at the very best, a poor second in producing it. Before World War II, the United States was the acknowledged leader in product quality exceeded only in certain areas by Germany. In those circles Japan was not even in the running. Japanese products, as they were imported into the U.S., had the deserved reputation of being only very poor facsimiles of the real thing. However, slowly, deliberately, in full view of us all, with our complete knowledge, understanding and even help, all that has changed. Today, task force after U.S. task force is being sent to Japan. They are all studying Japanese methods in efforts to upgrade the quality of our own products at least to their levels and to learn the secrets of their productivity.

Quality can obviously be upgraded with money, and therein lies the rub. In the mid-1980's, the U.S. car manufacturers could place a compact car on the market at a certain price. However, the Japanese could then ship to the United States a vehicle of equivalent size but with higher quality components, park it next to the domestic vehicle and hang out a $2,000 lower price tag.

There are many reasons for this dilemma. Most are recognizable; but the solutions are very elusive and, at times, totally beyond reach. Parity with Japan will eventually arrive; but it will require some new rules for the game, an upgrading on the one side and perhaps a deterioration, on the other.

Japan lost the war in the Pacific to the United States and the Allies. However, with the signing of the surrender documents on the battleship U.S.S. Missouri, on September 2, 1945, Japan's success as an industrial nation was assured because the U.S. and the other Allied powers would do everything possible to make that happen. During the latter stages of the war in the Pacific, Allied planes and bombs destroyed most of the Japanese industrial capacity. The culmination came on August 6, 1945, with the second atomic bomb, which was dropped on Nagasaki and which brought immediate surrender. General Douglas MacArthur was appointed the supreme commander of the Allied powers and thereby became Japan's governor and also the kindly uncle. He eventually came to be Japan's savior and one of its most respected heroes even to this day. MacArthur was responsible for the revitalization of Japan, for the healing of its wounds and for the rebirth of its industrial potential.

Of necessity, after the war, the Japanese started with all new factories. These factories included the most modern knowledge and theories about manufacturing techniques. The Japanese are also instilled with a vastly different philosophy about life and personal accomplishment. Their ways are conducive to the production of a fine product and even precludes the need for strong labor organizations.

In April of 1985, I visited the Mazda plant in Hiroshima, Japan. Amazingly enough it had survived the A-bomb blast mainly because it was located on the side of the hill away from the explosion. During World War II this plant produced many of the military vehicles which were used in the Pacific islands. These were sturdy machines, somewhat reminiscent of the British Rover, about twice as large as the American Jeep. Most of Japan's factories, aside from Mazda, were deliberately and almost totally destroyed during the last months of the war. Thus, the Japanese post-war industrialization began with a "green field", as it is said when a new plant is being built. The U.S. plants, on the other hand, were then already old and tired. Yet it was mandatory for the good of the nation's economy that they be converted back to peacetime production as quickly as possible without any extensive rebuilding, renovation or upgrading. They were to continue in that condition for another 30 to 40 years.

The Japanese had as a primary objective the physical rebuilding of their country. They wanted to restore national pride and morale which had hit rock bottom after the successive failures of their war lords, who were stopped and turned back at almost every turn following the first attack on Pearl Harbor, December 7, 1941. As the Supreme Commander, General MacArthur supervised the democratization of Japan and was, therefore, largely responsible for its rapid rise as an industrial and world power.

Carl Beckers, a senior vice-president of the St. Louis Union Trust Company, was asked to become honorary counsel to Japan and therefore went in with MacArthur. He later described for me the first official meal of MacArthur in his new assignment. The General left the U.S.S. Missouri right after the surrender was signed. He was escorted to one of the banquet halls for his very first meal on Japanese soil. An aide suggested that he not partake of any prepared food until other aides had first sampled it in order to assure that it had not been poisoned. However, MacArthur is described as placing his hands on the table, holding the utensils poised upright, and announcing, "These people have, up to now, been my enemy. They are now my friends, and one trusts his friends." He began eating in a hearty manner. The Japanese smiled and understood where he was coming from.

General MacArthur then began the massive undertaking not only of rebuilding the government but also of restoring a peacetime industrial economy sufficient for the Japanese population. He was directed to channel his authority through the emperor and existing government machinery as far as possible, but now following the principles of a democracy. One of the Allied objectives was the dissolution of the great industrial and banking trusts, the assets of which were seized in 1946 and later liquidated through MacArthur's organization. Other programs included land reform wherein tenant farmers were permitted to purchase the land they worked. An overall educational program, along democratic lines, was organized and implemented. Women were also given a voting franchise for the first time.

However, the rehabilitation of the Japanese economy was far more difficult than the reorganization of the government. The scarcity of food had to be offset by imports from the Allied powers, but mostly from the United States.

Industrial capacity was almost totally non-existent and, by the beginning of 1949, aid to Japan was costing the U.S. more than $1 million per day. This continued at various levels, until June 30, 1951, when the United States terminated all economic aid. On April 28, 1952 the peace treaty became effective and full sovereignty was restored to Japan.

In 1946, and thereafter, the State Department invited teams of Japanese to study the U.S. industrial systems. There was a great need for Japan to manufacture and export in order to rebuild its economy, its efficiency and the morale of the entire nation. In this war ravaged country MacArthur found a disheartened people. He quickly issued scrip, funny money, or shinplaster to give the Japanese people some buying or trading power. At that time the regular Japanese yen was worthless.

There was something splendid about the character of Japanese people. The welfare benefit syndrome was totally non-existent. No one waited for a handout. Everyone was anxious to do their part in rebuilding the country in whatever way they were qualified or able. General MacArthur introduced labor unions into Japan. However, these never became as popular, or as militant, as their U.S. equivalents. The Japanese unions were and are, in fact, only token organizations with very limited membership. Owen Bieber, the UAW president, made another effort at organizing the Japanese workers early in the 1980's and his efforts met with almost total failure.

Semon "Bunky" Knudsen, who once almost became GM president, told of his impressions of the Japanese manufacturing philosophy after a visit there early in that country's economic recovery period. The Japanese were then producing vehicles but had not yet been able to install any serious degree of automation or transfer equipment. Thus, engines were coming off the engine line and had to be delivered for installation to a chassis line, which was about 100 yards away. Logically for the Japanese, a long line of wheelbarrows was parked at the end of the engine line, somewhat resembling a taxi stand. Whenever an engine was ready to be delivered, whoever was nearest would grab a wheelbarrow, have the engine placed on it and go wheeling off, without demanding a hero badge.

Bunky wondered how many union classifications it would have taken to move that engine in the United States under similar circumstances. In the United States, the automotive labor movement became very strong with the GM sit-down strikes that began on December 30, 1936 in Flint, Michigan when a very effective and very militant labor union was organized under the leadership of Walter P. Reuther. The movement flourished in the war and, coupled with patriotism, became the "arsenal of democracy".

The United Automotive Workers took full credit for winning the war. The union grew in size and influence which led to vast increases in strength and bargaining power. The UAW then established some limiting work rules, which went hand-in hand with seniority. The number of job specifications proliferated and became not only a cause of higher production costs but also a limiting factor to innovation and the utilization of the latest technology. Most seriously, it made the U.S. products non-competitive with Japan, especially in the world market. This is the situation established in the 1980's and which will necessarily continue, to a degree, into the twenty-first century. As an example, in the mid-1980's each automotive employee in the United States produces an average of 15 vehicles per year. The Japanese employee produces 60 cars at less than half the wage.

Another important factor contributing to the non-competitive status of the U.S. automotive industry, and other industries as well, is that many of the factories are still of pre-war or early post-war vintage. Only in the mid 80's has a great movement started to bring the industrial capacity up to the level of the leading edge of technology. Application of current technology will require some very comprehensive appraisals by both the industrialists and labor. Completely new rules of coexistence will be required.

While the U.S. delayed industrial advancement, the Japanese industrial recovery has continued at a very steady and rapid pace, constantly integrating the very latest in technology and machinery into their manufacturing process. The Japanese never stop trying to learn and to improve their capabilities.

Harwood Rydholm, a Chrysler vice-president in 1961, was requested by the state department to show a team of Japanese plant engineers Chrysler's newest and most modern assembly plant. Chrysler had just completed the plant in Fenton, a suburb of St. Louis, Missouri.

I was there, attending a Financial Federal Analysts regional convention. The Japanese visit coincided with that meeting, so I was asked to accompany the Japanese on their tour which took place, at their request, even though the plant was shut down. They took voluminous notes, talked at great length about what they were seeing and took hundreds of photographs during the day. I thought that they had obtained all of the information that they could possibly use, when their leader turned to me and asked, "Might the building blueprints be available to us?" I telephoned Harwood Rydholm about the request, but I'm not sure if he honored it.

The Japanese were not just making courtesy visits, as is often the case in such international exchanges. They sincerely wanted to copy the best of what they saw and then, I am certain, even improve upon it. Thomas Mathues, GM vice-president in charge of manufacturing, paid a visit to Toyoda City in 1980 and was welcomed with the customary Japanese hospitality and grace. Eiji Toyoda invited Tom Mathues into his office and proceeded to expound on the greatness of GM with the usual Japanese politeness. At the end of their conversation, according to Tom Mathues, Mr. Toyoda commented that he had accomplished his life's objectives because at last, Toyota had surpassed GM in sales volume. In this he betrayed motives very similar to those of his American counterparts. Normally, a Japanese person would avoid saying anything which might appear boastful.

The success of Toyota at GM's expense can be extended to include the entire Japanese and American automotive industries. However, this has been confused and diluted somewhat in recent months. The Japanese are now building their own plants in the U.S., going into partnership with domestic producers on some vehicle types and even accepting U.S. partners in Japan. It is becoming increasingly difficult to analyze and evaluate the individual U.S. or Japanese potential.

Eiji Toyoda also developed and implemented the Kan-Ban, or "just in time" supply system. It is used today by some, and will be used tomorrow by all U.S. manufacturers. Kan-

Ban definitely includes heavy shortcomings but these are overshadowed by the benefits.

Stephan Sharf, in the mid-80's, was executive vice-president of Chrysler Corporation until Lee Iacocca put him in charge of world-wide supply procurement or, as the union would call it, "outsourcing". Mr. Iacocca was angered by President Reagan's decision not to ask the Japanese to continue voluntary quotas on auto shipments to the U.S. Lee Iacocca wanted protectionism but the country decided to move to a free market. Lee Iacocca's supply procurement officer held some interesting viewpoints on Japanese manufacturing philosophies, which he often discussed. Steve Sharf felt that Kan-Ban was just another name for fast inventory turnover. The more it is turned over, the less warehousing, less storage and less capital is required to operate a manufacturing facility. You are using the other guy's money to buy your own stuff; sort of an industrial credit card.

There was no need for Kan-Ban from the geographic viewpoint. However, the need is now growing from the standpoint of economics.   Kan-Ban is currently creating an uncertainty in the supplier body. Realistically, the automotive manufacturers are not much more than assemblers and merchandisers. As an example, in the mid-80's, Chrysler bought 70 percent of what it sold, Ford 60 percent and GM a full half. A change in those ratios, for whatever reason, will create widespread repercussions.

For decades now, suppliers were scattered far from the points of assembly, depending on an excellent railway and highway system. Trucks and boxcars were actually moving warehouses. A supplier was not required to be located next to an assembly plant and did not need to be concerned about deadlines. The manufacturer's warehouses, located next door, were usually full of identical parts, enough for weeks or months of uninterrupted production. That system is now slowly joining the dinosaurs.

Steve Sharf told me of his own idea of Kan-Ban. Chrysler transmissions were being built in the Kokomo, Indiana plant and had to be delivered to the assembly plant in Belvedere, Illinois. A truck loaded with transmissions would leave Kokomo for Belvedere while an empty truck, having delivered a load of transmissions, would leave Belvedere for Kokomo. Midway, the drivers would meet, exchange trucks and each would go back to get home in time for dinner and in time for an evening with the family or bowling. That, according to Steve Sharf, was "just in time" at its finest.

In my opinion, Steve Sharf was the true father of automation in the U.S., but Del Harder, a Ford vice-president, received credit for introducing automation onto the American manufacturing scene. He even gets credit for coining the word "automation" which eventually made its way into the dictionary. Automation, truly, is just a technologically advanced extension of Henry Ford's movable production line of 1913, in Highland Park, Michigan. Stephan Sharf, at the Buffalo plant of the Ford Motor Car Company, in 1946, had ideas for index machines, transfer machines and other equipment which did things and moved things automatically. However, he had problems in getting the unions to accept and work on these revolutionary ideas since the tasks required did not usually fall within the large inventory of job specifications.

However, Steve Sharf managed to overcome the grave problem of getting U.A.W. workers to build some of the innovative machines needed for automation. He persuaded the unions to establish a separate "automation department" wherein all skills could be blended to produce the kind of new machinery needed for automation. Mr. Sharf, in one fell swoop, advanced the cause of automation. He established a method of circumventing inviolate union rules for job classification which is being used even today in modern labor negotiations and new contracts.

In the late 1940's, Steve Sharf's department was a small example of what the Japanese total automotive industry was to become in the 1960's and 1970's. Now in the 1980's, the U.S. industry is striving mightily to reach parity along a very rough road.

At that time, the Japanese teams of engineers studying the U.S. manufacturing technique learned their lessons well. Now, some forty years later, the teacher becomes the student. In the interim, the teacher has become inefficient, complacent, non-productive and most importantly, non-competitive. The U.S. task forces being sent to Japan are making some remarkable discoveries about the Japanese work ethic. Some findings are practical, while others are purely astonishing in that they are examples of another culture, not akin to ours. Very noticeable to the U.S. observer is the exhibited sense of loyalty and pride. The workers all hate to make mistakes and will go to any length to avoid or rectify them since an error would be a reflection on their honor. They are, for the most part, proud of their job and proud of the company they work for. Absenteeism is almost non-existent.

Also very noticeable is the worker versatility. There are fewer job classifications. The individual employees are willing to do almost any work as long as it helps the overall effort of building vehicles. Work is accomplished by a team or committee effort. Individuals take pride in the accomplishments of their team. It is not unusual for the union to take management's side and discipline a wayward member. This would be an unheard of occurrence in the United States. There is also more employee involvement in planning the product and its execution. Suggestions are welcomed, not to build public relations statistics as in the U.S., but as a genuine belief that the worker may have something to offer. There is more emphasis placed on the basic involvement through a suggestion than there is placed on the financial savings and reward.

It is a common practice in Japan for workers to sing the company song every morning while they, as a group, do their daily exercises in the company gymnasium. It is also amazing that a large percentage of the vehicles sold in Japan are sold by door-to-door salesmen. These salesmen are often factory workers who are moonlighting. Some automotive workers even volunteer their time and energy in an effort to boost sales during slow domestic marketing periods. The computer aided engineering design program is considerably behind the U.S. counterpart. However, the Japanese industry is far ahead in computer tool design, computer aided model build and computer aided die build. These are all timesaving benefits, reducing the time requirements to design and release an automobile for production by as much as forty percent.

Many Japanese factories are truly integrated, each producing tooling, sheet metal, engines, transmissions, axles, and even assembling vehicles, all under one roof. The factories are also highly automated with a generous representation of robotics. The plants are usually small and clean, with extensive material handling facilities. Kan-Ban is utilized almost exclusively, making the presence of any storage facilities unnecessary.

The U.S. task forces visiting Japan are coming back with many suggested changes for the domestic plants. Many of these recommendations are being incorporated into the plans for the manufacturing facilities of the future, including GM's Saturn, Chrysler's Liberty and Ford's Alpha. However, these new facilities are not just copies of the Japanese methods. The Saturn project, especially, holds revolutionary promise. Roger B. Smith said, "Saturn is to a Japanese auto plant what a Japanese auto plant is to Henry Ford's assembly line. It is that big a leap."

Perhaps someday we will reverse the process and have Japanese task forces again studying our facilities. However, they may have a more difficult time now copying the U.S.

efforts. David Cole, an automotive analyst, and son of Edward Cole, one-time GM president, observes, "The Saturn concept really represents a major step forward, and one that is going to be very difficult for the Japanese to emulate. Software is the Japanese Achilles heel. They are fantastic at hardware, but computers are worthless without software."

The Saturn, Liberty, and Alpha are not a totally new concept. During World War II, as a Marine on Guadalcanal, I used to dream of sometime owning a car. That dream was nurtured by GM's announcement that a small car would be produced, at war's end, at Lordstown, Ohio. I wrote to a dealer and ordered a small Chevrolet. However, upon return, I learned from the dealer that Chevrolet would not be building a small car because market studies indicated almost no demand for anything but full size vehicles. I purchased, instead, a Chevrolet Aero Sedan for $1,208, delivered price.

Lordstown lay fallow until the late 1960's when the Chevrolet Vega plant was conceived and assigned to the newly formed GM Assembly Division. It was a true forerunner to the Saturn. The GMAD officials determined that a 100 vehicle per hour rate was possible utilizing robotics and very sophisticated automation systems. As a final flourish, a robotic arm swung up and deposited an O.K. sticker on the windshield if the vehicle was deemed satisfactory for delivery to the customer.

In 1973 the plant was completed and placed in operation. Andre Archambault, the president of the Chicago automotive analysts' organization, led a group of us through the new plant. We were very impressed by what we saw. However, the unions were not impressed and blue-collar blues took over the work ethic. The workers finally permitted a rate of only 85 vehicles per hour, robotics and automation notwithstanding. The 15 vehicles per hour represented the difference between a profit and a loss and GM abandoned efforts to advance technology, at least for the next 12 years.

In the meantime, Japanese observers walked through the Lordstown plant, made notes, took photographs, went back to Japan and soon had an arm stamping the Japanese equivalent of O.K. on 100 vehicles per hour, and shipping those to the United States.

From 1973 through 1985, Japan made some major advances in their automotive manufacturing capacity, while the domestic producers, GM, Ford and Chrysler, made only minor adjustments. The U.S. manufacturing potential, competitively, was falling further and further behind, with no hope, until January, 1985, when the Saturn project was announced. The hope grew stronger in July, 1985, when the plant's location was pinpointed to be Spring Hill, Tennessee.

This time, however, learning from the mistakes of Lordstown, Ohio, GM went first to the union, laid the robotic, automation and computer cards on the table and then proceeded to negotiate an agreement. Owen Bieber, the U.A.W. president, recognized the need for high technology at this point in the automotive history and it was still a matter of give and take before the GM Council and the U.A.W. agreed to the terms, on July 26, 1985.

It is a historic agreement, the first of its kind in the world. Principally, it introduces the Japanese manufacturing ethics into the United States, but with domestic overtones. According to the original agreement, Saturn production workers are to be salaried. There are to be no time clocks. Furthermore, after an established period, the workers are to be given the security of a lifetime occupation. Additionally, if all goes according to plan, the production workers will take part in profit sharing and will be given incentive bonuses for meeting production goals.

Another factor involves a team concept where workers in groups, and not necessarily on assembly lines, will be putting together entire sub-assemblies. Thus, there will be possible fewer worker job classifications. One worker could be capable of as many as 15 skills, by current standards, which is not as amazing as it appears. Finally, the union has agreed to accept high security in exchange for lower wages. This could be as much as twenty percent less than received by the automotive worker on a national average.

Without a shadow of a doubt, the Saturn project, soon to be followed by Chrysler Liberty and Ford Alpha, represents a whole new generation in industrial capability, at least in the automotive field. It far outdistances the Japanese and will, if fully implemented, lead the U.S. industry into the twenty-first century and far beyond. More than likely, the fifty-two assembly plants in this country today will eventually be replaced by only about twenty Saturn types. Much of the Saturn concept may not come to be, at this point in time, since it is ahead of the state of the art. However, it is intended to be, basically, a paperless operation where computers are integrated fully into administration, design, scheduling, ordering, marketing and even marketing surveys. Electronic mail will replace letters and memos.

Saturn customers will, perhaps, sit down at the dealership's computer terminal, punch in their choice of color, vehicle type and options. Computers in Spring Hill will receive this order and assign it an assembly sequence. Almost immediately the details of this order will be transmitted to the appropriate supplier plants, to start the fabrication and delivery process of tires, wheels, radios, radiators and other components, but only "just in time", or Kan-Ban. Obviously, this will need to be tempered by scheduling wholesale or volume orders.

The Saturn project also makes the monotony and incessancy of the traditional assembly line obsolete. In traditional assembly, the same worker installs the same part, sixty times an hour for eight hours. The Saturn cars will be assembled in modules, and the modules put together by groups of workers who will be spared, at least in part, the boredom of quick repetition. Modular concept also accommodates computer driven robots which will produce predictable quality at reduced costs. Robots are, and will be, a natural choice to replace workers in many of the less attractive, monotonous or strenuous operations, such as spot welding, fixturing, painting, applying sealant, parts loading, unloading and parts delivery. Extensive use of robotics is also planned in the manufacturing processes where robots can be used to load, unload and control repetitive production machines, such as lathes, grinders and milling machines.

Still another big stride planned in manufacturing technology of the Saturn project is machine vision, used in the sorting of sub-assembly parts and electronic inspection of components for quality and consistency. Lasers will be used as range-finding devices to inspect critical dimensions of Saturn bodies and assemblies to ensure consistent size and quality. As the vehicle rolls out the factory door, other computers will notify the dealer that the car is on its way. The finance organization will be notified to start collecting payments from the dealer or customer, and to pay the suppliers.

GM has been long preparing for Saturn and for other improved projects which will undoubtedly follow. The company now owns the GM Robotics Corporation, which has close ties with Fanuc Limited of Japan, one of the world's largest robot manufacturers. GM purchased Electronic Data Systems, the undisputed leader in computer technology. GM also owns Teknowledge Incorporated, an artificial intelligence system firm which will help to keep all the robotics, automation and computer systems on track. In addition to this technology, GM has most recently acquired the Hughes Aircraft Corporation and all its radar, navigational and space know-how. The technological potential is mind-boggling.

The Saturn project and its competitive counterparts are an effort to incorporate superior American techniques into the world's most efficient system of automotive production, a position we occupied until World War II. The American industry is currently convinced that the high-tech fix will be better, in the long run, than producing cars in developing countries. The latter is the only other alternative which would permit U.S. automotive manufacturers to become competitive with the Japanese and other importers.

However, inevitably, increased technology will result in fewer Jobs. In 1979, the average vehicle in the United States could be assembled in about 80 man hours. In the mid-1980's, that was reduced to 55 man hours. The Saturn project and others like it hope to reduce that to about 20 man hours. Thus, the manufacturers will be getting their reduction in costs and becoming competitive on a world-wide basis by reducing manpower requirements. But what about the labor force, what happens to it?

This is where my crystal ball and those of the other financial and automotive analysts become murky. At this time, there appears no clear-cut outlet or escape for the displaced workers. Although solutions to national economic problems have always been found, at this point, the solutions to autoworker displacement are quite elusive, even in theory. It is somewhat comforting to realize that the one most important factor to the well-being of the U.S. economy, the automotive industry, was non-existent just 100 years ago. The next 100 years may be equally as unpredictable.

The one aspect I am quite certain about is that the U.S. industrial age has now reached maturity.

CHAPTER FIVE

THE MODEST BEGINNING - 600 B.C. – 1900 A.D.

A journey of a thousand miles
must begin with a single step.
        - Lao-Tzu

As we approach the last decade of the twentieth century, the successes and failures of the Bricklins, DeLoreans, and Avantis, Checkers and developers of overseas imports into North America are fresh upon us. Additional newcomers include the Korean Hyundai and Yugoslavia's Yugo, both of which entered the field in the mid 1980's. Already the Soviets' Lada has attempted to penetrate the Canadian market, with an eye on the U.S. Others will undoubtedly follow.

At this point in time, the contenders for world automotive manufacturing supremacy bring forth into modern history such names as Roger B. Smith, Donald Petersen, Lee Iacocca, Eiji Toyoda and a handful of others from the automotive scene.

The automobile, a replacement for the horse, the buggy and the bicycle, was seemingly ready to be born long before the beginning of the twentieth century. It appeared to be waiting patiently for the development of suitable motive power. Only in the last small segment of recorded history has any portion of the available energy been utilized to help humans. First came the water wheel, followed by the steam engine, electricity was then harnessed; and finally in 1862 Beau DeRochas conceived a machine, which eventually evolved into the modern gasoline spark ignition engine. A successfully operating four-cycle engine was first constructed by Dr. N.A. Otto, a German, in 1876. In fact, the thermodynamic process by which this type of engine operates is called the Otto cycle in his honor.

In 1892 another German, Rudolf Diesel, found that if the piston was allowed to sufficiently increase the air pressure within the combustion chamber, the temperature of the air would ignite the fuel and preclude the need for spark ignition. Thus, the compression ignition or diesel engine was born. The thermodynamics involved in this process became known as the Diesel cycle.

However, long before the gasoline or diesel engine came to be, the steam engine existed. In fact, a steam engine was originally conceived in 130 B.C. and described by Hero of Alexandria in his "Pneumatica." It was called an aeolipile and consisted of a rudimentary reaction turbine, almost a water wheel, which was driven by steam escaping from a covered pot of boiling water, heating over a fire.

Recorded historical data is quite vague in this area and time period. However, it seems possible and even probable that the very first horseless carriage or self-propelled vehicle that the world had seen can be credited to a Jesuit missionary in China about the year 1655. Father Verbiest's impressive scientific talents earned him recognition even outside of the ecclesiastical field. He was not only the Astronomer Royal in Peking but also Superintendent of the Cannon Foundries during the reign of Emperor Shun Chih of the Ch'ing dynasty. He performed a number of experiments in steam propulsion before he came up with a practical answer in the form of a small four-wheel carriage with a very light body. The motive power was an ancient Aeolipile, but an improved version, built by Giovanni Branca, an Italian chemist. Branca's Aeolipile was a kind of steam windmill with a boiler cast in the shape of a man's head and shoulders. This was filled with water and heated until a jet of steam issued from the man's mouth through a tube and played directly on a paddle wheel.

Father Verbiest's revised and portable version of this engine included a water vessel heated by a pan of burning coals, all loaded on the wagon. A nozzle directed steam from the boiler onto a wheel equipped with four vanes. This wheel, in turn, was crudely geared to the wheels of the vehicle which moved at a "good speed" as long as the steam lasted. The vehicle could also be steered.

In about 1680 a quarter of a century after Father Verbiest, Sir Isaac Newton, the great English physicist, designed a steam carriage which took propulsion by steam one step further. A boiler was firmly attached to the wagon and had an escape pipe pointing backward. The vehicle was propelled directly by reaction from the escaping steam on the same principle as the modern jet. Newton is credited with having pioneered the propulsion of vehicles by the steam jet. This, no doubt, is due to the fact that he discovered the theory and formulated the law stating that "every action has an equal and opposite reaction". The arena of steam propulsion was very active until well into the twentieth century. Not only did this era bring about a variety of steam engines, but a variety of steam driven vehicles as well. The list of steamer names, beginning with Father Verbiest's in 1655, and extending into 1900, runs well into the hundreds, with just about as many varieties. Some were powered stagecoaches, some were boats, some were passenger-carrying wagons, some were carriages and some were even steam driven bicycles.

Around 1900 A.D. simultaneous progress was also being made in gasoline engines and in electrical power. At the start of the twentieth century, twenty-two percent of all motor vehicles were propelled by gasoline, thirty-eight percent were electric and forty percent were driven by steam.

The steam engine, as applied to automotive propulsion, remains an enigma. As the U.S. Motor magazine of July, 1926 wrote, in reviewing one of the last steam cars on the market, "It is reasonably certain that if even a fraction of the many millions spent in the development of the gasoline car had been spent on steam car development, there would be several successful steam cars on the market today." This understatement could easily have been reworded to conclude that "...there would not be a single gasoline car being sold today."

First of all, the gasoline engine is more violent and dangerous. It depends on explosions of gasoline for its motive power. Today's gas engines produce as many as a million explosions every hour at highway speeds. The steam engine uses only the calmer pressure of expanding steam, heated by any available source of controlled heat and can be made to run much more smoothly as explosions or sudden bursts of energy are not involved. Secondly, the thermal efficiency of the internal combustion engine may reach about thirty-five percent, while the steam engine is about 90 percent efficient, wasting only about 10 percent of the available energy. Finally, the low-end torque, or pulling power, of a gasoline engine at low speed is extremely poor requiring various types of torque multiplication devices such as axle ratios and transmissions. A demonstration of this quality of "low end torque" of a gasoline engine is the old "slipping clutch" test. One would drive one's car up until the front bumper was against a tree or telephone pole, shift into low gear and engage the clutch. If the clutch was good, the engine would stall. It would run only if the clutch was slipping and needed adjustment or replacement. On the other hand, the steam engine delivers full torque and does not easily stall. In a similar situation, the steam engine would continue running after it had twisted the propeller shaft into a pretzel or blew out the tires on the driving wheels. However, to build up a full head of steam from a dead cold usually required about ten minutes and a stationary engineer's degree. It also required huge amounts of water. Most motorists were not willing to accept such a delay and such inconveniences each time they wanted to use their car.

Henry Ford I not only built an automobile in his father's stable and had to have the bricks broken out to get the finished creation onto the street; but he also became the first automobile driver to go at thephenomenal speed of 60 mph.

Bridgehampton, Long Island, is known as a spot for beautiful summer vacations. It is also known for the famed Bridgehampton auto racecourse. Walter Hansgen called himself a "garage man". He lived in Bedminster, New Jersey and became known locally as a man who bought and sold road-racing vehicles. He was known internationally as one of the great drivers of his time. He befriended many Ford Motor Company people and especially Semon Knudsen, then president.

Walter often told his Ford associates about the Road Racing Drivers Club, which met monthly at Sardi's, off Broadway in New York City. Membership in this club was very prestigious. One had to be elected by the members, the world's leading road racing drivers. Curtain time for Broadway plays was at 8:30 p.m. and after the playgoers departed and the restaurant emptied, Vincent Sardi, himself a road racing buff, gathered with the professionals in his office. The drivers would partake of Wisconsin cheese and soft drinks.

Walter Hansgen became known as "King of the Bridge". He was virtually unbeatable on the Bridgehampton course and in the late 1960's, he also became recognized as the leader of the Road Racing Drivers Club. I acted as their secretary and heard all of their conversations. In those rooms, the joys and dangers of road racing driving came alive.

Walter, better than anyone else, tied together the high risk racing arena to the make-money automobile industry of Detroit. He loved to tell of how a simple "garage man" could have the attentive ear of an automotive giant such as Semon Knudsen. Shortly after I left my duty as secretary, I experienced the shock of learning that the "garage man," now driving for Ford Motor Car Company at LeMans, in France, had been killed in a practice run.

The motor sport grew out of the desire of drivers on our nation's highways to go, and go fast. The industry moved toward higher and higher speeds until in 1975, influenced by the fuel shortage as much as safety considerations, Congress mandated a nationwide fifty-five mile per hour speed limit. By the mid-1980's, there were strong moves to raise the speed limit once again. Meanwhile, motor sport, the very dangerous kind of competitive driving like the Indianapolis 500, became more and more popular.

As this is being written, I'm encouraging a modern day driving giant, Mario Andretti, to stop driving. I had encouraged Walter Hansgen, who once finished thirteenth at Indianapolis, to end his driving career. Walter did not stop driving until his death in 1966 from injuries incurred on the Le Mans racing circuit. Sadly, this dangerous sport continues to attract human emotions in the grandstands, in the pits, and behind the wheels of the cars. There is a national and international desire among the populace to go fast. Steam lost out to the gasoline engine for many reasons, but certainly one was the highly emotional reason that a gasoline engine could propel a vehicle very fast, something Henry Ford discovered early on with a mile-a-minute prototype automobile.

Meanwhile, the early gasoline engine was not without problems. To start an engine, one had to stand in front of the vehicle and turn the engine over with a crank until it decided to start. In frustration, at prolonged or frequent failure, some drivers vented their anger by pulling out the crank and using it to beat on the sheet metal parts of the vehicle. Sometimes the engine, upon being cranked, would sputter and backfire. This would wrench the crank out of the cranker's hand, spin it backwards, and break the cranker's arm in the vicinity of the elbow. The crank was also known to fracture thumbs frequently, wrists infrequently and was at times lethal. At best, cranking required great effort. At Ford engineering the code name for the crank was "hernia".

Byron T. Carter developed the Cartercar in the Michigan State prison and eventually sold his rights to William Durant who was building the GM Empire. One summer day in 1910, while driving across the Belle Isle Bridge in Detroit, Michigan, Carter came upon a lady motorist in distress. The engine in her car had stopped. He gallantly offered help. As he cranked vigorously, the engine coughed to life. However, both he and the lady forgot to retard the spark. He was holding the crank improperly; the thumb was not to be used as an opposing member but laid alongside the forefinger. The crank whipped out of his hand and cracked him in the jaw, breaking it. Gangrene soon set in and he died.

Breakthroughs were needed for both the steam and gasoline engines. This came for the gasoline engine when Charles F. (Boss) Kettering invented the electrically driven self-starter first used on the 1912 Cadillac. The breakthrough for the steam engine came about a decade later with the development of the flash boiler which reduced the startup time to about a minute. By then, however, the sweepstakes were won by the gasoline engine.

At various times, some one hundred or more makes of steam engine driven vehicles appeared on the North American horizon. Today, there are none. Probably the best-known and longest-lived steam driven vehicle in the United States was the Stanley Steamer. It was developed by the Stanley twins, F.E. and F.O. in 1896 and was on the market until 1925. During its tenure, the Stanley Steamer covered itself with respectable measures of glory. In 1899 it was the very first horseless carriage to climb Mt. Washington. Stanley Steamers became the first automobiles in the U.S. to be used by metropolitan police. This was in Boston, Massachusetts, in 1902. In 1906, a Stanley Steamer racer bopped along Ormond Beach, Florida, at a timed speed of 127.66 mph. In 1907, this same machine, at 190 mph, became airborne and an instantaneous scrapheap. Amazingly, the driver survived but this cooled the Stanleys' racing ardor and they turned their attention to more mundane machines. However, the steam automobile's popularity continued to decline steadily and the last Stanley Steamers were built in 1925.

Another steamer, the Locomobile, which could raise a full head of steam in a couple of minutes, still could not get started soon enough for the American buyer and lasted until 1929. Another brand, the Delling, lasted from 1923 to 1934; after that, no more steamers.

However, the steam engine may have lost the battle but not necessarily the war. In the mid-1980's, we have engines driven by gasoline and diesel oil, both fossil fuels in short supply and non-replaceable. These will be followed by electric cars whose batteries will be charged by coal-fired generators. At the same time, gasoline will be derived from coal, to continue driving our cars, but at about twice the cost of gasoline refined from crude oil. There is about two hundred years worth of coal in the bowels of the earth at the current rate of use and less if it becomes more popular. Then comes one of the ultimate fuels, nuclear fusion, where a cupful of seawater contains more energy than a supertanker full of petroleum. Nuclear fusion produces heat, not explosions, and back will come the steam engine.

The developments and progress in the steam vehicle area were paralleled by the evolution of the electric car which, then and even now, has obvious benefits. It was generally conceded in 1899 by the SCIENTIFIC AMERICAN that for passenger transportation in urban usage, the electric automobile was most acceptable. It was quiet, free from odor, simple in construction and gearing, easy to drive, clean, dependable within limits and flexible in performance. Electric vehicles are being built today in very limited numbers, and exhibit these same positive qualities. On the negative side, around 1900 was the short range (under 80 miles), long battery recharge time, scarcity of charging stations, high cost, heavy weight and short life of the batteries. The same drawbacks exist today. The weak link is still the battery.

For many years Thomas A. Edison had been promising the world an improved storage battery that would make the electric vehicle more practical than the gasoline automobile. At the beginning, Edison was taken seriously but later was ridiculed for his failure to produce. "Motor Age" finally commented, "Mr. Edison's bunk has come to be somewhat of a joke – a real joke." This was one of Edison's very few public failures.

The first electric vehicle is believed to have been built in 1839, by Robert Anderson of Aberdeen, Scotland. Since it was quite primitive, this vehicle was in no way competitive with the steam vehicles that had then been traveling the roads and rails of England since 1825. In England in 1870, Sir David Salomons developed an electric car with a light electric motor. However, this vehicle used very heavy storage batteries and the resulting power loss due to the extreme weight of the batteries resulted in range and speed performances far inferior to that of the widely used steam engine. In 1886, the first electric powered taxi was introduced in England. It used a 28-cell battery and a small electric motor. The top speed was about eight miles per hour, and the range was less than 50 miles.

From 1890 to 1910, a number of researchers made significant improvements in the types of batteries used in electric cars. The modern lead-acid battery, developed by H. Tudor, and the nickel-iron battery, developed by Edison and Junger, made the electric car a much more viable alternative and resulted in a substantial increase in the manufacture of electric powered trucks and electric powered family Automobiles. During this same period, Walter Bersey became known as a designer and builder of good and dependable electric vehicles. Because of his advancements, the London Electric Cab Company, in 1897, inaugurated regular service using Bersey's electric cars. A 40-cell battery provided power for the 3-horsepower electric motor, and the cabs could be driven about 50 miles between charges. A 3-horsepower motor is about the size used in today's power lawnmowers. The Pope Manufacturing Company of Hartford, Connecticut, in 1897, began producing electric powered road vehicles and manufactured some 500 units over the following two years. Thus the electric vehicle was introduced into the United States before the turn of the century.

By 1900, some fifty automobile plants in the United States, large and small, were turning out about 4000 cars annually. Of this number, more than three-fourths were driven by either steam or electricity, and in about equal numbers. The electric car was generally viewed as the most practical automobile but its short range and heavy batteries were severe limitations. Steam engines were also well developed, but steam engines required frequent stops for water at horse troughs, leaving horses thirsty.

The year 1985 celebrated the one-hundredth anniversary of the gasoline-powered automobile. Karl Benz; a German manufacturer of stationary gasoline engines, is generally credited with pioneering and developing the automobile to the stage of commercial feasibility. The first Benz car, built in 1885, was a tricycle, powered by a one cylinder, 0.8 horsepower engine. Carl Benz and other producers were soon starting to offer motor vehicles for sale to the public. In 1891 Benz came out with a vastly improved four-wheel automobile that featured Ackermann steering and a redesigned engine capable of 700 rpm. This automobile was fairly reliable and did well in sales. It was also widely imitated. However, aside from minor changes, Benz retained the same basic design for ten years and his car was thereby soon surpassed technically by other manufacturers.

The early automobiles all resembled wagons or coaches, representing the natural transition from the horse drawn to the engine powered vehicles. They all were relatively tall, and the people sat high above the ground. In the process of transition from horse to horseless carriage, the vehicles were encountering some strange phenomena which, today, fall into the category of vehicle handling. As long as a heavy horse was pulling the wagon at a slow speed, directional stability was only a matter of the wagon following the horse, regardless of where it went, even straight up the side of a mountain.

However, when one or more of the vehicle's wheels were asked to provide the traction and the vehicle had to be steered around impending doom, and at a faster speed, various problems came to the forefront. If two solidly connected wheels were asked to provide the drive, there was the problem of different distances traveled by the wheels at either side in going around a turn. One of the wheels was forced to skid, contributing to instability. Inventors experimented with single wheel, to be used as a drive wheel, at either the front or rear, in a tricycle arrangement. That also proved to be unstable at any speed. Some inventors even went to five wheels, with a fifth, the drive unit, centrally located within the vehicle's periphery.

Horse drawn wagons had the step ring, solid front axle centrally pivoted and the wheels were small enough to tuck under the wagon in a turn. Such an arrangement proved incredibly unstable in self-propelled vehicles and soon experiments were being conducted in more precise steering systems. Eventually the Ackermann steering system was developed where the wheels turn at different angles in relation to a common pivot point.

Steering control varied with the individual creation. Some inventors used tillers, some used cranks, and some used bicycle-type handlebars and a few used horizontal wheels, a forerunner of today's universally-accepted steering control. In retrospect, each of the systems makes as much sense as any of the others, and a wheel, by no means, holds any clearly defined advantages. One vehicle, the 1886 Hammel, went one step further. The driver turned the wheel to the left to steer the vehicle to the right.

I am reminded of a recent incident which happened in Chicago, Illinois. Tractor-trailer types of fire rigs, known as hook and ladders, usually have a steerable rear axle to make the vehicle more maneuverable in city streets. However, to be fully effective, the wheels have to be steered in the opposite direction in order for the vehicle to straighten out and complete the turn as quickly as possible. My fireman acquaintance spent a very hectic day as the tiller man, which is the name for this rear driver. Every turn the fire truck made he steered, ostensibly, in the wrong direction. Finally, his shift was over and he got into his car to go home. He did well going straight forward but soon he had to make a right hand turn. Instead, he made a left, right into a drug store.

In the 1870's one of the first to recognize the automotive potential was George B. Selden, a patent attorney and amateur inventor, in Rochester, New York. In November of 1895 he was granted a U.S. patent for an improved road machine. He originally filed an all-encompassing patent for a self-propelled road vehicle in 1879. He then used evasive legal tactics to delay the patent's acceptance and also to keep down the competition until he could commercially exploit his rights. However, in 1895, the Patent Office revised the rules on delayed applications, and Selden was forced to get off the fence.

Everyone soon realized that the horseless carriage was not just a passing fancy but rather an irresistible force. Selden was able to sell shares of his patent rights to the American Association of Licensed Automobile Manufacturers. This organization included many prestigious producers and their main activity was divided between making and selling horseless carriages, and in extracting royalties of one and a half percent on gross sales from other non-member car builders. They met very stubborn resistance but sued manufacturers and won. Eventually, however, this entire ungainly structure was destroyed by the stubbornness of Henry Ford, who chose to contest it. The Selden patent was eventually declared totally worthless since a working model was never created according to the patent description.

Other U.S. inventors, in the meantime, had progressed far beyond Selden's paper accomplishments in building road cars. In 1893, Ransom E. Olds, a Lansing, Michigan machinist, made history's first sale of an automobile, a steam powered unit for $400. Directly in the face of the Selden patent, the Duryea brothers, J. Frank and Charles E., bicycle mechanics of Springfield, Massachusetts, built their first gasoline-powered car in 1893. Others who followed were Elwood G. Haynes, Edgar and Elmer Apperson, Jonathan D. Maxwell, Hiram Percy Maxim, Charles B. King, Ransom E. Olds, Alexander Winton and Henry Ford.

At this point, the automotive scene literally exploded, not only from the standpoint of inventors and inventions but from the standpoint of interest in cars expressed by people in general. This was the very beginning of a love affair with the automobile, which is as strong as ever almost one hundred years later. Over five hundred applications for patents relating to the automobile were filed by September 1895. Most of these applications were submitted that very summer.

The American automotive industry was effectively formed in the closing years of the 19th century. The Duryea brothers organized the Duryea Motor Company in 1895, made their first sale in February 1896 and produced twelve more vehicles that year, about five minutes worth by the manufacturing standards of the 1980's. The production of twelve Duryeas marked the first time the same design was used to build more than one vehicle in the United States.

The parade of new car manufacturers continued. Elwood G. Haynes and the Apperson brothers formed the Haynes-Apperson Company of Kokomo, Indiana, and began to produce vehicles in 1898. Alexander Winton organized the Winton Motor Carriage Company in 1897 and produced this country's first truck, a panel van, in 1898. In 1899, there were thirty active manufacturers producing self-propelled vehicles in this country and by 1900, 8000 automobiles were registered in the U.S. The first truck was not registered until 1904, although many had been made.

At this point the automotive manufacturing companies were failing almost as fast as were their creations. The failures were soon replaced by others who also either failed, were absorbed by others, or became limited successes. None of the 19th century manufacturers are a part of the four manufacturers of today, although Ransom E. Olds and Henry Ford were active in that era.

The 1900's arrived and maintained the automotive enthusiasm which had been generated in the closing years of the preceding century.

CHAPTER SIX
STEADY GROWTH – UNTIL W.W.I – 1900-1917

The world's a scene of changes, and to
be Constant in Nature was inconsistency.

- Abraham Cowley

Early in the twentieth century, a fair portion of the country's interest was centered on passenger-carrying automobiles. Various speed contests and reliability demonstrations maintained the levels of recreational exposure for the self-propelled vehicles. However, it took a massive disaster to demonstrate their utilitarian capabilities.

The San Francisco earthquake of 1906 provided a most demanding and intensive test for the motor vehicles of that era. Quickly afterwards a caravan of trucks was organized to carry the needed supplies to the devastated areas. Additionally, some two hundred automobiles, privately owned by residents of the city, were pressed into use by the military and civic officials for a variety of emergency usages. As an example of the magnitude of the operation, these cars and trucks, in just a few days, burned some 15,000 gallons of fuel donated by the Standard Oil Company. This equates to about 1000 miles per vehicle and these were relatively short runs. After tires overheated and exploded from usage, the vehicles continued to be driven on their rims for days, just to keep them in service. They were driven as fast as possible over the debris-strewn streets. For additional capacity, passenger cars were even towing horse-drawn carriages after many of the horses began to expire from the stresses of their labor. Surprisingly, automotive mechanical failures were scarce.

The fame of the automobile's role in the San Francisco disaster spread throughout the land. All of the reports contained ecstatic words of praise and both the War

Department and other government agencies quickly made plans for extensive use of the automobile. The average citizen could also now see that the horseless carriage was stronger than the horse, smelled better, left no solid emissions on the road, and could be put away wet. An additional benefit, which would grow with the years, is that it took people to build the vehicles. Horses, more or less, proliferated without human assistance. As early as 1902, some ten thousand skilled workmen were already employed in the various phases of building automobiles and trucks. The numbers would grow dramatically with the years.

Henry Ford I was then the driving automotive force in the United States. In October 1908, he produced the amazing Ford Model-T. This car was an extremely uncomplicated and almost totally indestructible vehicle. It was offered at a price which brought reliable transportation within the reach of nearly everyone in the country who had the inclination of owning one. Ford reduced the price and increased production for nearly every year that the car was being built. In 1909, he sold 18,664 units at an average price of $950. This price didn't require too much averaging because there were very few options. In 1917 and 1918 he sold 785,432 vehicles at $360 apiece.

When the Model-T was discontinued in 1927, more than 15 million had been produced. The Model -T was not Henry Ford's first vehicle produced and offered for public sale. He named his cars after the letters of the alphabet, went through it all, and then started over again in 1928. The first Model-T was created in 1903. The vehicles did not progress in ascending order of letters because many prototypes which carried designation letters were never released for sale.

However, it was the Model-T that took the country by storm. The very early popularity of the Model-T left Henry Ford with some enviable problems. He did not need to worry about sales because customers were waiting in line to purchase his cars. His problems were centered on the need to make enough of his Tin Lizzies to satisfy demand. Most of the early Model-T's were assembled in Detroit, at the Piquette plant, using floor assembly methods. This was the only system known to the automotive industry at that time. The vehicle would stand in one spot on the factory floor, surrounded by workers. The assemblers would keep on getting in each other's way while installing their components in some semblance of order. This involved a lot of wasted time in waiting for something to be finished before the next part could be attached. However, this was not totally ineffective because, in the late 1980's, manufacturers are considering some concepts of modular build as an assist to worker's morale and vehicle quality.

About 18,000 Model-T's were manufactured in 1909, although many times that number could have been sold, if available. The qualities of durability, reliability and performance of the Tin Lizzies were making them legends in their own time. The Ford Motor Company moved into its new and larger quarters in Highland Park, Michigan in 1910. Production volumes increased dramatically, up to 72,500 units in 1912, even though floor assembly methods were being utilized. By that time, the new Highland Park plant was bursting at the seams and something had to be done. It turned out to be the assembly line system which was destined to revolutionize all manufacturing, not only in the U.S., but in the world as well.

Some meat packing houses had already been using overhead conveyor lines for moving heavy animal carcasses, and assembly line techniques had been involved in quantity production of such items as rifles, sewing machines and bicycles. Thus, the assembly line was not an invention or development but rather an evolvement, the taking of existing methods and improving upon them. The idea is quite simple and very logical. Instead of bringing parts to a group of men moving around a stationary object, the object moves and the men remain in place. A basic element, such as a chassis or an engine, is moved slowly along a line of workers who each add to the total build. As it passes, the workers each perform a specialized operation. The work progresses until the completed unit emerges at the end of the line. In this way, the number of man hours or time needed to produce a car is drastically reduced. The unskilled labor can be taught to perform a single part of a highly skilled operation in almost no time. There are, of course, disadvantages to this process as well. The innate repetitiveness of the assembly line system very often leads to worker boredom and dissatisfaction.

Assembly line production was first applied to the Model-T magneto fabrication; but ,before the end of 1913, complete cars were being put together by this new method. The first efforts were very crude. Ropes were being used by workers to pull the vehicles from one worker station to the next. The vehicles remained stationary until one operation was finished. Then, the car was pulled to the next station. However, the rope system proved unwieldy and workers usually just pushed the vehicle along as needed. At that point in the assembly line progress, it took 250 assemblers and 80 parts-bringers, working 9 hours a day for 26 days, to build 6182 chassis assemblies, for an average of twelve and one-half man hours of work for each unit. That happened to be the lowest time average for all of the vehicle factories in operation.

Nevertheless, Henry Ford decided the system would be improved and he installed a motor with a capstan which could pull heavy rope. The chassis were each attached to this rope and progressed like a train, more or less continuously along the line, including six assemblers for each vehicle who would move with it, pick out parts from trucks driven to the line and assemble them to the vehicle. When it came to the heavy engine it was lowered, with a chain-fall, into position.

This was a vast improvement, reducing the average time to a little less than six hours per chassis.

Next, the assembly line was lengthened to 300 feet, more workers were added, and the time required for each chassis was reduced even further. It now took two hours and thirty-eight minutes to assemble a chassis. At the end of 1913, another identical assembly line was added. In early in 1914, four were set in motion, one of which was driven by an endless chain. The management improved the working techniques, keeping each assembler generally in the same position installing the same components, while the chassis moved past and on to the next person. The tasks were then further subdivided and the work teams increased in size. Yet the average man-hour time for each chassis was reduced to one hour and thirty-three minutes. In fiscal 1914, ending September 30, 248,307 Ford cars came off the lines. The methods were being constantly improved and only three years later, in the fiscal year 1917, 730,041 cars were produced. Some ninety percent of all Ford cars being produced were pre-sold and carried cash-on-delivery bills. The other ten percent barely had time to be unloaded from the railway cars before they were also purchased.

Henry Ford was in a very unique economic position. First of all, his factory produced but one specialty article for sale. Secondly, the article was coveted by nearly everyone and, as a result, sold as soon as it was assembled. Finally, as a manifestation of the axiom that "success breeds success", these desirable articles were being built by very expensive machinery, which only Ford could afford. And, he could afford it only because he was selling such huge numbers of cars at such relatively low prices.

In 1913, a factory worker was being paid $2.34 per 9 hour day, or 26 cents per hour, so it took about 80 percent of his gross annual wage to buy a $500 car. On Monday, January 5, 1914, the Ford Motor Company made American economic history by announcing a minimum wage of $5.00 per day for "even the lowliest laborer, and the man who merely sweeps the floor." The working day was also reduced from nine to eight hours. Soon, car prices were reduced further and a worker could buy a car for about 23 percent of his gross annual wage, a more favorable percentage than exists now in the late 1980's.

Ford assembly line production at Highland Park continued at a very successful level until April 1917 when the United States entered the conflict of World War I, which had begun on July 28, 1914. The U.S. automotive industry had to mobilize for the war effort. After the war, the Ford Motor Company resumed its successful ways. It flourished and expended until it became the world automotive power that it is in the 1980's.

The end of the Model-T came about as a result of several factors. Ford was consistently bringing down the prices of his cars so that by the middle of the decade, one could purchase the vehicle for $295.00. Furthermore, Ford was paying comparatively high wages and would have nothing to do with Eastern bankers. When the downturn came he began to register some losses.

Secondly, Henry Ford refused to change design. He was now in competition with others, especially with General Motors' Chevrolet. General Motors adopted a policy which specified frequent changes to incorporate improvements and that made the Tin Lizzie appear only second best.

The end of the Model-T was some eighteen months in coming. Finally, on May 26, 1927 it was announced that the Model-T was being discontinued. That morning the 15 millionth unit was produced. When the news reached the public it brought in enough orders so that the existing high inventory was exhausted and Ford had to produce almost a half-million more. The final count was 15,485,781 Tin Lizzies. At the end many customers, who could afford it, bought two vehicles, one for now and one for the future. A New Jersey woman bought seven and a wealthy man from Arizona bought ten so that he would not have to learn to drive another car. Considering the durability of the Model-T, he probably never had to if he lived to be a hundred.

For six months thereafter Henry Ford refused to approve plans for a new car. However, he slowly weakened in the face of a promise by his designers that the new vehicle would be all that the old car was, and better.

The Tin Lizzie, during its period of popularity, had more than 200 competitors. Of that total, only a few recognizable names managed to persevere late into the twentieth century. The survivors in the 1980's include Cadillac, Buick and Oldsmobile, and these, ironically, are now all a part of General Motors. GM also got its start very early in the twentieth century, but its story is quite different from that of Ford. Whereas Ford was almost always a single enduring company, General Motors was a combination of various organizations, because this was Durant's idea of what it should be.

William Crapo Durant, aka Billy, inherited wealth; however, he started making his own living when he was sixteen. Eventually Billy became head of Durant-Dort Carriage Company, the largest of a group of companies that made Flint Michigan the "carriage capital" of the country. Durant eventually became the founding father of General Motors. It all began when Billy took over an ailing and foundering car company, started in 1899 by David D. Buick. Under Durant's leadership Buick flourished and by 1902 became one of the Big Four of the automotive industry. The others were Ford, Reo and Maxwell Briscoe. Billy Durant was an extrovert, an incurable optimist and a big thinker. He envisioned a tremendous future for the automotive industry. He saw endless prospects for a company which would produce several varieties of automobiles. Heretofore, a single bad year usually meant financial ruin for a company producing a single product. Durant theorized that if one company made and sold several different types or brands, then if one model failed to sell, the others could pull the firm through the economic low spot. Durant also had the idea that a large combine should include parts supplier divisions. In 1907, Durant, in conjunction with Benjamin Briscoe, made an effort at uniting his Buick organization with Maxwell Briscoe, Reo and Ford. Negotiations went quite well, and a price of $8 million each was established for Ford and Reo. However, at the last minute, Ford wrecked the project by demanding cash. At Ford's lead, Reo also then wanted cash. The amount was unavailable to Durant/Briscoe, so the deal was then abandoned.

Billy Dunant's next move was in September of 1908. He then determined to incorporate the General Motors Corporation in the state of New Jersey. His early negotiations involved the empire of J.P. Morgan to help with financing. The Morgan House suggested that the name of the organization should be International Motors Company. For unknown reasons the deal then fell through and Durant, in a fit of pique, scratched out "International" and scribbled in "General." It then became General Motors Company and continued as that until 1915, when the name was changed to General Motors Corporation.

When GM was born, Durant used Buick as the foundation. He later added Cadillac, Oldsmobile and Oakland, which was later to become Pontiac. Durant then embarked on an aggressive whirlwind buying spree. He purchased an assortment of other companies without paying much attention to the actual value or earning power of what he was buying. The purchases included Cartercar, Elmore, Ewing, Marquette, Randolph, Welch and several others. None survived, and their passing eventually brought Durant trouble. He also bought two truck companies, the Rapid

Motor Vehicle Company of Pontiac, Michigan and the Reliance Motor Truck Company of Owosso, Michigan. By 1912, both companies merged to form GMC Truck and Mach Division. That, in turn, became the Truck and Bus Group in 1982.

William Durant's almost desperate expansion efforts brought problems in just two short years. By 1910 General Motors Company was in deep financial trouble. The rate of expansion had depleted the cash and credit resources with which Durant had started. Purchases were financed mostly by the issuance of securities. The accumulation of unprofitable subsidiaries, purchased at inflated prices, had burdened the company with a debt far in excess of its earning power. Durant then turned to the financial sector for help. He offered to relinquish his personal control of the company in exchange for a loan that would keep General Motors from receivership. It was not easy. He was turned down in Kansas City, Chicago, New York and St. Louis. Finally, in desperation, he went back East and practically gave away the store to get help. A bankers' syndicate, including J. & W. Seligman of New York, and James W. Storrow of Lee, Higginson and Company of Boston, intervened and saved GM from the dissolution which appeared imminent. GM was saved by the convincing arguments of Cadillac's president, Henry M. Leland, who pledged all of his own and the company's resources to the cause. The syndicate issued $15 million in 6 percent notes which were covered by mortgages on all of the company's real assets. To do this they advanced $12.75 million. Additionally, they received a bonus of $6,169,200 in GM stock. The syndicate has often been criticized for the harshness of their terms, and it was deals such as these that made Henry Ford distrust "money men" so much.

For the favor of advancing 12.75 million, this bankers' syndicate from New York and Boston received back over $21 million, plus the 6 percent interest on the $15 million. There was little risk of default. GM real properties, if liquidated at market value, would have more than covered their investment.

The syndicate eventually made GM healthy again and was responsible, indirectly, for the hiring of Charles W. Nash and Walter P. Chrysler into the management fold. In 1910, Nash became head of Buick, largely because the Buick division owed Nash's carriage company several million dollars. Nash asked Durant for a chance to rectify the situation. In 1912, Nash became the president of General Motors. Later he went on to form what is now American Motors.

Chrysler was a railroad master mechanic. The banking syndicate asked him to join GM, and specifically Buick, to lend that division the technical expertise which Nash lacked. Chrysler accepted the offer. When Nash moved up to the presidency, Chrysler replaced him as president of Buick Motor Car Company. He later, of course, left GM to form what is now Chrysler Corporation. General Motors survived and, indeed, began to flourish, with the banking syndicate providing the direction. William Durant continued as vice-president and member of the board of directors. He considered the events of the immediate past as only a minor setback, and went about preparing a personal resurrection. This is where Chevrolet enters the picture.

Louis, Gaston and Arthur Chevrolet were French race drivers who came to the United States to drive for Buick. Louis also had talent in automotive design and development. Soon thereafter Billy Durant began quietly and surreptitiously backing Chevrolet in the development of a smaller car. In this he had financial help from the Chatham and Phoenix Bank in New York, which owed Durant a debt of gratitude. Its major stockholders had made a fortune on the shares of GM stock received from Durant in exchange for the Heany Electric Company and a worthless patent for a tungsten lamp.

The Chevrolet car was introduced in 1912. It became an immediate success and was instrumental in Durant's return to power. William Durant had issued Chevrolet stock, and after the car went into production he offered stockholders a trade of five shares of Chevrolet for one share of GM which provided the stockholders an immediate paper profit. Louis Chevrolet, by this time, had faded from the picture and turned his attention to building Frontenac race cars.

By 1915, the trusteeship of the bankers' syndicate had expired, and a new Board of Directors was to be elected for General Motors. In what must have been the power play of the century, Durant marched into the meeting and announced that he now controlled the company. His stock trades had indeed given him control.

Today Chevrolet is GM's largest and most profitable property, but in 1915 GM was actually owned by Chevrolet which held a portfolio of 450,000 shares of the 625,000 outstanding.

Perhaps the most important transaction that Durant made for himself, for GM, and for the entire industry, was the acquisition of two small related companies, Dayton Engineering Laboratories and Hyatt Roller Bearing Company. From the standpoint of mechanical and financial potential, these were relatively insignificant additions. However, along with Dayton, GM received Charles F. Kettering and along with Hyatt, Alfred F. Sloan, Jr.

While GM flourished, it could also have been otherwise. William Durant's former associate and partner, Benjamin Briscoe, tried at the very same time to build his own automotive empire, a rival to GM. He called his organization the United States Motor Corporation. Founded in 1910, it was based on one prosperous company, Maxwell-Briscoe, just as GM was based on Buick. Also, like Durant, Briscoe embarked on a vigorous program of acquisition of other companies. These, however, turned out to be a collection of lame ducks, including the Columbia Motor Car Company which was formed from the remains of the Electric Vehicle Company. In 1912, U.S. Motor went into receivership. Benjamin Briscoe ran out of money. Unlike the Durant situation, a bankers' syndicate did not come to the rescue. Instead, Walter Flanders, formerly of Ford and also of Everitt, Metzzer and Flanders, (EMF), sometimes referred to as "Every Mechanical Failure", was called in to salvage what there was of value. He reorganized the company as the Maxwell Motor Car Company. This, in time, would become the parent of the Chrysler Corporation which, in the 1980s, is the third of the Big Three, or Four, in the U.S. automotive arena.

Chrysler Corporation, formed in 1928, is a relative newcomer on the automotive scene. Of Chrysler's current brand names, only Dodge existed in the early 1900s, having been founded by brothers John and Horace Dodge in 1914. The Dodge brothers were uneducated factory hands who worked their way up to the operation of their own machine shop which specialized in automotive transmissions.

Henry Ford's early beginnings included Alexander T. Malcomson as partner. The latter signed a contract with the Dodge brothers to produce 650 complete automotive chassis, including engines, transmissions, frame and axles, for the Ford product. The brothers were to receive $250 per chassis but sometimes had difficulty in collecting. Business was at the mercy of Ford, who was then buying their entire production run.

The Dodge brothers played a major role in the rise of the Model-T to prominence. However, success changed Ford's personality for the worse, and the Dodge brothers were not the most even tempered individuals themselves. They had a difference of opinion and in 1914 cancelled their contract with Ford to make a car of their own. Others who left Ford at that time were James Couzens and William S. Knudsen.

Knudson, soon thereafter was to go to work for General Motors as head of Chevrolet. Walter P. Chrysler continued as the head of Buick operation until irreconcilable differences with Durant over policy in 1920 caused him to walk out, slam the door and never look back.

The major competitors to Ford and General Motors at that time were Willys and Maxwell. Both were in financial difficulty as a result of poor management. John North Willys, like Durant, had overextended his company's resources. At Maxwell, the authority was divided between two men.

Hugh S. Chalmers was a former National Cash Register employee and a super salesman who knew very little about production. Walter E. Flanders, who took over the failing company from Benjamin Briscoe, knew a lot about production but very little about engineering. The Maxwell Company was in trouble again.   Interested bankers brought ex-GM executive Waiter P. Chrysler into both companies to take charge of reorganization.

However, the Willys effort was a Chrysler failure. That corporation was put into receivership, eventually liquidated, and the component parts allowed to resume their corporate independence. However, in Chrysler's defense it must be pointed out that he did not have a free, autonomous hand in his efforts at reorganization. He was opposed at every step of the way by the still powerful figure of John N. Willys, who refused to admit and accept failure and defeat. Willys did, in fact, make somewhat of a recovery. With the help of wealthy friends in Toledo, Ohio, he regained control of one segment of the former corporation, the Willys-Overland Company. In time he succeeded in building another Willys empire, banking heavily on the popularity of the low priced Overland.

Chrysler's efforts of restructuring at Maxwell were not opposed, and the Maxwell automobile continued to be well accepted by the buying public. Chrysler was also driven by the fact that he wanted a car of his own and his own company.

The Maxwell organization produced an excellent foundation for both ambitions. With the help of three bright, young engineers, Carl Greer, Fred Zeder and Owen Shelton, Chrysler set about designing his car. They decided to take advantage of the lessons learned by the aviation industry about high compression and high performance engines and to install this type in the Chrysler car. Chrysler put the Maxwell Motor Car Company into receivership in 1921 and reorganized it under his total control. However, he kept the Maxwell name for another four years until his Chrysler car had reached the marketplace and achieved a modicum of success. The Chrysler car was ready in 1923, but neither Chrysler nor the Maxwell Company had the capital to produce it. Walter Chrysler hoped to attract the attention of money men by exhibiting prototype models at that year's New York Auto Show. However, by the rules, since the car was not in production, it was not allowed in the show. Undaunted, Chrysler rented the lobby of the Commodore Hotel around the corner from the Grand Central Palace, the site of the auto show, and held his own private presentation. It drew considerable interest, mainly because of the high compression engine which was well ahead its time.

One of those interested happened to be Ed Tinker, the president of the Chase Securities Company. Chrysler and Tinker entered one of the new Chrysler cars, locked the doors and proceeded to bargain, surrounded by a sea of curious hotel lobby visitors. Tinker offered to underwrite the Chrysler venture, giving the company ninety-two cents on the dollar. Chrysler wanted ninety-six. Tinker countered with ninety-four and a bonus for Chase. Chrysler was adamant, so Tinker got out of the car and went home. Chrysler panicked, and with B.S. Hutchinson, who later was to become treasurer of Chrysler Corporation, took the subway to Wall Street to accept Tinker's offer. Tinker, however, was not at the bank. The two tracked him down to a barber shop. The deal to establish Chrysler Corporation was made through a mask of lather.

The Chrysler car was introduced to the public in 1924 and, by 1927, had climbed to the fourth position in sales volume. Unfortunately, it could not be produced cheaply enough to compete with Ford and Chevrolet which now became Chrysler's ambition. DeSoto was brought out early in 1928, but it was a close relative to the Chrysler and, therefore, not cheap. Production facilities were being constantly expanded, but the components purchased from outside suppliers were expensive and precluded a low vehicle price. Chrysler needed his own parts supply capability. To that end, he looked longingly at the Dodge Brothers Manufacturing Company which included extensive forge and foundry installations.

The Dodge brothers became victims of the influenza epidemic that followed World War I and died within a few months of each other in 1920. Their company continued to operate humbly until 1925 when the New York bankers, Dillon-Read and Company, approached the widows with an offer of $150-170 million in cash and stock, an offer they quickly accepted.

The bankers bought the company with the idea of a quick resale and a quick profit, but for two years they had no offers, and, when in 1927 the company lost money, Clarence Dillon approached Walter F. Chrysler. Chrysler was anxious to buy, and Dillon was just as anxious to sell. Each knew of the other's inclination but neither would admit his own desire. Both played it nonchalantly, both claiming that they did not have too great an interest in a transaction, but each would be willing to enter into an agreement only to help the other one out.

They finally took a suite at the Ritz-Carlton hotel and negotiated for five days and nights. Finally, they hammered out a deal wherein Chrysler bought the entire Dodge Brothers Company for $170 million in Chrysler stock. He also assumed the liability of $56 million in Dodge bonds. The Dodge

Brothers' organization also included a dealer network which numbered 12,000 strong and was considered the best sales organization of that type in the U.S. This network could now be used as an outlet for the other Chrysler products. Chrysler immediately called K.T. Keller with news of the deal. Keller then dashed around to all the Dodge plants to drape huge canvas signs which pronounced to the world "Chrysler Corporation-Dodge Division". Late in 1928, out of the Dodge stables, the Plymouth made its debut as a low-priced car which could compete with Ford and Chevrolet. Chrysler's ambition was fulfilled, and the third of today's Big Four was born.

The fourth member, American Motors, was not formed until 1954, but its roots go back to the era of the very birth of the automobile.

In 1902, Thomas B. Jeffery abandoned his bicycle building business and started to mass produce automobiles. He was in on the ground floor, along with the Popes, Wintons, Fords, Duryeas and Oldsmobiles. He named his cars Ramblers, the same name he used for his bicycles. After he died in 1910, the car was renamed the Jeffery in his honor.

Meanwhile, Charles W. Nash came up through the Buick Division before becoming president of General Motors. When Durant returned to power, Nash left, considering himself too conservative and cautious to ever be able to work with him. In 1913, with the help of James W. Storrow, the same man who bailed out GM, Nash bought the Thomas B. Jeffery Company. He soon restructured it as the Nash Motor Car Company and started building and selling the Nash automobiles.

In 1904, Roy D. Chapin and Howard E. Coffin left the Olds Motor Works and tried partnerships with two other manufacturers, E.R. Thomas and Hugh Chalmers. Finally, they got their own company started in 1909, with the financial help of J.L.O. Hudson, the owner of a department store in

Detroit, Michigan. They named the car after him and organized the Hudson Motor Car Company. Chapin performed the management chores and Coffin the engineering.

With World War I upon the country, Chapin headed the Highway Transport Committee for the Council for National Defense but also found time to plan the introduction, after the war, of a low-priced car named the Essex. The Essex later sprouted the Terraplane.

In 1954, Nash and Hudson were combined to form American Motors under the direction of George Romney. There were only two original automobile manufacturers involved, the Jeffery Company and Hudson, but before the American Motors merger, they produced nine different cars: Rambler, Jeffery, Hudson, Nash, Essex, Terraplane, Lafayette, Ajax and Dover. None remain. American Motors Corporation, in the late 1970's, embraced the remaining product of still another of the automotive pioneers, John N. Willys. This product was the Willys Jeep, currently available in several models.

Willys, a bicycle manufacturer, assumed control of Overland's automobile production in 1907. He continued building Willys-Overland models, and even branched out into the Willys-Knight models but ran into financial trouble in the 1920's, and Walter Chrysler was appointed by the creditors to rescue the company. Chrysler failed, but John Willys again regained control of the Willys-Overland Company in 1921. However, in 1929, the company was again in financial trouble and went into receivership. By this time John Willys had retired from active management and was serving as the U.S. ambassador to Poland. The company's crisis brought him back and, before he died in 1933, he did have the satisfaction of seeing his company solvent again, although the Knight affiliate which had become outdated had to be eliminated.

At the beginning of World War II, the Willys Company was asked to manufacture the Army Jeep and, by war's end, had produced some 660,000 units. After the war, the company produced only civilian versions of the Jeep until being taken over in 1953 by Kaiser and by the Kaiser-Jeep division. In 1972 it was taken over by American Motors. In the late 1980's the Jeep is still that company's most popular and profitable product.

Today, in the late 1980's, there are at least three and one half members in the Big Four. General Motors is the largest, followed by Ford, followed by Chrysler, followed by small American Motors, which is constantly losing money.

CHAPTER SEVEN

WORLD WAR I

Accurst be he that first invented war.

- Christopher Marlowe

World War I began as just a local European conflict between Austria-Hungary and Serbia on July 28, 1914. However, it expanded and was quickly transformed into a general European war by the declaration of war made by Germany against Russia on August 1, 1914. It gradually evolved into a global conflict involving thirty-two nations, twenty-eight of which were known as the Allies or the Associated Powers, which included Great Britain, France, Russia, Italy and eventually the United States. The opposition was known as the Central Powers consisting of Germany, Austria-Hungary, Turkey and Bulgaria. The United States remained a neutral nation until April of 1917. The U.S.'s entry into the conflict was opposed by many prominent citizens, the most notable of whom was Henry Ford I. Until the U.S. actually declared war and began to take an active role, the automotive industry was completely unaffected by the events taking place in Europe. It was totally absorbed by the introduction of the assembly line, the reorganization of General Motors, the appearance of new cars like Chevrolet and Dodge and the common mergers and bankruptcies of its various members.

Henry Ford I was an outspoken proponent of isolation. In 1915, he chartered a "Peace Ship" which carried him and other individuals of similar convictions to Europe where they attempted, without success, to persuade the belligerent governments to end World War I. He also made the announcement that his company would refuse war contracts. These were Ford's personal beliefs and were not in the least an indication of selfishness or lack of patriotism on the part of the automotive industry.

Automotive production of the civilian market continued unabated right through the year 1917. Ironically enough, some of Ford's Tin Lizzies were finding their way to the Allied front lines where they served with distinction. The White Motor Company built 18,000 trucks for the Allies and did so well they never built another car again. For the most part, the American government condoned the business as usual attitude and no thought was given to bolstering the U.S. security systems.

Serious mobilization began only after the U.S. declared war, but it was many months before any slow-down in automotive production became apparent. In fact, passenger car production continued into 1918, until the War Industries Board ordered the automotive community to cut its output in half. Then, while the automotive production diminished, the production of trucks doubled. The workers now had to learn to make guns, bullets, gun carriages, tractors and aircraft engines.

The Ford Motor Company built forty-three submarine chasers, known as Eagle boats. Apparently, after America had declared war on the Central Powers, Henry Ford withdrew his objections to war work and, caught up in the patriotic fervor of the times, even announced he would refund to the government all the profits he made on war contracts, a promise he conveniently forgot once his profitable war business began in earnest.

The war also provided the U.S. with concrete evidence of the value of the highway transportation system. After all, the war came only some fifteen years after the birth of the automobile, and a networking road system had not been built prior to the automobile's development because long distance travel by horse was not practical on a mass scale. The road system was, in fact, quite rudimentary in 1917, but it was imperative that it be used as much as possible to relieve some of the burden on the railroads.

Secretary of Transportation Roy Chapin cut through government red tape to boost this budding highway system to its maximum potential during the war years. As an example, new trucks were being loaded onto railroad cars to be transported to the Atlantic seaboard where they were put on ships for delivery to Europe. With careful planning of routes and by involving local authorities to keep these routes open and in reasonable repair, Chapin devised a plan which permitted the trucks to be driven to their ports of embarkation. Each new truck also carried a load of freight, thereby further assisting the overloaded railroads. Until this time, trucks were not used on long hauls, and this was the beginning of the feud between the railroads and the trucking industry, a feud which has continued into the 1980's.

The automotive industry was also asked to delve into aircraft manufacturing. That effort was less than satisfactory. The airplane was an American invention, yet, until the war, the country did nothing to stimulate interest. An aviation industry scarcely existed as such. By 1915, the total output of military aircraft stood at twenty six. The consensus was that facilities and techniques that produced motor vehicles in quantity could do the same for aircraft when and if the necessity arose. This reasoning, of course, was faulty because airplanes are far more complex than are automobiles. They are also made of different materials and assembled differently. The same faulty thinking about mass production techniques for aircraft was to be repeated twenty-five years later at the onset of World War II when it was also assumed that a civilian auto-based industrial complex could rapidly adapt to meet the air transport needs of the military.

In point of fact, the auto industry could not meet such radical needs, and airframes did not roll off modified automotive production lines. Rather, special aircraft facilities had to be built and many automobile men did have a hand in building the considerable numbers of aircraft that were eventually produced.

John N. Willys gained control of the Curtiss Aeroplane and Motor Company. This was done at the urging of the U.S. government since Glenn Curtiss, the owner, was more interested in design than in production. The other major manufacturer of air-frames was the Dayton-Wright Company, the creation of a syndicate coming from the automotive industry and headed by Edward A. Deeds of Delco. Deeds was eventually made responsible for all U.S. aircraft production and in that capacity he became the scapegoat for all of the real or imagined faults of the aircraft industry. The recently completed Panama Canal was still fresh in American minds, a success which was hailed as the greatest technological and engineering feat of all time. Americans were overconfident and a bit naive. They did not understand why America could not produce military goods in huge volumes overnight. They didn't understand that the nation's manufacturing capability needed time for preparation. Aircraft engines were another story. These were similar enough to automotive versions that it was practical to build them in automotive engine plants. However, this was also not without problems.

The easiest way to get into production quickly was to utilize tested and proven allied designs. However, these types of engines required a substantial amount of hand machining by skilled craftsmen and were not adaptable to American high-volume production methods. Eventually, some Italian Bugatti and Spanish Hispano-Suiza engines were produced in quantity. For reasons of efficiency, a decision was made to design an aircraft engine compatible with U.S. techniques and facilities. The famous Liberty engine was conceived. It was designed principally by E.J. Hall of the Hall-Scott Motor Company and J.G. Vincent of Packard. The two locked themselves in a Washington, D.C., hotel room for three days at the end of May, 1917. They carried instructions to design a unit that used only tested and proven devices and was adaptable to mass production.

The result was an excellent but very conventional engine. It originally had eight cylinders but later increased to twelve for more power. The power output ranged from an original 220 horsepower to a later 440. A total of 24,475 Liberty engines were built during the war, almost all in automotive engine plants. The Liberty engines used nearly 300,000 cylinders. Ford produced the cylinders with a mass production method. Until then the process had required hand machining.

The biggest error of the wartime production effort was the failure to understand that military aircraft could not be built by volume production methods as were automobiles. The production line system as established for the automobile industry did not contain provisions for easy incorporation of changes. Changes often became necessary for the military aircraft industry based on combat experience and advancing technology. The war ended before these problems of production could be solved.

Armistice came on November 11, 1918. Immediately after the war, there was considerable labor unrest. There were serious and far reaching strikes in the coal and steel industries. Because of these strikes and because of material diversion to the war effort, shortages of various goods caused some temporary problems before the automobile industry could again reach full production. Also, there were some transportation problems. Railroads had difficulty in converting their systems and methods from government employment to private engagement. Nevertheless, the U.S. automobile industry had never completely converted to war production, so the road back was not a very long one. Even in the face of great difficulties, the vehicle production for the first post-war year exceeded the 1917 figure.

The automobile manufacturers were correct in their assessment of the post-war market potential. There was not only an increase in the demand for passenger cars, but also for trucks. Roads were now adequate for long distance travel, and trucks had proven their capabilities during the war effort. However, the most inviting challenge appeared to be effort to invade Ford's Model-T market. In 1919, the $800 Overland, produced by John N. Willys, was the second best-selling vehicle in this country. He also was then building the Willys-Knight, using the sleeve-valve Knight engine which operated more smoothly and quietly than any of its contemporaries.

Roy D. Chapin's Hudson Motor Car Company also made a run for the prize with the Essex. Several years later, in 1922, Chapin made a bold move in offering a closed sedan for only $100 more than an open touring car.

General Motors was also active in the automotive arena. In 1918, the travesty of Chevrolet owning General Motors, a Durant ploy, was eliminated by the formation of the General Motors Corporation, which was formed from both the General Motors Company and Chevrolet. Also included was a parts conglomerate, United Motors Corporation, which included Delco, with Charles F. Kettering and Hyatt Roller Bearing Company, with Alfred P. Sloan, Jr.

Sloan eventually acquired the reputation as the real builder of General Motors. After graduating from the Massachusetts Institute of Technology, he went to work for John Wesley Hyatt, who produced roller bearings but was a poor businessman. The company was saved by a $5,000 loan from Sloan's father, and Sloan became president. Afraid that GM and Ford would begin producing their own bearings, Sloan joined Durant's United Motors. In the reorganization of GM, he became a vice-president.

William C. Durant continued his expansion and acquisition program. For $30 million he bought the Fisher Body Company which was the creation of six brothers who were originally wagon and carriage producers in Norwalk, Ohio, but converted to the production of automotive bodies in 1905. Durant also picked up Frigidaire, a one-man operation, for $56 thousand. Durant was also responsible for the formation of the General Motors Acceptance Corporation which facilitated the process of buying a car by advocating and popularizing deficit spending.

Fisher Body and Frigidaire continued for decades as financially successful members of GM before going out of business. GM's financial arm continues to flourish and grow into the late 1980's.

Henry Ford I also joined the post-war expansion parade. He saw that the demand for his cars would exceed the production capacity of even his high-volume Highland Park plant. Already, in 1916 he began planning for a vast facility in River Rouge, Michigan which would include its own steel mill. With the coming of peace, the project was pushed to completion at a cost of $116 million.

Henry Ford I was also looking around for new areas of challenge. In the 1918 Federal election, he was a Democratic candidate for U.S. Senator and narrowly lost to Truman S. Newberry. Had Ford won, the Democrats would have controlled the Senate in the formative post-war years. Ford's ardor for politics and public life cooled in 1919, after his libel lawsuit against the Chicago Tribune came to trial. In 1916, the Tribune had disagreed with Ford's outspoken views in favor of neutrality and isolationism, calling him "an ignorant idealist" and "an anarchistic enemy of the nation". When the case was tried three years later, Ford was quoted as saying, "History is bunk." In context, Ford actually said that as a student he had felt that the subject of history was bunk. However, when a movement was being organized to give Ford the Republican presidential nomination, in 1924, he declined.

The truck industry came into its own in these post-war years with many manufacturers, such as White, Mack and Autocar concentrating exclusively on the manufacture of trucks. Others, such as Ford and General Motors, were looking at trucks as an additional area of interest to coexist with, and perhaps borrow from, the passenger cars. My own emergence in this chronology, incidentally, coincides with the Chevrolet truck. We both began our lives in 1918.

We moved from three horses pulling a plow in the 1920's to our first tractor, a Fordson, in 1929. By then I was eleven, and my father and older brothers were bidding on putting a gravel or aggregate surface on the road towards Kaleva. My father and brother John bid $1.55 per cubic yard to put gravel on the sand road, but lost to a lower bidder. Later on, my father was a successful bidder on another portion of that same project, allowing us to purchase a Chevrolet truck, a truck which could hold two tons after a 2 x 6 temporary frame had been installed on top of the steel frame, to secure the steel dump box.

We had a good life in the country, and cars and trucks came to be freedom vehicles for us. Without them, we could never have developed the land to its full productivity. We, and hundreds and thousands of us along the sand roads of the nation, became a market for the automobile and the automobile industry.

The giants were busy. Elmer Sperry did miracles with the gyroscope. Alfred P. Sloan, Jr. married industry and finance into a productive unit which helped to build not only the United States, but the free world as well. Henry Ford I, the pioneer of the world in the car age, was having his influence on his grandson, Henry II. In Wall Street, intellectuals Pierre Bretey, Len Jarvis, Kenneth A. Ward, Gerald Martin Loeb and others were forging a research profession in which a car buff kid from Kaleva, who in the 1920's hardly realized that there was a frontier beyond a cleared line of pine stumps, eventually found his vocation.

CHAPTER EIGHT

THE ROARING TWENTIES

Let us therefore follow after the things which make for peace.
- Romans 14:19

The decade following World War I is referred to today as the Roaring Twenties, or the Jazz Age. Beginning early in the 20th century, several hundred companies entered the automobile arena. By 1929, only eleven survived, and this would be reduced even further. The end of the decade was marked by the great stock market crash, with the beginning of the Great Depression. Nevertheless, the mid-1920's were indeed one of the most festive eras in the United States history and also marked the advent and full acceptance of the automobile, the blossoming of advertising, women's emancipation, prohibition and the creation of time payments, especially in combination with automobiles. It was memorable, too, for the existence of such luminaries, man and beast, as Rudolph Valentino, Al Capone, Babe Ruth, Jack Dempsey and Man O'War. Radio was the new diversionary gadget; Mah Jong was the new game. President Coolidge's "prosperity" followed President Harding's "return to normalcy."

The war had accelerated the process of equalizing men and women. During World War I women had taken over many jobs usually held by men and even formed the League of Women Voters to exert unified political pressures. In 1925, Nellie Taylor Ross was elected the first U.S. woman governor in the state of Wyoming. About two weeks later, Miriam (Ma) Ferguson became the governor of Texas.

Before World War I, railroads were the principal national transportation system of the United States. Coal fired steam locomotives pulled trains over thousands of miles of rails to link the widely scattered cities of this nation. With the onset of the war, however, the various companies representing the railway system were unable to coordinate efforts. As a result, the lines were temporarily appropriated by the government, first by Presidential proclamation, and, shortly thereafter, by Congressional mandate.

The government was quite successful in getting the nation's transportation needs satisfied during the war. This made an impression on many. In fact, when the war ended, there was strong sentiment that the government should take over ownership from the individual companies, nationalize the system and continue to operate the railroads. The railway labor unions favored this as did some of the users. The owners, however, wanted their property returned, plus compensation for its use. The Transportation Act of 1920 effectively submerged any idea of government ownership and placed more power in the hands of the Interstate Commerce Commission, an organization which grew to be reckoned with, even in the 1980's. Curiously, before the war, the government maintained a general anti-trust attitude which precluded the merging of railroads. Now the opposite was true, and the ICC was instructed to formulate consolidation plans which would bring about higher efficiency.

In the 1920's, the railroads were also facing their first serious threat since their beginnings. During the war, military trucks proved that they did not need to be carried by the railroads to their destinations. The trucks carried both themselves and a portion of the cargo normally assigned to the trains to the ports of embarkation. Trucks also proved their capability and durability on the war fronts. At the same time, the automobile was beginning to cut heavily into rail passenger traffic. By 1927, passenger travel on the railroads had decreased by one third. The war had only temporarily halted the rise in the ownership of private automobiles. Now, in the Roaring Twenties, most families either had an automobile or were planning to buy one. More and more people were beginning to consider the automobile an integral part of their lifestyle. They were using the automobile to travel longer distances to earn their livelihood. Cars also became a recreational tool for Sunday drives and even vacations. The automobile was becoming a necessity, almost as important as a home. In fact, some people preferred to own a more modest home in order to be able to afford an automobile as well. A survey, conducted at this time in a Midwest city, indicated that a large number of families who owned autos did not yet have bathtubs. The suitor who did not own a car, or who could not borrow the family flivver, often went dateless. Girls did not like to be taken out on streetcars or subways. The automobile, in fact, became a very strong social force, changing the dating and courtship rituals. Previously, young couples spent hours together in the parlor, usually in the girl's home. The automobile now was becoming a mobile parlor which could take the young couple to more distant, more exciting places and away from parental supervision.

This newly-found way of life involved many changes. Service stations and roadside restaurants were built at every intersection. The filling station and repair garage became a major element in the small business community. Rudimentary tourist cabins became the forerunners of the plush motels of the 1980's. The increasing numbers of automobiles demanded more and better paved highways. The better the roads got, the more people and automobiles they attracted, and the more people bought automobiles.

The United States, during the 1920's, spent nearly $2 billion annually on streets and highways. By 1927, there were in existence some fifty thousand miles of paved roads. In 1928 a person could travel by automobile from New York to Kansas, all on paved highways. Automotive travel farther west was not advisable during periods of heavy rain or snow.

The astounding popularity of the automobile created traffic problems within the cities which, by the 1980's seem part and parcel of city living. New types of roads were needed, as were bridges, tunnels and some degree and form of accepted traffic control. The first traffic signals were manually operated "stop" and "go" signs. These signs were introduced in New York City early in the decade. Soon after, red, yellow and green timed lights, patterned after the railroad signal system, were introduced and accepted nationally as a feasible method of traffic control. The first expressway-type road was the Bronx River Parkway in New York, shortly followed by the Long Island Parkway and Connecticut's Merritt Parkway. Chicago constructed a double-decked roadway in 1925, the Wacker Drive which, for some reason, did not gain universal acceptance. The Holland Tunnel, under the Hudson River was completed in 1927. It was the first underwater tunnel specifically designed for automotive use. Tunnels were cut through rock in Pittsburg in 1924. The George Washington Bridge, spanning the Hudson River and linking New Jersey and New York City, was begun in 1927. At that time, with a span of 3500 feet, it was the longest suspension bridge in the world.

In 1910, there were some 458,000 automobiles in the United States. By 1920 the number of passenger cars and trucks had mushroomed to 9,250,000 units. By the end of the decade, that number had reached over 26,500,000. That meant that the entire population of the United States could go for an automobile ride at the same time. On some Sundays it seemed that they all did.

In this era, General Motors and Ford were already the two giants of the industry with Chrysler being third. There were still a goodly number of smaller independent companies such as Nash, Willys-Overland, Hudson, Packard and Studebaker. The post war depression was to wipe out most of all the others.

I happen to have some excellent second hand knowledge of Ford's efforts at dealing a real motorcar. I came to know Arthur Klann in the 1970's, about the time that he became blind. He asked me to put on tape a book about Henry Ford written by Bill Klann, his brother. Bill had written only this one book, a copy of which went into the Ford Motor Company archives when Bill retired from the company in the 1940's. Art Klann called himself a garage man. He had been the sales representative of Michigan for a wheel alignment and balancing company headquartered in St. Louis. Now Arthur and his brother Bill's book became my pipeline to the early Henry Ford. Henry, according to the book, became dejected by the failure of the Model-T in 1926. He began spending almost all of his time in the famous Highland Park plant in Michigan. This is where the moving production line had been invented and where the five dollar automotive earning day became a reality in 1913. Henry Ford was then near financial ruin. The vehicles of Walter P. Chrysler, Alfred P. Sloan, Jr., Charles W. Nash and others were outperforming the Model-T on the road and in the marketplace. Arthur told me more of the inside story than was in his brother's book. Apparently, after two days of total seclusion in the plant, Henry Ford suddenly came out. He had found a fresh desire to develop a new car, and began working feverishly with Bill Klann and others on plans for what was called the Austrian Ford. That was simply a code name for a new car which would become the Model-A. Bill took a briefcase with the Austrian Ford plans, unlimited bank notes, and lines of credit from Henry Ford to England. There are some interesting insights into the personality of Henry Ford that came forth in his exchange of cables with Bill Klann. Bill was a master car maker and things went quite well. He had found a shop willing to do some of the work. On one occasion, Henry cabled Bill, "Need anything?" – Henry.

Bill cabled back, "Lonely." Henry cabled back, 'Sending wife." And he did. Soon a prototype of the Model-A was finished. It was put on the deck of the French liner Normandy and brought to America as a successor to the Model-T. In August of 1927, Edsel Ford, Henry's son, announced that the Model-A was an accomplished fact. Production did begin early in 1928, but it was not until 1929 that production could begin to match the heavy demand.

The automobile industry was helped in its development by very ordinary people. In the 1920's, my own older brothers were among those who went to Detroit after the fall harvest to work in the automotive plants, returning home in time for spring planting. The automobile industry was growing very fast. Indeed, by 1929, car sales had reached the phenomenal total of 6.2 million units. There were many tales of workers staying at the machines or on the assembly lines for as many as 18 hours at a stretch. The streetcar conductor would awaken the riders or workers when they got to work and again after work when they came near their rooming houses. Workers, usually single men or married men who left their families behind, established small communities in Metropolitan Detroit based upon ethnic backgrounds. Highland Park, Michigan, for example, became a favorite boarding room area for people of Finnish extraction from the Upper Peninsula and from my own small Finnish community of Kaleva, Michigan.

Meanwhile, General Motors was working through problems of its own. The career of William C. Durant at General Motors came to an end on November 30, 1920 when he resigned as president. At that point, he had already assembled the automotive divisions which form the nucleus of General Motors Corporation, even in the late 1980's. Buick and Chevrolet were created by the power of his own personality and doggedness. Oldsmobile and Oakland, which became Pontiac, were rescued by Durant from the clutches of oblivion. Durant bought Cadillac, the most successful car after Ford, with cash on the barrelhead. Durant's downfall came about by his own management policies. He failed to realize that the Corporation had outgrown the autocratic leadership of a single individual. The problem crested with the resignation of Walter P. Chrysler. Prior to this crisis, at the lowest ebb of the economic downturn, Durant had also been personally buying GM stock in order to sustain its value on the open market. Now Durant was very near personal insolvency. Bankers, 10 years before, had invested some $15 million in the company. Now they feared that the GM president's personal failure might bring about the collapse of the entire Corporation.

GM Chairman Pierre duPont and John Raskob, Chairman of Finance were astounded and shocked by the turn of events. They decided to talk to other duPont executives to plan a course of action. This eventually led to decisions that the Durant insolvency should be corrected and that the duPont empire should invest in the Corporation up to $10 million in cash and extend trade credit for millions more. This led to some intensive negotiations involving Durant, Raskob and duPont, as well as the House of Morgan. Morgan had, earlier, made a substantial purchase of GM stock. The final settlement included the $10 million investment by the duPont Empire to pay Durant's obligations and the negotiation of a $20 million loan for GM by the Morgan Company with some New York banks. Under the final terms of the agreement, the duPont Company received 60 percent of the GM stock held by Durant while he retained 40 percent.

Morgan and Company received nothing but the satisfaction of being instrumental in saving GM and eventually getting their money back with interest.

In early 1971, John Coleman, a lawyer, came into my office while I was research director of the investment firm William C. Roney and Company in Detroit, Michigan. The Roney Company had been one of the 40 correspondent firms of the old Hayden, Stone Company. We of Hayden, Stone sold our assets to C.B.W.L. (Cogan, Berlind, Wyle, Levitt) on Friday, September 10, 1970 just a few minutes before Hayden, Stone would have declared bankruptcy. C.B.W.L., incidentally, has grown into today's Shearson-Lehman/American Express.

Mr. Coleman commissioned me then to do a study for the Internal Revenue Service which was contesting the low evaluation of GM stock declared by Christiana Corporation, one of the duPont related companies. The Christina Corporation had been ordered by the U.S. district court to divest itself of the combined 23 percent holding of General Motors stock.

The Roneys and I worked approximately one month steadily on the project ending up with more than 90 pages of text and tables and with a specific valuation of the am stock on the distribution date. I concluded that the $10 million investment by duPont, plus credit, actually saved General Motors in the 1920's. I also concluded that the market for GM stock was strong enough that it could easily absorb the Christiana divestiture without major damage to other holders of the GM stock.

The IRS needed to know what the "expert opinion" market value was. I concluded that GM was worth its most recent 12 month earnings multiplied by a figure derived by subtracting two from the prevailing price-earning ratio of the Dow-Jones Industrials. This formula generally yielded a reasonable market value.

After my study was received by the Justice Department, Mr. Coleman, acting for the IRS, called and questioned me at length about whether I knew Dr. S. Friendly, head the Warden School of Business in Philadelphia, Pennsylvania. Dr. Friendly had also been engaged by the IRS to make an independent appraisal. Our separate figure for the GM stock price on distribution day was within 25 cents of each other. I was able to assure John Coleman that I did not have the privilege of ever meeting Dr. Friendly.   I assume that he believed me.

On November 30, 1920, William C. Durant finally resigned. GM directors quickly elected Pierre duPont as president on an interim basis since he was most reluctant to serve. However, his "interim" term lasted two and one-half years during which GM grew and prospered as a direct result of his business acumen. In this success, he was assisted by the short duration of the post-World War I recession.

Another helping hand for General Motors at this time came from the dictatorial type of management practiced by Henry Ford. He was driving away many of the outstanding men he had developed in his organization. In this manner, Norval Hawkins came to General Motors. He had been the author of the Ford sales organization which was then capable of distributing three-quarters of a million cars annually.

In another display of poor judgment, the Ford Motor Company fired William S. Knudsen who had built most of the Ford assembly plants in the U.S. and Europe. Pierre duPont was a business executive of remarkable luck and skill. During his short tenure at GM, he provided the Corporation with men of such caliber as Sloan, Haskell, Kettering, Raskob, Hawkins, Knudsen and many other promising young executives. With Sloan as the driving force, duPont also established the General Motors operational philosophy which successfully carried it into the 1980s. Mr. Sloan's method of management included eight very important ingredients: facts, an open mind, courage, equity, confidence, loyalty, search for progress, and hard work. None was more important than the others.

Alfred P. Sloan, Jr. became GM's president in 1923, and Pierre duPont eventually became the Chairman of the Board. William S. Knudsen became the head of the Chevrolet division. Under his leadership Chevrolet provided Ford with some excellent competition in the low-price field, finally surpassing Ford when the Tin Lizzie faltered. The fierce competition between Ford and Chevrolet continues into the late 1980s and, amazingly enough, they annually remain too close for anyone to predict the victor in either passenger car or truck sales.

General Motors and Ford continued throughout the decade as the two giants in the industry out-producing the rest of the manufacturers combined. Both were now international businesses. Ford established manufacturing subsidiaries in Europe before and during World War I. General Motors purchased British Vauxhall and the German Opel companies. Chrysler, at this point, was far behind the two leaders but definitely ahead of the rest of the field. As of 1928, Durant Motors, William C. Durant's third effort at an automotive empire was ostensibly the fourth power in the industry. However, Durant Motors was in trouble even before prosperity ended.

Next down the ladder, sharing about a fifth of the market, were the combined efforts of Hudson, Nash, Packard, Willys-Overland and Studebaker. Finally, behind these, struggling for the remaining ten percent of the market was an assortment of smaller manufacturers. Some of these smaller companies produced some fine automobiles. Among these were Reo, Peerless, Franklin and Hupmobile. Another was the twelve and sixteen cylinder Marmon; a splendidly designed vehicle which matched the Rolls-Royce in luxury and smoothness. Still another was the boat-tailed Stutz whose "Bearcat", along with raccoon coats, became the symbol of the Jazz Age.

There were still other small manufacturers. The Auburn Automobile Company was a small producer of high priced cars that came under the control of Errett Lobban Cord in 1924. Simultaneously, he also acquired the Duesenberg Motor Company. The Duesenberg was a huge automobile equipped with a straight-eight engine and four-wheel hydraulic brakes. Erret Cord decided to produce an additional vehicle which would bear his name. The Cord was technically innovative with a front-engine, front-drive configuration which was expensive to build and service and about six decades ahead of its time.

The outlook for small producers of passenger cars going into the end of the decade was bleak. This was mainly because of competition with the higher volume manufacturers. Between 1923 and 1927, after the little and before the big depression, the number of automotive producers decreased from 108 to 44. Casualties included such other historic names as Haynes and Winton, which went back to the birth of the industry. Small survivors with the best prospects were firms such as White, Autocar, Mack, Fageol and Twin Coach Company which had chosen to concentrate on trucks.

As with other aspects of the economic life in the United States, 1929 was the turning point for the automotive history. Production that year reached 5,337,087 units. This was a record for that time and one which would not be matched for several decades. Then came Black Thursday, October 24, 1929. With the stock market crash the Great Depression began. It was to have a profound effect on the United States, its inhabitants, and the rest of the world as well.

CHAPTER NINE

CRASH/DEPRESSION

Your system was liable to periodical
convulsions...business crises at
intervals of five to ten years, which
wrecked the industries of the nation.
- Edward Bellamy

Black Thursday, October 24, 1929, was the day on which the stock market crashed. In actuality, this was only the catalyst which led to the Great Depression and all its ramifications. Theories abound as to the reasons for the crash. Basically it was caused by an inexplicable loss of confidence in the market which precipitated panic selling. In fact, several days after the crash, on Black Tuesday, October 29 the ticker tape signed off for the evening announcing a total sales of 16,383,700 shares, a volume which represented a loss in share value on Wall Street alone of some $10 billion, more than twice the value of currency in circulation in the United States at that time.

Eventually, the stock market losses in the period of the crash were placed at $50 billion which, in 1929, was a mind-boggling figure.

The stock market crash influenced, to varying degrees, the entire world. Germany was strongly affected. Germany had its own economic crisis which had started earlier. The loss of aid and investment from the United States forced the German crisis to quicken its pace. Unemployment grew, banks began to fai, and, because of this, the fortunes of Adolph Hitler prospered. Indirectly, the crash aided and abetted the circumstances which eventually led to World War II.

Other European nations were affected to different degrees. France, for the most part, ignored the crash and, in fact, benefited, because it now attracted the floating world capital which would have otherwise gone to Wall Street. Italy took notice of the U.S. problems but carried on with almost no effect. Holland's stock exchange, however, suffered the same fate as its New York counterpart. Switzerland, as always, stood neutral and financially as solid as a rock. Belgium suffered a slight decline in its own market. Spain displayed, at first, no interest in the crash but, soon thereafter, Spain's gross national product declined when deprived of foreign investments, and this was followed by political instability and the seeds of a revolution grew into a civil war.

The 1929 crash reverberated instantly in the halls of the London Stock Exchange and brought about unsettled conditions. Stock values declined; lending money values increased. Credit became more difficult to obtain. Unemployment began to rise.

New Zealand experienced no ill effects. South Africa was of the opinion that the U.S. got what it deserved. However, Australia's economy depended strongly on exports to the U.S. and on Wall Street loans. When both decreased, Australia headed into its own version of the Depression. India salvaged what it could from Wall Street and reinvested on the Shanghai stock market.

The stock market crash had an immediate effect on Canadian shares being traded on the New York Exchange. These collapsed, as did the American stocks on the Toronto and Montreal Exchanges. The consequences were not immediately catastrophic, but Canada depended heavily on export to its southern neighbor and to Europe. True to Murphy's Law, a drought in the prairies in 1929 reduced Canada's wheat crop by fifty percent. This put Canada was on its way to a recession of its own.

Domestically, the effects of the crash on individuals and on companies ranged from totally devastating and suicide provoking to "who cares". As an example, one of the most active, respected and well-known financiers of that era was James J. Riordan. Among other involvements he was president of the New York County Trust Company and a major investor in the Radio Corporation of America. On Friday, November 8, 1929, he sat in a chair, placed a revolver to his head and pulled the trigger.

James J. Riordan had been a Roman Catholic, and his death created a dilemma for the Catholic Church. The Church followed the dogma that suicide victims could not be buried by the Church unless there were unusual and extenuating circumstances. New York Bishop John Dunn conducted an inquiry into the matter and ruled that Riordan had taken his life while in a state of "mental aberration caused by his own losses in Wall Street and the losses of his friends for which he perhaps felt a moral responsibility." James Riordan's suicide was one of many, since it is now estimated that at least one million investors became instant paupers.

GM's William C. Durant was badly battered by the stock market crash. A large portion of his savings went, perhaps as much as $40 million. He even commandeered his wife's trust fund, some 187,000 shares of GM stock, reinvested on Wall Street, and promptly lost it. His final attempt at a comeback in the automotive industry ended in 1933 when the sluggish Durant Motor Car Company failed. In 1935, Durant opened up a grocery market in Asbury Park, New Jersey, lived an almost hand-to-mouth existence and was even reduced to sweeping and mopping his own floors. He made a last effort at big-time by opening up a bowling alley in Flint, Michigan which was to be a forerunner of a chain of high-class establishments. That never happened. In 1942, he suffered a stroke and lived the remainder of his life confined to a wheelchair. On March 18, 1947, he died, at age 85. Meanwhile, the crash had no immediate effect on Henry Ford I and his company. In fact, Ford was of the opinion that Wall

Street and the crash deserved each other, a short-sighted viewpoint.

The weeks following the crash saw a steady decline in freight loadings, steel production and automotive manufacturing. Bank deposits shrank and many banks were faced with a sudden surge of depositors who were desperate to withdraw cash. Some banks were forced to close their doors. There was then no insurance on deposits, and the withdrawal panic had a tendency to snowball. There were long lines at the bank doors, and many more banks failed. Finally, on March 3, 1933, President Herbert Hoover's last day in office, the country's entire banking system failed. Will Rogers, the era's popular homespun philosopher, remarked, "We are the first nation in the history of the world to go to the poor house in an automobile."

The government made efforts to restore confidence. The federal income tax was reduced and public works projects were increased to provide work for the army of unemployed. However, the numbers of workless grew faster than the government could put people to work. President Hoover called Henry Ford I to the White House to ask him if he could offer any help. Ford promised to raise wages from $6 to $7 per day even though, at that point, the automotive market was nearing the point of saturation. New cars were simply beyond the reach of most people. Even used cars were unaffordable. Lots were jammed with vehicles no one could buy. Many cars were not being driven because their owners could not afford the gasoline. Gold flowed out of the country. Speak-easy and blind pig prices fell. By December, 1929, retail stores were reporting a 50 percent drop in the sale of radios and other items not in the category of necessities.

Into 1930, some very unusual measures for economizing were being put into effect throughout the country. Some newspapers disconnected their electric clocks to save on electricity. Bethlehem Steel laid off some six thousand employees, evicted them from company houses, then tore the houses down to save on property taxes. Hilton hotel rooms were being offered at rates below cost. Entire floors of hotels were closed to save heat. Telephones were removed from guest rooms to save the fifteen cents per month rental fee. Stationery was doled out sheet by sheet.

Former financiers and executives were selling apples and pencils in the streets. Soup kitchens flourished. Movie houses were giving out free dishes and holding money drawings. The economy forced the introduction of a limited barter system. One could see a movie in exchange for canned goods, frankfurters or foot ointment. A popular Midwest newspaper would accept payments of ten bushels of wheat for a year's subscription, eighteen bushels for two years. Newsboys hated collection days.

Fuel economy was never more important than during 1932, the bottom of the Great Depression. My father, Isaac Jouppi, was the county road maintenance supervisor. His "county" or "company" car was a Whippet. We were not allowed to use the car for family business, but, occasionally, Father would use it to take us to the Lutheran Church in Kaleva, Michigan.

Father kept meticulous records on the costs per mile of that automobile. Gasoline then sold at 16 cents per gallon, and oil was about 15 cents per quart. Numbers have always fascinated me. I remember, almost as if it were yesterday, the cost of my father's operation of the Whippet. It was 2.62 cents per mile, including the original cost of the vehicle. Today, that cost is in the vicinity of 40 cents per mile, even with the great strides made in the direction of fuel efficiency.

There did not exist, at that time, an inexpensive, permanent type of anti-freeze. Father used alcohol in the cooling system, but there was a tendency for it to evaporate and boil out of the water with which it was mixed. When the level got low, he would have to drain out the ineffective mixture at night so the engine would not freeze up. In the morning, he had to heat a teakettle of water over the wood stove to fill the radiator, because unheated water was likely to freeze before the engine started. He'd have to do the same thing whenever the car was parked for any extended period of time until he managed to buy more alcohol. He even placed cardboard in front of the radiator grille to retain heat when he thought he could get away with it. Even so, sometimes the radiator would freeze while he stopped to examine maintenance projects around the county.

I remember Nass Myers, who once came in and asked me to check the oil in his ragtop Model-T Ford. The Model-Ts then had a long vertical oil tube, with a petcock at either end. To check for oil you first tried the upper level petcock. If oil flowed from there, all was fine. If none was evident at the upper level, then one tried the lower level. If some flowed it was still safe, but more oil could be added. If there was none flowing from either petcock, the engine was in dire need of oil.

The oil in the Myers' car flowed from the bottom petcock, but not from the top, so we had a happy discussion. I put a quart of oil into his crankcase to bring up the level, and away he drove. In three or four days, he came to see my brother John and said, "My car is without oil." John looked at the engine and discovered that I had neglected to close the upper petcock and thus allowed all of the oil to escape. He took the engine apart, replaced the bearings, pistons and valves and returned the automobile to Nass. That was my first disaster in the automobile industry, but far from the last.

The Great Depression however, was not the worst thing that happened to the automotive industry. Looking at it from the viewpoint of the market itself, the early automobile industry reached a high point in 1929. Then came Black Thursday, and from that day in October of 1929 until December of 1932, the auto industry suffered only its second worst downturn. The worst period for the auto industry, in terms of loss of sales and duration, came from March of 1979 through June of 1982. That was a 39-month slide. The slide down from Black Thursday was only 37 months in length.

In November of 1932, with the nation in the midst of the Great Depression, Franklin Delano Roosevelt was elected president, succeeding Herbert Hoover who was being blamed for the nation's ills. The automotive sales rose in November, right after the election. There seemed to be a renaissance of the national spirit, shared by both the Democrats and Republicans even though the Republicans were not to put one of their own into the White House again until 1952.

Auto sales increased in 1933 as compared to 1932 and continued strong until 1938 when there was another recession. This downturn in auto sales was an enigma at the time; in fact, there was a demand for cars but not an ability to buy. This 1938 recession in auto sales did not repeat itself until 1958, when economists and automotive people were saying, "This is just like 1938." In 1938, we must remember that the U.A.W. had already been formed, and there were some major fears that the union organizing events of 1936 and 1937 would seriously hurt the auto industry. America, toward the end of 1938 began to prosper as a noncombatant supplier for France and England during the beginnings of World War II. Detroit began building cars in large volume once again until 1942 when all production stopped and Detroit turned to the production of war materials.

The 1930's were a great testing period for the American automotive industry. Ford Motor Company was coming on very strongly with the Model-A. Walter P. Chrysler was introducing the Plymouth and DeSoto. In spite of the depression, there was much due largely to the competition that was taking place between the Big Three. Alfred P. Sloan Jr. was of the opinion that GM should no longer be content as merely Ford's major competitor, but rather should strive to be number one. Chrysler Corporation, while noting Sloan's successful efforts, adopted a policy of not trying to match either GM or Ford, dollar for dollar. Chrysler tried to produce and merchandise automobiles that were perceived to be more valuable, and thereby charged approximately five to ten percent more for an equivalent unit. Chrysler Corporation also brought forth the Airflow DeSoto in 1936. This car became the pattern for many automobiles of the future, as increasing speeds made aerodynamics an important consideration in automotive design.

By November 1985, Ford Motor Company had carried this concept to the ultimate in its Ford Taurus and Mercury Sable models by designing the door windows flush with the door metal rather than at the center of the door thickness, an innovation which created very serious technical problems for Ford. This brought into competition two supplier companies, one in France and the other in Cleveland, Ohio. In this case, Cleveland and the Standard Products Company, headed by James S. Reid, Jr., won the contract. James Reid Sr. was a surgeon who became an inventor after World War I and founded one of the early pioneer automotive suppliers, which eventually became the Standard Products Division.

When I first arrived on Wall Street, there were those who spoke of the harsh times during the Great Depression. One of my later Wall Street mentors, William C. Roney, formed his own company in 1925. Chrysler Corporation was formed also in 1925. In that era, less than a million shares a day were traded on the market. By the late 1980's, volumes of 100 million a day were common.

People like Kenneth A. Ward, the father of Wall Street stock charting with whom I worked at Hayden, Stone, told of how graduates of Yale University would shine their shoes, put on spats and go to visit the country banks selling bonds. People who survived in the financial district in the 1930's became the giants of the industry in the 1950's and 1960s. They included such people as Gerald M. Loeb, one of the three founders of E.F. Hutton Company; Pierre Bretey, who became such a great railroad analyst that he was the chief witness for mergers and consolidations in the railroad industry in the 1960's. Many felt N.L. Jarvis was the shrewdest trader of them all at that time.

Another financier, who came along somewhat later was David B. Stone. David followed in the footsteps of his grandfather Galen Stone, who founded Hayden, Stone in 1875. David B. Stone was very interested in the ocean and became deeply involved in the Woods Hole activity. In 1985, the Woods Hole activity was instrumental in discovering the whereabouts of the sunken Titanic. A product of the late depression era, David was born rich but continued to work in Wall Street with great humility and force until he left to manage the family interests in 1968. After he left, Hayden, Stone Company, for reasons other than David Stone's departure, went into a decline from which it never recovered. David Stone started out managing only his own family estate. By 1985, he was managing 22 of the family's major estates, and fortunes for 21 other families, largely in the East.

Ford's success in the Depression era or, more precisely, lack of failure during this period, was due principally to past performance. The company was an excellent example of how really big business can absorb an unbelievable degree of mismanagement. Henry Ford I had become an aging dictator whose subordinates were in constant conflict with one other. He hired Harry Bennett, a former prizefighter, to be his executive officer. Some Ford executives found that their employment was terminated when they were locked out of their offices and found their belongings thrown out in the street.

Ford bitterly opposed unionization. This eroded his popularity with the masses. He became, at times, unreasonable and insisted on seemingly unprofitable ventures. For instance, he purchased the Fordson tractor manufacturing facilities. The venture eventually became profitable but was still expensive to Ford due to patent claims arising from the casual nature of Henry's agreement with Henry G. Ferguson, the tractor's designer.

The one bright new Ford development of that era was the first V-8 engine installed in a low-priced car .Innovations in foundry techniques allowed for casting of the entire block and crankcase as a single unit. This kept costs low enough to permit installation in a low-priced car. The Ford V-8 could match the speed of most other cars it met on the highway and temporarily put Ford back ahead of Chevrolet in sales in 1932. Ford's competitive position versus GM began to decline once again the following year. This downward spiral continued into the 1950's when Ford dropped for a time to third place in total sales, behind Chrysler Corporation.

The Chrysler Corporation during the Great Depression was a bona-fide success story. During the worst period, it was operating at only forty percent of capacity, but careful management kept the company healthy and it actually improved its market position. Chrysler introduced many important technical innovations during these recession years and established the deserved reputation of producing a well-engineered car. Walter P. Chrysler retired in 1935 with the company on solid footing. He died in 1940.

General Motors saw its fortunes decline during the Great Depression but had financial planning and management of sufficient horsepower to prevent a repetition of the crises of 1910 and 1921. GM even managed to expand into new areas, such as diesel engines.

The diesel engine had been a viable force since its development by Rudolph Diesel in 1892. Despite its high thermal efficiency, the diesel engine inherently called for a very high weight-to-power ratio. It required rugged and heavy construction to withstand the extremely high compression forces. To a degree, that is still true in the 1980's.

In the 1930's, diesel engines, because of their mass, could not be installed in cars or trucks and were mainly confined to stationary applications and for use on various ships. The weight problem was being researched not only by General Motors, but also by the Winton Engine Company and the Electro-Motive Corporation. The latter company was attempting to combine diesel power with electric drive for railroad use. General Motors, at the urging of Charles Kettering, bought both companies and made extensive progress in diesel engines.

To reduce the unit weight, Kettering pioneered the two-cycle diesel engine. This version was immediately accepted by the railroads. It proved so efficient that it eventually displaced the steam-driven iron horse. Further engineering refinements adapted diesel engines to highway tractor and bus use, but widespread acceptance in this area did not materialize until after World War II. In the 1980's almost one hundred percent of over-the-road highway hauling is accomplished by diesel power, most of it four-cycle.

The second major venture of General Motors during the Great Depression era was entry into the manufacture of aircraft engines. Among other aviation properties, GM, in 1929, purchased the Allison Engineering Company in a relatively minor transaction, involving only $592,000. Allison was a machine shop which had first specialized in racing cars and then moved to the manufacture of bearings for aircraft engines. During the early 1930's, GM and Allison turned to the design and manufacture of in-line, liquid-cooled aircraft engines. With the coming of World War II, GM's Allison division was expanded to become a major producer of aircraft engines. Today the division also includes diesel engines, turbine engines and large automatic transmissions.

Alfred P. Sloan, Jr. resigned as GM's president in 1937, but continued on as chairman of the board. William S. Knudsen became president but served only four years before being drafted by Washington to take charge of the U.S. war production effort. By 1937, General Motors controlled forty percent of total domestic vehicle annual sales and thirty five percent of worldwide vehicle output. It was also building refrigerators, diesel-powered locomotives and aircraft engines.

GM's domestic automotive offerings at this time included Cadillac; a cheaper Cadillac called the LaSalle, Buick, Oldsmobile, Pontiac (which had replaced Oakland) and Chevrolet. GM also had established GMC, the division which produced various sized trucks and buses. The Chevrolet division also manufactured light-duty trucks. This is essentially the same GM organization which has carried on into the 1980's, with the exception of the now discontinued LaSalle. During this period, General Motors established the overseas division which produced the Vauxhall in England and the Opel in Germany.

Thus General Motors weathered the Great Depression to become the world's largest privately-owned manufacturing empire, the largest the world had ever seen. The duPont force then owned about twenty-three percent of General Motors. However, this was not an individual ownership, but included the duPont Company and duPont family members.

The Great Depression was also an era when the first generation of the automotive "giants" was being replaced by a new wave of candidates. Henry Ford I seemed unable to adjust to new realities. Charles W. Nash and Ransom E. Olds gave up the presidencies of their companies; William C. Durant went broke; and death took Roy D. Chapin, Hiram Percy Maxim, John N. Willys, Henry M. Leland and Alexander Winton. These men were the pioneers, the people who began with a blank piece of paper. They were giants, but their successors are also giants in their own right and have proven capable of maintaining the automotive industry as a major economic force, not only nationally, but also on a worldwide basis.

CHAPTER TEN

DEPRESSION/WORLD WAR II

Great emergencies and crises show us
how much greater our vital resources are
than we had supposed.
-William James

The automotive Big Three weathered the stock market crash, the collapse of the banking system, and the Great Depression without any permanent scars. However, the same cannot be said for the individuals of the labor force and their families. After the crash, unemployment rose to seven million. At the height of the depression, there were thirteen million workers without work, or approximately forty percent of the labor force. Even by 1937, when the economy was ostensibly on the upturn there were still ten million without work.

Many of the unemployed became homeless. Some slept on park benches. Others rode the subways all night where they were at least reasonably warm and could get some sleep, however fitful. The night travelers washed up in train stations and then embarked in search of a breadline where one could get, perhaps, some coffee and doughnuts. As noon approached, the new poor would get into the breadline for lunch, repeat the process for supper and then seek a place to sleep. The words, and later the song, "Brother, can you spare a dime?" became the symbol of the era.

The Great Depression continued unabated, to varying degrees, throughout most of the 1930's. President Franklin Delano Roosevelt took office on the day after the collapse of the U.S. banking system and quickly implemented the various aspects of his New Deal platform designed to curb the staggering rise in unemployment. His National Recovery Act (NRA) was a measure designed to increase jobs and thereby buying power and required employers to pay higher wages for shorter hours. It drove up prices and profits, but with more people working it also created consumers. The Supreme Court eventually ruled the NRA an invalid experiment since it violated Constitutional Rights.

However, all of the combined efforts of the President and Congress were not enough to extricate the United States from the clutches of the Great Depression. It took World War II to do that.

Adolph Hitler rose to power in the German Republic at almost the same time President Roosevelt took office in the U.S. Hitler quickly began building military might for his own purposes while involving an unbelievably cruel anti-Jewish Nazi philosophy.

Italy, under the leadership of Benito Mussolini, also began to rattle its saber and in 1937 attacked and defeated Ethiopia. The United States immediately placed an embargo on Italian olives, and everyone was soon drinking olive-less martinis. Mussolini was to become a partner with Adolph Hitler, and their alliance became known as the Axis Powers.

Hitler occupied the Rhineland in 1936 and then annexed Austria in 1938. Czechoslovakia fell to Hitler in March of 1939. On September 1, 1939, Hitler invaded Poland. This precipitated World War II which for the next several years was confined to Europe. The United States maintained a policy of neutrality and isolationism until December 7, 1941, when the Japanese attacked the U.S. naval base at Pearl Harbor in the Hawaiian Islands. On December 8, President Roosevelt declared war on Japan. Shortly thereafter, Italy and Germany announced declarations of war against the United States. On December 11, 1941, Congress declared war against the Axis Powers, and the country was now involved in a conflict in two widely-scattered parts of the world. The U.S. at this point in history, was almost totally unprepared for war, and a large portion of its fleet was now at the bottom of the ocean, courtesy of the Japanese.

By this time, however, Detroit had a very strong production capability with high-volume automotive manufacturing and supplier plants. It quickly became the Arsenal of Democracy, the manufacture of cars and trucks being almost immediately suspended for the duration of the war. The 1941 models were the last to be made in substantial volume, although about 200,000 units were produced in 1942. The war ended in Europe on May 8, 1945, and on, September 2, 1945 Japan also surrendered. The automotive industry lingered in armament production only as long as necessary and Henry Ford II drove the first post-war Ford off the assembly line on July 3, 1945. However, the volume of cars produced in 1945 was quite low, and it was not until 1946 and later years that the industry fully recovered in the face of almost unbelievable pent-up demand: a demand compounded by the returning servicemen who had matured in the service, saved some money and now were anxious to get some wheels.

CHAPTER ELEVEN

WORLD WAR II/POST WAR PERIOD

We make war that we may live in peace.
-Aristotle

The automotive industry made some very important contributions to the war effort. First of all, it gave up large numbers of its young to military service. Thousands of engineers, technicians and other highly qualified young people volunteered for, or were conscripted into, the Army, Navy, Marines or Air Force. Many of them never came back.

Secondly, the automotive industry was able to convert its tremendous potential in high volume production, manufacturing facilities, and technical know-how to the war effort, with an invaluable savings in time and expense. Even though the United States was totally unprepared for war when it came, it quickly caught up to speed and eventually out-produced the Axis powers.

The automotive industry continued automotive production into 1942, even though materials were becoming scarce. Much raw material was, instead, going to our European Allies, since they were in such desperate straits. The automotive executives were being criticized by the U.S. public for using even the slightest amounts of valuable materials for making automobiles, but not as unreasonably as were the aircraft manufacturers. Before the U.S. declared war, the aircraft industry was called a warmonger for making any military aircraft at all. As soon as we were in war, they were being criticized by the same people for not making them in large enough numbers and quickly enough.

The automotive industry continued to make trucks, both for civilian and military use, producing about 2.5 million units for the war effort. Military vehicles, obviously, had special requirements but these were not too far removed from the domestic variety. Also produced were small numbers of automobiles, destined as staff and scout cars for the military. The remainder of involvement for the auto industry was into areas totally removed from its normal operations.

One of the better known automotive products manufactured during World War II was the military Jeep whose production continued, almost unchanged, into the mid-1980s. It was a four-wheel drive, four-cylinder, short wheelbase, general purpose vehicle, and from the abbreviation of G.P. came the name "Gee Pee" which was finally corrupted to "Jeep". The Jeep replaced the mules of World War I and became an indispensable workhorse, being used for every conceivable purpose. The Jeep was designed by Captain R.G. Howie of the United States Army. He was helped in the design by Arthur Herrington, a four-wheel drive expert, who was co-founder of the Marmon-Herrington Company, whose products included four-wheel drive automobiles.

The first Jeeps were built by the American Bantam Car Company, but demand quickly outpaced their capacity, and soon Willys-Overland and Ford were asked to help. With Willys as the major producer, almost 700,000 Jeeps were built for military use during the war. After the war, many were declared surplus and ended up being driven on dates by the same G.I.'s who drove them during the conflict in less pleasant circumstances.

The war department logically turned to William S. Knudsen and the automotive industry for help in building tanks; however, this turned out to be a much more complicated process than simply converting the automotive assembly lines. New factories had to be built, and the tanks designed, produced, assembled, and tested by men who had never seen a tank before. The first manufacturer to be approached was Chrysler, and a new plant was built in Warren, Michigan, just outside of Detroit. After groundbreaking in September 1942, tanks were rolling off the line the next September. Other manufacturers were drawn into tank production, but Chrysler remained the principal supplier, right up until the mid 1980's when the facility was sold to General Dynamics which, even today, produces tanks for the military.

The automotive industry was also venturing into areas where the products did not include some form of wheels and were not driven by gasoline or diesel powered engines. These products included artillery shells, gun mounts, machine guns, small arms ammunition, fire-control systems, anti-aircraft guns and other highly specialized military equipment never seen by civilians in peacetime.

Automotive manufacturers also took part in the production of naval military hardware. As an example, Packard engines were used in Patrol-Torpedo (PT) boats which were capable of speeds up to 85 miles per hour. But the most publicized, most controversial, and probably the most important contribution was the industry's quantity production of military aircraft, in spite of the proven facts that aircraft manufacture did not lend itself to high-volume production techniques and that the airframe and engine required a higher degree of precision than found in motor cars.

In spite of its inexperience, the automotive industry was called upon to join forces with the aircraft manufacturers to produce the 50,000 planes that President Roosevelt called for in the first year of mobilization. Henry Ford I quickly announced that he would have no trouble in producing a thousand identical planes per day if the government and the unions kept their noses out of his business.

The two factions entered into an uneasy alliance, each doubting the capabilities of the other, and, in the end, both succumbed to patriotism and worked together quite well. Initially Ford was asked to produce Rolls-Royce engines for the Royal Air Force. Ethel Ford and Charles E. Sorenson,

Henry Ford's production manager, approved, but Henry Ford's decision to make a moral stand for pacifism and isolationism surfaced at just this time and he would have nothing to do with the endeavor. So the Rolls-Royce engines were made by Packard. Later Ford relented and joined forces with General Motors to produce the radial Pratt and Whitney engines. GM was already producing Allison in-line engines for some aircraft.

The original assignment for the auto makers to produce engines soon had to be expanded to other aircraft components as well. A program was quickly put into practice whereby Ford would manufacture assemblies for the Consolidated B-24 Liberator bomber; General Motors would have a major function in the building of the North American B-25 bomber and the Grumman torpedo bomber; and Chrysler, Hudson, and Goodyear were to assist in building the Martin B-26 bomber. Final assembly, in most cases, was to be done by the respective aircraft manufacturers in plants built by the government.   Aircraft manufacture by the automotive industry was not a smooth transition with instantaneous results. Most manufacturers had problems to varying degrees, but none as serious as did Henry Ford I in his efforts or perhaps, more aptly, in his reluctant effort to build the B-24 Liberator bomber.

A large factory was being built by the government at Willow Run in Ypsilanti, Michigan, and Ford's lieutenant, Charles E. Sorensen, was in charge of the aircraft production operation. Sorenson envisioned the full utilization of mass production techniques, and, in that, generated all sorts of problems with the aircraft's designer, Consolidated, and its engineers. To Sorensen's credit, Consolidated eventually adopted many of his proposed techniques. Sorensen was adamant in his opinion that Consolidated knew nothing about mass production, and he was probably right. Conversely, Sorensen knew nothing about aircraft.

In addition to mass personality clashes, the operation in Ypsilanti, Michigan was soon plagued with material shortages. Reliable pipelines were yet to be established. Furthermore, Ford Motor Company was divided by internal struggles, especially between Sorensen and Ford's fair-haired boy, Harry Bennett. Henry Ford's unpredictable attitude about war and war material increased internal conflict as did the company's poor labor relations.

At one point, the Air Force was contemplating a recommendation to have the government nationalize "Will-It-Run" which would have pleased many left-wing advocates and even Walter P. Reuther, who was in favor of a joint venture for aircraft production which would include the government, the automotive manufacturers, the aircraft manufacturers and the UAW. This "Reuther Plan" found very little support and was never adopted. By late 1943 and in 1944, in spite of all these problems, Willow Run was producing Liberators at the rate of four or five hundred a month. This was a triumph for Sorensen's methods but he paid the price for the early failures. After forty years as a loyal employee, Henry Ford I dismissed him after the war. Sorensen then became president of Willys-Overland, but retired shortly thereafter.

All in all, the American industry very nearly met President Roosevelt's 50,000 units per year production quota with 47,000 aircraft in 1942. This number was surpassed in subsequent years. A grand total of over 250,000 units were compiled for the entire war effort.

The automobile industry has always had a fascination for airplanes. General Motors had, in its roots, a company which today is part of Rockwell-International. Ford produced the famous Tri-Motors and later made an effort to introduce a Flying Flivver. Chrysler, in 1985, became the owner of an aircraft company, the Gulfstream.

My own involvement with the automotive/aircraft aspects, on an intensive basis, began in World War II. I, as a member of the U.S. Marine Corps, became engrossed in an effort to find and photograph Japanese radar installations and then, working through the military system, to have them eliminated as being dangerous to our health. Toward the end of World War II, my commanding officer felt that I should receive the Distinguished Flying Cross for an episode I was involved in over the China Sea. Later I received Air Medals to account for thirty-five air missions over enemy territory.

Little did I know then that the airplane and the automobile industries would meet once again, in peace time, after World War II. During the war, it was all airplanes and no cars. Immediately after the war, it was cars and almost no airplanes but with one exception. General Motors had a plant in Kansas City which was known as the guns and butter facility. In one part, it produced automobiles and, in another, it continued to produce some airplanes, but not many, since there were very few government contracts to be had in the 1950's. The plant was under the direct supervision of John F. Gordon, a naval academy graduate, who later rose to the presidency of General Motors.

In 1986, I came upon a successor to the torpedo bombers which had flown so well in World War II. It was Grumman which joined General Motors in World War II to develop and build the torpedo bombers. These were labeled TBM's if built by General Motors and TBF's if produced by Grumman. They were almost identical, and both planes were outstanding workhorses, especially in the Pacific. They were equipped with folding wings and a tail hook for aircraft carrier operation.

Grumman evolved into the Gulfstream Aircraft Corporation, headquartered in Savannah, Georgia. It was purchased by Chrysler in 1985 for $681 million. Many of the older Gulfstream employees had come from Grumman. The purchase was due, at least in part, to a desire on the part of Lee Iacocca not to be upstaged by GM's Hughes Aircraft purchase early in 1985. General Motors paid slightly more than $5 billion. Lee Iacocca told a Savannah, Georgia group that Chrysler had also bid for Hughes but offered a more realistic amount which, in Iacocca's estimation, was $3 billion.

I had the opportunity to go through the Gulfstream plant in February of 1986. I was astonished at the high quality and slow pace at which airplanes were built. The production output of this plant is about 3.5 aircraft per month. Every detail of each plane is subjected to the most rigorous kind of testing. Each aircraft required seven thousand man-hours of labor at Gulfstream. These twin-engine jet powered aircraft are used for executive transportation. The price, in my view, is also astonishingly high. The Gulfstream IV which was, just then, in the late stages of development, would sell for $17 million each.

A small incident at the time of my visit to the Gulfstream plant concerned Lee Iacocca's involvement with Washington, D.C., with regard to the Statue of Liberty. He had been summarily dismissed as chairman of a committee which determined what should be done with the money being collected for the restoration of the statue. Lee Iacocca was also successful as a fund raiser for that project, but Washington claimed a conflict of interest and canned him. He resented the fact that he had been fired from a post which was basically honorary. In typical forthright Iacocca fashion, he graphically explained to a small group of us visiting automotive analysts the difference between Savannah and Washington. Holding aloft a large key, given to him by the mayor, he said, "See how nicely Savannah treats me? It gives me a key to the city. In Washington, all I got was the shaft."

Before the onset of World War II, and before the full commitment of the United States to the war effort, the automobile had permeated almost every aspect of American life. When Pearl Harbor brought the war to our doorstep, it was accompanied by the realization that the free-wheeling use of automobiles could not continue. Americans who were not joining the military began to be made aware of the fact that they could not jump into their car whenever they wanted and go wherever they chose. First of all, there was the need to conserve the machinery since new cars were not being made, and no one knew when, or even if, they would ever be made again. Secondly, materials necessary to keep an automobile in operation were becoming scarce. Spare parts were becoming difficult to obtain. Japan had invaded Malaya and the Netherlands Indies, cutting off almost our entire supply of rubber. Synthetic rubber was still on the drawing board. Thus, if the rubber wore out on the family flivver, new tires were not to be had. At one point, the government even considered the tires on the 35 million vehicles in the United States as a national rubber reserve, to be nationalized if necessary.

The rubber shortage was followed by a petroleum crisis. This crisis primarily affected the heavily industrialized parts of the country. Even then, the U.S. was not self-sufficient in petroleum production. We depended on imports, via tankers, to supply the Eastern seacoast areas. The German submarines took a heavy toll in oil tankers along the Atlantic seaboard, and even in the Gulf of Mexico. Will Rogers was once asked how he would deal with the German submarine problem. He told the questioners that he would boil the ocean. "How can that be done?" they asked. Will Rogers replied, "I'm giving you the overall solution. You have to work out the details on your own."

Despite the shortages of petroleum, rubber and replacement parts, it was important to keep the automobiles running. Americans had geared their lives to the motor vehicle. Now cars were needed for all sorts of normal, vital activities, such as getting to and from work. Additionally, the new plants to produce war material, for the sake of expediency, were often being built where there was not established housing or public transportation.

The government responded to the rubber shortage by establishing a national highway speed limit of forty miles per hour, later reduced to thirty-five.

Petroleum shortages were dealt with by establishing a rationing system, where the basic allotment for pleasure driving was two gallons per licensed driver per week. Larger rations were possible, depending on proof of urgent need and degree of involvement with the war effort.

The Midwest and West produced enough oil for their own needs. There was no real shortage in these areas. Only the Northeast, until then dependent on easily available imported oil, was experiencing shortages. The government demanded equity throughout the country. Even Texans, who owned oil wells, were given ration books. Eventually, there were more than 25 million gasoline ration books issued in the country. The system was rife with corruption and abuses, but there seemed to exist no alternative, and the approach did work to the desired degree.

After Pearl Harbor, the automotive industry became almost totally committed to the war effort. To expedite the transition, the Automotive Manufacturers Association was instrumental in the formation of the Automotive Council for War Production. Alvan Macauley, president of the AMA, and of Packard Motor Company, became chairman of the ACWP. George Romney, another AMA official, became the managing director. Romney later became the president of American Motors and, still later, the governor of the state of Michigan, with unsuccessful presidential aspirations. At war's end, the industry made the transition from swords back to plowshares more smoothly than anyone had reason to expect.

In the middle of the war Roosevelt campaigned for, and was elected to, his fourth term. The populace was not about to change horses in midstream, especially since things were finally beginning to go well for our side. However, Roosevelt did not live long enough to see peace. He had been afflicted, early in life, with infantile paralysis and did not have the full use of his legs at any time as President. Furthermore, he was otherwise in poor health, worn out by the length of his servitude, the extremely heavy burden of the country's problems and the awesome responsibilities of his office. He died shortly after his fourth inauguration, on April 12, 1945, of a massive cerebral hemorrhage. The war in Europe ended less than a month later on May 8, 1945. President Roosevelt was immediately succeeded by Vice-President Harry S. Truman, who became the thirty-third President of the United States.

The war with Japan continued unabated after the cessation of hostilities in Europe, but now the United States could concentrate on a single front. Huge fleets of B-29 bombers were taking a terrible toll on the Japanese mainland, and, on July 26, 1945, representatives of the United States, the United Kingdom and China met at Potsdam, in conquered Germany, and issued an ultimatum, the Potsdam Declaration, calling upon Japan for unconditional surrender. Japan quickly rejected this offer.

President Truman was left with one of the most overwhelming decisions that any individual human being has ever had to make. He ordered the use of the atomic bomb on Japan. The first was dropped over Hiroshima on August 6, 1945, destroying about sixty percent of the city, totally flattening an area of two and one-half miles in diameter which was located directly under the explosion, and eventually killing an estimated 140,000 Japanese. However, Japan still refused to capitulate. On August 9, a second atomic bomb was dropped on Nagasaki with similar destructive effects. Japan then quickly decided to accept the terms of the Potsdam Declaration on August 14, 1945, and the official surrender took place on the battleship U.S.S. Missouri on September 2, 1945.

President Truman was a feisty gentleman who never looked back or agonized over his decision to employ the atomic bomb. He is credited with the statement, "If you can't stand the heat, get out of the kitchen." Truman was of the opinion that the use of the atomic bomb actually resulted in a smaller loss of lives than would have occurred had the Allies invaded the Japanese mainland.

When the war ended with the surrender of Japan on August 14, 1945, so did gasoline rationing. The American public quickly demonstrated their system of priorities. Every community in the country became quickly littered with torn up gasoline ration books. Owners then quickly jumped into their jalopies, which were by then held together with baling wire, powered by rebuilt engines and rolling on re-treaded tires. They drove ecstatically to the dealers to add their names to the long lists of people ordering new cars. They were joined there by the millions of returning veterans who also wanted to buy automobiles, many for the first time. This was a strange era in which there was no used car less than four years old. Everyone wanted, and could afford, new cars. It was years before the assembly lines could catch up with the pent-up demand. Again, as after World War I, there were shortages of materials and interrupted supply lines. However, the prospects of the automotive business were unbelievably alluring and, for a time at least, the cars would sell themselves.

General Motors entered the new era with a new president, Charles E. Wilson, who had replaced William S. Knudsen. GM was in an excellent position to retain its leadership, having diversified products and excellent leadership. At this point in time, the Ford Motor Company seemed to be less endowed with capable leadership. In May, 1943, Edsel Ford, Henry Ford's son and president of the company, died. Company historians attributed his death to stomach cancer, undulant fever and a broken heart. The cancer followed a stomach ulcer. That, and the broken heart, were apparently caused by frustrations and the persecution at the hands of the elder Ford and his lieutenant, Harry Bennett.

The vacant presidency was taken over by Henry Ford I, then already eighty years old and the victim of two strokes. Fortunately, the government released Henry Ford II, Edsel's oldest son, from service in the U.S. Navy to assist in the management of the company. Henry II became vice-president in 1943 and quickly ran into the same antagonism from the elder Ford and Bennett as had his father, Edsel. But Henry Ford II was not going to be anyone's puppet, as he was later to prove to the world on numerous occasions.

Furthermore, the Ford women all became his allies. It took time and effort to wear down Henry Ford's reluctance to step down in favor of his grandson. However, pressured by all around him, with the exception of Bennett, he quit, on September 21, 1945; and Henry Ford II was elected the president of the Ford Motor Company with full authority to do as he wished. He fired Harry Bennett the very same day. Meanwhile Henry Ford I went into complete retirement. He died just two years later, bringing a sad end to a phenomenal career which had greatly affected the course of U.S. history.

Henry Ford II quickly found that the health of his company was worse than he had first anticipated. Ford Motor Company was losing money at about a $9 million-per-month rate. Henry knew that he needed help quickly. He decided on Ernst R. Breech who had been a GM executive and was now the president of the Bendix Aviation Corporation. Since he had also previously been president of North American Aviation, Breech had both automotive and aviation experience. He was reluctant to become associated with an apparent loser, but accepted the challenge of trying to rebuild the Ford Motor Company. He became its executive vice-president and later its president. Henry Ford II was very capable, but he was also very lucky. At that time, ten ex-Air Force officers wanted peacetime positions, but also wanted to be hired as a group. They ranged in age from twenty-six to thirty-four and, in the service, were involved in logistics as well as financial and statistical controls. The ten men applied en masse at the Ford Motor Company. They were immediately hired and became known as the Whiz Kids. They provided some high-level talent and eventually made good presidents and vice-presidents. One of them, Charles B. (Tex) Thornton, eventually left Ford and became the founder of the Litton Industries. Others included Robert S. McNamara and Arjay Miller.

After the War, I was torn between continuing an engineering career, into which the U.S. Marine Corps had launched me, and returning to the media. I undertook graduate studies at the Engineering School of the University of Detroit while also working the 2 to 10 p.m. shift at the Associated Press. It was then that I came to know Henry Ford II, but only peripherally. It was not until decades later that I felt I really got to know him more intimately.

Henry Ford II had taken control of the company early in 1947. At that time, a group of us writers were at the Ford Motor Company headquarters in Dearborn, Michigan for a 2 p.m. press conference at which Prince Iben Saud would meet with Henry Ford II. The Prince was intending to purchase some vehicles for Saudi Arabia. All had been readied for the two o'clock meeting. However, just as the hour approached, one of the Prince's entourage stepped forward, raised his arm and brought out the prayer rug. Soon every turbaned member of the Prince's party was kneeling on a rug, facing Mecca. Allah took precedence over Henry Ford II, over a press conference, or over any other business - a simple matter of priorities.

Chrysler, as GM, seemed to make the transition from wartime to peacetime without unusual problems. The management remained unchanged. K.T. Keller became president when Chrysler retired and remained in that position until 1950. Chrysler also continued as the country's leading producer of military tanks well into the 1980's.

The independent automotive producers after World War II included Hudson, Nash, Packard, Studebaker and Willys. The unprecedented, post-war seller's market was of great benefit to the independents, but only until the Big Three got into high gear, at which point the smaller independents were forced to abandon the low-price market entirely. Willys, with its civilian Jeep, was an exception.

The post-war automotive boom even lured some newcomers into the automotive realm. Henry J. Kaiser was a California businessman who acquired national prominence as a result of his wartime production performance, especially in merchant shipbuilding. During the war, he joined forces with Douglas W. Frazer, president of the Graham-Paige Motor Company, with the idea of producing motor vehicles when peace came. In 1945, they formed the Kaiser-Frazer Corporation and absorbed Graham-Paige a few months later. Manufacturing facilities were acquired by lease or purchase of idle government-owned facilities which had been built for war production. One of those plants was Willow Run, where Henry Ford I had such a difficult time getting the first Liberator bombers off the production line. Willow Run eventually ended up with General Motors.

The Kaiser-Frazer effort was destined for early success. All automobiles which were produced could be sold, at least until the post-War, bottled-up demand was eased. The first cars of Kaiser-Frazer were produced in 1947, and included a Kaiser line, a Frazer line and a small compact, the Henry J. They were extremely innovative automobiles, markedly different from the vehicles then being produced by the Big Three.

For a time, it appeared that the Kaiser-Frazer effort would represent the first successful entry into the automotive arena since Chrysler's in 1925, but reality soon came to the forefront. In 1948, the Kaiser-Frazer line accounted for five percent of domestic new car sales. However, within five years, all three models had disappeared from the scene. In 1953, Kaiser-Frazer became the Kaiser Motors Corporation which also included Willys-Overland. Several years later, Kaiser withdrew from the passenger car field entirely to concentrate on Jeeps and small commercial vehicles which were produced in Toledo, Ohio.

Several other manufacturers made a run at the post-war automotive sweepstakes. One was Preston Tucker, a Chicago businessman, who was ready to produce an extremely innovative, rear-engined automobile with sports car styling, tentatively called the Torpedo. Tucker ran into financial disaster and went out of business after producing a small number of his cars which are, today, mostly in museums.

Another effort involved a very small car produced by the Crosley Corporation, manufacturers of radio and television equipment. This was a lightweight car with a four-cylinder engine. It was originally introduced in 1939 but did not have time to take a reasonable share of the market before the war stopped production. The Crosley survived until 1952 when the company was bought by General Tire and Rubber. The Crosley car at this point was discontinued. Had it been brought to the market ten or fifteen years later, when people were turning to compacts, it undoubtedly would have been a success. As with the 1934 Chrysler Airflow, the Crosley was just too far ahead of its time.

The first post-war automobiles gradually going into production at the manufacturing facilities of the Big Three were almost totally carried over from the pre-war design. There was no time for major changes, except perhaps for changed grilles. The same old dies were pulled out of storage, dusted off, and production was begun. The independents also began producing almost the same vehicles that had been produced immediately before automotive manufacture ceased for the duration. The one exception was Studebaker, which was the first manufacturer to get back into full-scale operation with an entirely new product. One of Studebaker's new models was the Starlight Coupe which had a rear window which resembled a windshield. It appeared double-ended, and was soon accused of not knowing whether it was coming or going.

General Motors and Ford brought out all-new models in all their lines in 1949. The GM offering included the Rocket engine for the Oldsmobile line. This was a high-compression V-8 engine developed by Charles F. Kettering which was the forerunner of the engine design used into the late 1970's. This was also the year in which the Cadillac began to develop tailfins which were to grow to larger proportions in subsequent redesigns.

In 1949, the industry's output reached more than five million automobiles and one million other units which included trucks. This finally surpassed the production record set in 1929, and it was once again possible for a buyer to approach a dealer and buy whatever kind of automobile and equipment he or she desired.

In 1950, automotive and truck production surpassed eight million units, but war clouds again gathered over the United States when North Korea invaded South Korea. Once again, U.S. military forces and military supplies were required in large numbers thousands of miles away. The automotive manufacturers began to carefully monitor the situation, trying to remember the conversion efforts and procedures of ten years earlier. Many lives again were lost, but automobile production and automobile use continued unrestrained.

CHAPTER TWELVE

THE 1950-1954 ERA

Peace, peace is what I seek, and public
calm endless extinction of unhappy hates.
- Matthew Arnold

The decade of the 1950's, in its early stages, did not produce any great changes in American automotive design. A sellers' market continued to exist, as the automotive industry was satisfying the pent-up demand created by World War II. Manufacturers were very reluctant to invest time, effort and money into automotive redesign and improvement, especially in view of the fact that they were selling every vehicle that they could possibly produce. Furthermore, the Korean War at that time brought about only a minor industrial interruption, and the slight curtailment of civilian production was hardly noticed by anyone. However, the automotive industry was rapidly becoming an oligopoly which included, as members, only General Motors, Ford and Chrysler. The independents, despite the high demand for cars, were finding it more and more difficult to compete and consequently sought refuge in mergers.

In 1954 Nash-Kelvinator and Hudson combined their individual assets and formed the American Motors Corporation, which still exists into the late 1980's, and all manufacturing operations were concentrated at one plant, located in Kenosha, Wisconsin. In 1950, Nash-Kelvinator had acquired as the general manager, a man who served successfully as manager of the Automotive Council for War Production, George Romney. When American Motors was formed, Romney became its president. He was well aware of the fact that he could not compete head on, model for model, with the Big Three, so he gambled on the idea that a market existed for a smaller, lower priced car than what General

Motors, Ford and Chrysler were then offering. The name "Rambler" was revived. The Rambler became the principal product, while both Nash and Hudson vehicles were discontinued in 1957. The entire endeavor passed through some critical years, never did seem to gain full vital health and strength, and even in the late 1980's, AMC seems to be absorbing losses year after year.

Also in 1954, two other independents, Studebaker and Packard, combined forces as the Studebaker-Packard Corporation. However, this time the merger of two weak automotive producers did not result in a stronger entity. Packard never had been a large-scale producer and always concentrated on the luxury car market. In the 1950's, Packard began competing poorly as a prestige vehicle against GM's Cadillac. In 1956, the Packard plant in Detroit was closed. All its production was transferred to the Studebaker facility in South Bend, Indiana. In 1958, Packard closed its doors. Studebaker alone continued until 1964, when it discontinued U.S. operations and moved to Hamilton, Ontario, in Canada and, shortly thereafter, into oblivion. From then until today, the automobile industry consists of the Big Three, General Motors, Chrysler and Ford with their various lines, and of struggling American Motors. Every now and then, some optimistic American entrepreneur enters the automotive arena, struggles mightily for a time and then disappears. Some stay to produce specialty cars in low volume. Included are such makes as the Avanti, the Bricklin and the ill-fated DeLorean. In the 1980's, established foreign manufacturers such as Volkswagen, Toyota and Mazda began building plants for their products in the U.S. These found greater measures of success.

The truck production industry was undergoing similar birth and consolidation efforts. The established members of the Big Three were also involved in the manufacture and sale of trucks of all weight categories. White Motor Company was an independent truck producer. In 1953, White's expansion efforts included the acquisition of Autocar, another independent truck company. In 1957 Reo was established and Diamond T was started in 1958. Other well-known firms in the 1980's, such as Kenworth and Peterbilt, entered the serious market at a later date. Further reorganizations and consolidations continued well into the 1980s.

The early 1950s also represented a strangely liberal period. Automobiles continued to be in high demand until later in the decade when the market reached a point of saturation. Manufacturers were all concentrating on higher production techniques and put little effort into engineering efforts or expense on product research, development and improvement. Consequently, the vehicles of the early 1950s were not much more sophisticated than were the pre-war versions. Very little was being done in the areas of safety, reliability and economy, especially compared to today's emphasis on these aspects. As an example, in Michigan and in other states, there was absolutely no speed limit on the county and state roads outside of urban areas. I remember, on many an occasion, driving to work at the GM Technical Center in Warren, Michigan, at speeds well over 100 miles per hour, as fast as the car would go. This was also on two-lane roads, since expressways did not yet exist, and I did this without collapsible steering columns, seat belts, shoulder belts or air bags. This was not wise, but I don't think that unusual at the time.

Another incomprehensible detail by today's standards existed at the General Motors Building in Detroit, Michigan and, I assume, at other office buildings in the country. The GM Building was then the epitome of decorum and conservativeness but any employee who wanted one was issued a spittoon, also known as gaboon or cuspidor. The brass pots stood by individual desks on large diameter rubber mats to accommodate expectorate near hits. Full misses were frowned upon. The issuance of a spittoon also included full nightly service.

The late 1940's and early 1950's were not distinguished by any spectacular or even interesting developments in automotive design. That is not to say, however, that the manufacturers were not preparing for the immediate and the long-term future. General Motors, for example, on July 24, 1945, announced plans for a great new Technical Center to be erected in the city of Warren, on the outskirts of Detroit. The Center was intended to consolidate the research efforts which were, heretofore, scattered among the various divisions. The plan was to minimize uplication of effort. This was a very ambitious project at that time and was conceived as a way of assuring, in the post-war years, continuing progress in research, engineering and design. The objective was not only improving the quality of the product, but also improving the overall standard of living for the public.

Work on the first buildings at the center got underway in 1949. The last of the 25 originally planned structures was completed in 1955. The final landscaping was accomplished in the spring of 1956. When completed and fully staffed, the Technical Center comprised the functions of Research, Manufacturing Development, Engineering Staff and Styling, later to become known as Design Staff. To the credit of the Technical Center's original concept and design, it must be stated that it was intended to be a showcase for the industry in 1956, and, for more than three decades, it has maintained its leadership qualities. Updated physical plants and functions remain a showcase even in the late 1980's.

In 1954, Anthony G. DeLorenzo was a rising vice president at General Motors. He had come from the Kudner Advertising Agency to General Motors, having first attracted the attention of Harlow H. Curtice, who was vice president and general manager of the Buick Division.

Tony was a very imaginative and innovative public relations person, who followed Paul Garrett. Paul, in his time, had been brought into General Motors and the automotive industry by Alfred P. Sloan, Jr. from the New York Journal of Commerce where he had been a financial writer. It was Alfred P. Sloan, Jr. who decided that GM plants and products would have to be better understood by the public in order for GM to succeed. Paul Garrett, in my opinion, was the true founder of the public consciousness of the automobile companies which he pioneered at General Motors. GM became the pattern for both Chrysler Corporation and Ford Motor Company in dealing with the public on matters apart from selling automobiles.

The automobile industry in the early 1950s was in need of massive capital expenditures. The pre-World War II plants were already obsolete. In the reconstruction period from 1946 through 1952, the industry had little time, or even inclination, for spending substantial amounts in modernizing and improving the plants. It was in this period that Charles E. Wilson, GM president, made the remark (we're referring here to the post-war period prior to 1950) that General Motors was selling cars to its dealers in the same manner as if they were charging $8 for $10 bills. Dealers were able to make immense amounts of money for each car that they were able to sell because there was such a demand and shortage of automobiles.

Tony DeLorenzo was responsible for some important public relations activity in the bottom of the 1954 recession. General Motors, at that time, was feeling its power, and Tony noted that GM was going to spend $1 million for capital investment and tooling. That kind of investment was extremely major in 1954. A typical DeLorenzo inspired headline was, "GM bets $1 billion, no recession." But, in 1954, as in later years, the auto industry too often became the victim of a recession rather than being instrumental in holding it back, or turning it around.

In 1954, Tony also sparked the move of General Motors into a marriage of the Electro-Motive and the earth moving

Terex operations with the automotive divisions and inspired an event which took place at Soldier Field in Chicago, Illinois. It was called Powerama and was intended to dramatize power equipment. One of the individual performances was to have the earth moving equipment of General Motors emulate dancing girls on an immense stage, or field in front of a stage. The crawler tractors did the Rumba, which was a popular dance at that time.

Early in the 1950's, Charles E. Wilson was the president of General Motors and Albert Bradley was the chairman of the board. However, President Eisenhower nominated Wilson as Secretary of Defense. When the Senate committee was investigating his qualifications for service in a national post, he told the Senators, as stated earlier in Chapter four, that the country and General Motors would each benefit from the other's windfalls. Those words may have appeared pompous but they did contain a large element of truth. This is especially true, in essence, for a country whose well-being, historically, depends largely on the well-being of its industrial community. Charles E. Wilson was accepted by the Senate and replaced as president of General Motors by Harlow H. Curtice. Albert Bradley continued as the chairman.

John Campbell was then the principal administrator in the research laboratories of General Motors. He was extremely interested in education. He assigned me to head up the educational relations activities of General Motors in 1955. My job was to enhance contacts with all of the major universities and colleges in the United States. Earlier, General Motors, through Kenneth A. Meade, then director of educational relations, had developed extremely good relationships with the engineering schools of more than thirty of the major universities. One of Kenneth's tools was a summer conference for engineering educators. One engineering professor from each of the schools was invited to come to Detroit, Michigan, with all expenses paid, for a two-week seminar. The professors were requested to study General Motors and to visit a specific division. At the end of each conference, the professors would gather their ideas and make a presentation to General Motors executives for their guidance, giving them whatever insights they had gathered from the meetings. Much later, I came to realize that the services which the professors performed for GM were of far greater value than the expense accounts which they accumulated during their stay. Here was the best brainpower that any company could have hired. It was available to GM for the cost of the educators' travel, room and board – a smart move.

In 1952, the year when I first joined General Motors, William Shockley invented the transistor or semiconductor, and this device of the Bell Laboratories revolutionized the electronic industry. Vacuum tubes became passé and, by the late 1980's, there was an international race for the super-chip. Chips became capable of storing and making connections with hundreds of thousands of bits of information.

I was, at that time, editor of the General Motors Engineering Journal, which was a bimonthly publication of highly technical papers. In one of my assignments, I had the pleasure of working with Bertram A. Schwarz, the Chief Engineer of Delco Radio. He had been most familiar with vacuum tubes and became fascinated with the transistor patent which he studied carefully. He even telephoned Shockley on several occasions to discuss it. Schwartz then developed a paper for the Engineering Journal on the very promising future of transistors. I had become aware of high technology advances while employed at Sperry Gyroscope, before joining GM, and I felt that GM was concentrating too much energy and resources on iron and not enough on electronics. It was not until the 1980s that GM made a serious effort to become a leader in electronics. It was indeed that desire which led to the acquisition of Electronic Data Systems and later of Hughes Aircraft Company.

John F. Gordon influenced my thinking greatly as I labored on the Engineering Journal. He was an executive vice president of General Motors Corporation when I met him in his fourteenth floor office. Jack was on the advisory board of the Journal. I had just been brought in from the Engineering Division of Sperry Corporation in 1952 right after I had taken part in the successful campaign for the presidency of Dwight D. Eisenhower.

Before meeting Jack, I had imagined that all of the General Motors' vice presidents were from some other world – untouchable by someone merely from an engineering laboratory. Not so! Jack urged me to get to know as many of the General Motors executives, engineers, and facilities as I could. He especially wanted me to study GM's guns and butter plant in Kansas City where military airplanes and cars were being built at the same facility. He had been involved in General Motors tank building during World War II and then later headed Cadillac Motor Car Division.

Jack's main lesson to me was: "Don't get too bogged down in the details, but let the Journal act as an integrator, pulling together the many facets of General Motors and making the whole mean something to society." And I had been led to believe that all General Motors really cared about was money!

Jack and I got along handsomely. Much later he, called me to his office to discuss a technical paper on transmissions which I had asked him to review. The papers published were first read for technical accuracy and then for appropriateness by a member of the advisory board, each of whom was a vice president.

In this visit, he was very brief. "This paper is not very good, do we really need it?" "No." With that, he dropped it in the waste basket. I had a difficult time explaining to the author of that paper what had happened and why his paper was deleted from the Engineering Journal.

GM did not concentrate exclusively on automotive and truck transportation. Richard M. Dilworth came to my attention in June of 1955 when he was issued a patent for a cooling and ventilating system for diesel electric locomotives. Specifically, the patent had to do with the control of exhaust fans and air intake shutters for regulating the circulation-of cooling air through the cab and engine compartment of that type of locomotive.

Mr. Dilworth, who was then retired, had served for a quarter century as chief engineer of Electro-Motive Corporation which later became a GM Division. Richard had virtually no formal education, which was typical of most automotive pioneers; yet, he became a chief electrician in the U.S. Navy, serving before World War I. Later, in civilian life, he rose from a construction machinist to engineer with General Electric where he took part in the development of gasoline/electric rail cars. He also worked on various electric power projects in the Philippines. In 1926, he became chief engineer of Electro-Motive Corporation, where he directed the application of an internal combustion engine to train propulsion until his retirement in 1955.

Dilworth was an unsung hero of sorts. If it were not for him, it is entirely possible that the steam powered locomotive would not have been replaced by the highly efficient diesel engine. Diesel power eventually became the mainstay of railroad and truck freight hauling in the U.S.A. and in other countries as well. If General Motors had not become known as a car company, it probably would have been known as the company which transformed the rails from coal to diesel through its Electro-Motive Division, which it had purchased in 1930 on the recommendation of Charles F. Kettering.

In the early 1950s, the Ford Motor Company, with Henry Ford II as president, continued making steady progress. The Ford car, annually, staged a furious sales race with the Chevrolet Division of General Motors, with Chevrolet usually finishing first. GM held a secure hold on almost one half of the total domestic market and sometimes more, but Ford remained a strong second, and maintains this position into the late 1980s. The Ford stock did not go public until late in the 1950s. Prior to that time, there was no chairman of the board, and Henry Ford II remained the company's top officer.

Of the Big Three, Chrysler Corporation experienced the greatest difficulty in maintaining its share of the market. There existed no tangible reason for this condition since Chrysler also was offering models which were basically pre-war in design, as were Ford and General Motors. Chrysler models also covered the entire range of customer preference. An indicator of trouble, however, was the fact that the Plymouth nameplate, in the 1950's, lost its usual third place sales position behind Chevrolet and Ford.

The decade began for Chrysler with the able K.T. Keller as president. In the fall of 1950, he moved up to Chairman of the Board, with Lester Lum (Tex) Colbert assuming the presidency. However, the changing of the guard did not bring about wholesale management changes. The one major executive move was the appointment of Virgil Exner as the chief stylist. Exner had trained under Harley Earl of GM and was hired specifically to alter the overall Chrysler line appearance which had become known as the "three-box styling". This implied that one box was used for the front end, a bigger, higher box for the passenger compartment, and a smaller box for the trunk and rear end. Exner soon teamed with Ghia of Italy to produce some spectacular prototype or show cars which rivaled those being built by GM. Exner quickly and totally redesigned the 1953 Dodge and Plymouth lines. In 1954, Chrysler also began offering its first fully automatic transmission, Powerflite, as an option in all its lines.

Several other occurrences distinguished this period for the Chrysler Corporation. The first was the opening of the Chrysler Corporation Proving Ground, a 4,000 acre facility at Chelsea, Michigan. The second was the $250 million, borrowed from the Prudential Insurance Company, which permitted Chrysler not only to purchase Briggs

Manufacturing Company, but also to finance its all-new 1955 line of cars.

In 1962, now as a Chrysler employee, I was squiring Monroe Chappelear, one of the East's most famous financiers, through some Chrysler Corporation facilities. Monroe was one of the three people in the Prudential Life Insurance Company of America, the Rock, who had brought forth in the early 1950's the $250 million, 3.5 percent, one-hundred year loan, which was at the very base of changing Chrysler Corporation from a loser to a winner. The first loan installment of $62.5 million was delivered on June 30, 1953. Each year thereafter, in 1954, 1955 and 1956, Chrysler received the additional $62.5 million, for a total of a quarter billion dollars, a very large loan in those times.

In the 1950's, the entire automobile arena changed from a catch up effort of the lost production during World War II to innovative cars, such as the compact cars which were brought forth at the end of that decade. It was the Prudential loan to Chrysler Corporation that dramatized the need for capital. Chrysler Corporation, in August of 1952, was having its automotive bodies produced and delivered by Briggs Manufacturing Company, which then came upon irresolvable labor problems. Chrysler Corporation, until now, had simply demanded delivery without regard for supplier difficulties. Chrysler finally decided to buy Briggs Manufacturing Company. With the $37 million purchase, however, Chrysler also inherited the labor problems which they, themselves, had helped create by imposing unreasonable delivery schedules. Labor at that time was riding the crest of its strength and it proved extremely difficult for Chrysler Corporation to develop competitive labor contracts with the union. Indeed, it was not until the Lee Iacocca era of Chrysler Corporation's history that the matter of proper competitive balance was struck among General Motors, Ford and Chrysler, with respect to the degree of union representation in the workplace.

As General Motors was going through its major capital expenditures programs, Chrysler Corporation was figuring on how to wisely spend the rest of the quarter billion dollars it had borrowed from Prudential Insurance. Chrysler had begun losing its share of the market to General Motors after the period of government enforced steel allocation had expired in 1952. Prior to that time, Chrysler Corporation had been able to get steel, which was in short supply, because of a steel allocation policy based on the military requirements during and prior to World War II. In fact, the Chrysler Corporation was getting enough steel to produce more than its share of the market, even though it had done very little to upgrade the design of its cars; but after automobiles became much more available, and the steel quota was lifted, Chrysler Corporation began losing ground.

These factors created a great personal opportunity for me later in 1961. Chrysler Corporation felt that, since I was getting along well with Monroe Chappelear and others at Prudential, I should be assigned to New York. I was soon transferred there and my primary assignment, not written into any job description, was to keep the Prudential creditors so well-informed about Chrysler that Monroe and others would not think more ill of Chrysler than the facts would bear.

All in all, the period of time from the early to mid-1950s was very unspectacular for the automotive industry, but it was also a very important period and well established the hierarchy. During this period, the pipeline of post-war pent-up demand for cars was filled and stepping stones were laid for spectacular progress in the decades to come.

CHAPTER THIRTEEN

THE 1955-1959 ERA

Progress is a comfortable disease.
- Edward Estlin Cummings

The second half of the decade of the 1950's was one of the most important eras in the history of the automotive industry. It marked the time that the market finally returned into the hands of the buyer and, thereby, forced the automotive manufacturers into product improvements, product refinements, and even innovation. In 1955, every member of the Big Three spent huge amounts of tooling money to bring out extensively restyled and redesigned models throughout the various lines.

General Motors came out with products which featured all-new styling, the principle feature of which was the curved, wrap-around windshield. GM promoted this as a great aid to side vision but, in truth, its outstanding positive point was that it appeared stylish to the American public. Difficulty of manufacture and sealing problems were also part of this innovation. GM also introduced revised engine line-ups, including the first V-8 for the Chevrolet Division since the ill-fated, air-cooled version of 1919. Automatic transmissions, air conditioning, power brakes and power steering were now available in all lines.

1955 also saw the introduction of completely redesigned light and medium-duty General Motors trucks. The market willingly accepted these new offerings and this led not only to a record year for General Motors, but for the entire industry as well. Yet GM was not to rest on its laurels. A completely new line was introduced in 1958 and again in 1959 when huge, winged leviathans became the styling theme.

In 1958, air suspension was introduced in passenger cars but was plagued by problems and high costs, with no apparent benefit to the customer. The system was discontinued after several years. Customers were chagrined to walk out and find their suspensions flat with the car's chassis almost resting on the ground. Air suspension has its merits and is being used in the 1980's on tractors and trailers which carry delicate loads. Air suspension probably has a place in the cars of the future.

In 1957, GM introduced fuel-injected engines but this feature lasted only a short time. Fuel injection was expensive and about thirty years ahead of its time. In 1955, Chevrolet brought out a V-8 engine for its two-year old fiberglass-bodied Corvette which made it more popular than ever.

GM, in this period, also decided to diversify and strengthen its sources of engineering talent. Before the Russian space satellite, Sputnik, in 1958, the Chairman of GM, Alfred P. Bradley, came to the conclusion that GM would need to expand the origins of its engineers beyond the reaches of General Motors Institute, which then provided seventy percent of GM's engineers, and beyond the Purdue-Michigan State axis, which produced the rest of the company's technical talent. By 1952, when I arrived at General Motors from Sperry Engineering, GM had become regarded as a mid-western engineering organization and was determined to change that image, to reach engineering schools all over the country and not rely so heavily upon the General Motors Institute.

When Roger B. Smith became chairman in 1981, General Motors Institute was finally moved into the private sector; and GM began to look for its engineering and scientific talent far and wide in earnest.

In 1955 I had an unusual assignment in assisting David Wagoner of the personnel departments in interviewing candidates for engineering and business administration at General Motors. In one interview session at the University of

Michigan, I found across from me a former member of the Japanese Imperial Air Force who had helped install the first basic radar systems on Japanese "Betty" bombers. He was astonished to learn that ten years earlier, in 1945, I had been aware of this project. He was on the island of Rabaul in January and February of 1945 and had been installing these radar systems. The sophisticated listening equipment which my Marine unit was using had detected this soon after the "Betty" bombers started flying with the new radar systems..

This gentleman from Japan had heard of U.S. technology being in the forefront of Japanese electronic science, so he asked to come to the University of Michigan. When he graduated, he decided to stay in the United States rather than return to his homeland.   Many other foreign students remained after graduation.   In the case of Japan, many students did return. They, along with graduates of Japanese universities, successfully made Japan into an industrial giant and a thorn in the side of our domestic automotive industry.

During this period, the Ford Motor Company also came forth with some dramatic new products. In 1955, a production record of nine million vehicles was established which was not exceeded again until the 1960s. Historically the months of July, August and September, were low sales periods for the automotive industry since the plants were shut down to begin work on vehicles for the new model year, but in 1955 car sales stayed up very strongly. A young man was just making his mark in Philadelphia for Ford Motor Company as a zone sales manager. His name was Lee Iacocca and, in 1956, he kept his sales at a high level in the Philadelphia region because he took the unprecedented step of challenging the styling department of Ford Motor Company and adding a silver stripe on the cars after they were delivered in his zone. These cars became known as the Philadelphia Fords. Customers came from as far away as New York City to buy that particular automobile. The Philadelphia Ford caused Lee Iacocca to be noticed by Henry Ford II who had seen a listing of the sales figures which were lower for all of the zones except Lee Iacocca's. Iacocca's sales were holding to the 1955 rate, and Henry Ford II asked, "Why?" As far as I have been able to determine, that was when Henry Ford II began to consider that Lee Iacocca might have a brilliant future as executive in the automotive industry. Henry Ford II, who first noticed Lee Iacocca, also helped him to develop his career right up to the point he fired him in 1978.

The Ford Motor Company, in 1955, brought out a completely new line of cars. The Ford offerings included the Thunderbird, introduced late in 1954. It was a steel-bodied two-seater, equipped with a 4785 cc. engine which became, for a time, even more popular than the Chevrolet Corvette. The Ford models included the hardtop line which featured a deep accent molding across the roof, making the car look like an Easter basket. A little later Ford introduced the Sunliner, featuring an extremely complicated metal roof which folded in sections and stored itself in the trunk, all automatically. In 1956, the Lincoln Continental Mark III was introduced, carrying an extremely high price tag for that period, just under $10,000. In 1958, Ford introduced the Edsel, along with completely restyled Ford models.

In the case of the Edsel, Ford had conducted a market survey which indicated that there was intense interest in a car which would be placed between the Lincoln and the Mercury. The result was a $250 million investment in the Edsel, a well-engineered but strangely styled vehicle which quickly became the subject of derogatory names and jokes. Introduced in 1958, the Edsel lasted only two years.

The Chrysler Corporation did not stand idly by but also introduced a completely restyled line of cars. Chryslers designs continued to be somewhat boxy. They could not compete with GM or Ford in appearance even though

Chrysler's engineering was as good or better. One of Chrysler's styling highlights was the availability of three-toning on some Dodge models.

Chrysler advertised its 1955 models as the "Forward Look", but this was only a prelude, and the actual forward-looking models did not arrive until 1957.

In 1956 Chrysler introduced the 3008 model equipped with a 300 cubic inch V-8 which delivered 340 base horsepower and 355 horsepower optionally. This Chrysler could be equipped with various axle ratios, including one of 6.17 to 1, which must have given that vehicle an acceleration capability from 0 to 60 miles per hour somewhere in the neighborhood of five seconds. Needless to say, it dominated NASCAR racing.

This vehicle could also be equipped with something called Highway Hi-Fi, a distant relative to the tape players in the 1980's. It was actually a record player which accepted special disks, about the size of the 45 rpm variety but which played at 16 and 2/3 rpm. The tone arm was designed to stay in the groove but was less than satisfactory over rough roads. GM and Ford had their own versions of the record players with an equal lack of success. Other strange options included a vacuum ash tray which emptied itself at the touch of a button into a reservoir under the hood.

In 1957 Chrysler's Virgil Exner brought out tailfins, which were an immediate success. There was even a claim made for aerodynamic qualities where the tailfins supposedly aided vehicle stability at speeds over 60 to 70 miles per hour. Torsion bar suspensions were also introduced on Chrysler models, with advertising claims made for a softer, smoother ride. At the same time, Packard brought out torsion bars which linked both the front and rear suspensions.

Chrysler was also responsible for the introduction of the compound curve windshield which went GM one better. Chrysler did well in this era until 1959 when GM also brought out some incredibly exotic fins which seemed to attract that portion of the buying public which bought cars on the strength of this feature. The entire industry, however, was suffering from shrinkage in the middle-priced field which included the Ford's Mercury, GM's Olds, Pontiac, Buick, and Chrysler's Dodge, DeSoto and lower-priced Chrysler. This loss of consumer interest in this area, coupled with bad timing of introduction, and their appearance quickly killed the Edsel line of cars.

In the early 1950s, I began hearing of a Wall Street financial analyst coming to Detroit, Michigan. This took place at General Motors when a particular analyst from Massachusetts Financial Services, named Harrison Condon, befriended Richard Gerstenberg, the GM chairman of the board. Condon and Gerstenberg had a special relationship which was the forerunner, in my view, of friendships between and among executives of car companies and Wall Streeters.

The belief developed in the early 1950s that the auto industry would continue to grow at a very rapid rate. However, in 1952, when the steel rationing ended, the automotive market became very competitive. The market reached its climax in 1955 when there was a great race between Ford Motor Company and General Motors, a race heightened by the fact that both GM and Ford had now brought forth new V-8 engines. General Motors, because it owned the GM Acceptance Corporation, was the first to come forth with thirty-six month time payments on automobiles, and Ford managed to follow suit. The combination of the still lingering shortage of cars caused by World War II, the availability of extraordinary new automobiles, including not only the V-8 engine but, for the first time, air-conditioning in volume, and the extended payments, created a peak in car sales in 1955.

In 1955, Chrysler Corporation was far behind General Motors in styling but not, by consensus, in engineering.

General Motors was bringing forth highly-styled, smooth vehicles, lower in overall height than the Chrysler products. Chrysler Corporation, at that time, was dominated by K.T. Keller. Walter P. Chrysler had much earlier set the size standard for his automobiles when he insisted that all Chrysler vehicles have enough headroom to permit him to go to the New York Opera without having his opera hat touch the ceiling. This Chrysler feeling that the cars should be tall became very costly in 1955 because General Motors and Ford beat Chrysler badly in the marketplace, but K.T. Keller refused to alter Chrysler's criteria.

In the race for styling leadership, Virgil Exner made a mark in the Chrysler Corporation. In 1955, the high box design was still prevalent, but he quietly began developing what became the 1957 car. In late 1956, Virgil Exner's low-slung automobile with tailfins captured the imagination of the motoring public, and, even though Chrysler Corporation was not able to get the leaks out of the doors, that car sold very well in 1957. Indeed, Chrysler Corporation captured nineteen percent of the market that year, and General Motors moved from a forty-nine percent share of the market back down to forty-two percent.

General Motors acted as a leader should. They accepted the defeat by immediately massing its engineers and stylists under Harley Earl and came forth in the early 1960's with styling leadership. Harley Earl was to GM design and styling what Eliji Saarinen and his son, Eero, were to appearance of the General Motors Technical Center. Harley was the role model for most automotive stylists of the period, from the 1930's into the 1950s. Indeed, he pioneered the field.

By 1986, stylists had as much encouragement as Harley Earl had in the 1930s. In the early automobiles, the main styling note was Henry Ford's "you can have it any color, as long as it's black." Utility engineering was king. But in 1928, Alfred P. Sloan, Jr. came to the conclusion that styling appeal could sell automobiles and he was instrumental in bringing in Harley Earl to restyle the General Motors fleet of cars.

Harley's first assignment was to make the 1929 Buick attractive. The size of this vehicle was such that it became derisively known as the pregnant Buickby the competition.

In 1986 stylists again had an opportunity to show their prowess. From 1975 to 1985, engineers had consumed most of the available product money, and generic Detroit had done a superb job in meeting the Rachid-Down MPG requirement of the 1975 energy act. By 1986, stylists again had money to spend, and they spent it well.

At Chrysler Corporation, in the early 1960s, the analysts were seeing a brilliant vice president and economist, William Flaherty, who was fond of saying that Chrysler Corporation may have made a mistake in challenging General Motors so vigorously with the 1957 tailfins. He expressed that opinion to the analysts I was bringing into his office. While employed at Chrysler, I functioned as host to the Wall Street financial community, along with Robert H. Savage who was the director of investor relations at the time. I was also writing the annual report, writing material for the Chrysler fact book and generally gathering facts and figures that would be used by others in speeches and presentations.

William Flaherty mentioned that in an oligopoly, such as existed in the automotive industry among General Motors, Ford and Chrysler, it behooved numbers two and three to be very careful about challenging number one in any aspect, because if number one was embarrassed in any way in the market place, it would come back at the smaller member of the family of oligopolists in the same manner as a big brother might bring the back of his hand across the cheek of a recalcitrant small brother. Chrysler Corporation happened to be the small brother; and, indeed, General Motors had seized the styling leadership.

Much later in the history of the automobile industry, Lynn A. Townsend, Chrysler chairman, who recalled the comeback of General Motors in 1961, was telling Wall Street analysts that Chrysler Corporation would never again move very far from General Motors' styling leadership. This attitude hurt Chrysler in later years, because their vehicles became known as "me-too" automobiles, and, as a result, the corporation suffered loss of sales. This was indeed a factor in the company's failure in 1978 when John Riccardo, then chairman, went hat-in-hand to Washington and triggered the famous Chrysler Corporation Loan Guarantee Act which brought Chrysler Corporation and Lee Iacocca to the forefront of the auto industry in 1980.

During this period of time, General Motors also had problems with the judiciary arm of the United States government. The Supreme Court of the country decided in 1958, after prolonged study and contemplation, that the Dupont Company must divest itself of all GM holdings, which then amounted to about twenty-three percent of the outstanding stock or some 63 million shares. The decision was made based on a section of the Clayton Act of 1914 prohibiting stock holdings which might restrict competition.

The Dupont Company was the pioneer and principal producer of quick-drying automotive finishes, and the Court decided that this could cause a problem. Several obvious realities carried absolutely no weight with the judges. The first was that Dupont saved GM from bankruptcy and thereby GM, the industry and the entire country owed them a debt of gratitude. Secondly, there existed not even a suggestion that Dupont had ever exercised any improper influence over GM in their former alliance. And, thirdly, Dupont was the biggest and best producer of automotive paints. As such, it would have held a preferential business position with any automobile manufacturer regardless of its financial holdings. Nevertheless, the majority of the court held that Dupont's interest in GM might give it a preferential position in the sale of automotive finishes.

This decision produced all sorts of problems. A sale of 63 million shares would produce reverberations on Wall Street, regardless of who the participants were. In addition, this stock was acquired about forty years before this order to sell. There existed a monumental and critical capital gains liability which could have been disastrous to Dupont, regardless of how large and wealthy it was. A proposal that the stock be placed in a non-voting trust was rejected by the court. Finally, a special Act of Congress was required to minimize the capital-gains liability and made possible the stock sale without debilitating losses. By 1964, the stock was all sold, and the courts were satisfied. Whatever capital-gains were involved fell upon the shoulders of the Dupont stockholders. General Motors and its stockholders were totally unaffected. During this period, the Ford Motor Company was also involved in some dealings which were not directly related to the design and sale of automobiles. The Ford Foundation, in 1956, had decided that it was unwise to have its entire enormous resources represented by common stock in the Ford Motor Company. They recommended that some of its stock be offered for sale to the public so that the Foundation could diversify its own holdings. The Ford Foundation had originally been formed in 1936 to avoid the possibility of the Ford family losing control of the company because of death and inheritance taxes. The wisdom of this move was seen shortly after the deaths of Henry Ford I and his son, Edsel. The Foundation then came into the possession of ninety percent of the Ford stock, becoming the world's largest private philanthropic organization.

The problem with the stock was that it was non-voting. The Foundation depended on Ford management for its well-being but had absolutely no control over the choices or decisions. Ultimately, this led to the Ford family's decision not to have all the eggs in one basket. A huge transaction such as this requires some delicate legal and financial maneuvers. First of all, the stock had to be reclassified so that the future stockholders would have a voice in the company affairs, however small. It was also imperative that the Ford family not lose the proper controlling interest.

When the stock went on sale, it was quickly gobbled-up by Wall Street. Brokerage houses were swamped with orders for the available ten million shares, which were first offered at $64.50 but quickly went as high as $70.00 per share. Subsequent offerings left the Ford Foundation with fifty percent of the total, individual Ford family members with eleven percent and the public with thirty-nine percent. Ford was still clearly in charge, and the Foundation now had pocket money for other endeavors.

The 1950s marked the beginning of the era that equated vehicle size with quality and prestige. This concept carried forward into the 1960s but was tempered, somewhat, in the 1970s and 1980s. In the 1950s and beyond the lower-priced smaller cars became bigger and more ostentatious so the higher-priced, larger cars had no choice but to become even bigger and gaudier. This almost amounted to reverse snobbery and propelled the Volkswagen Beetle to sales records. The automobile was becoming almost an extension of the ego of its owner.

The late years of the 1950's also saw the beginnings of the foreign car influx. In 1957, the imports of foreign cars amounted to 700,000 units, or about ten percent of domestic production. Almost half of the total was the Volkswagen Beetle. The United Kingdom ranked next, followed by France, Sweden and Italy. Japan also exported a few automobiles to the United States but was, at this point, still gearing up for the onslaught of future years. The compacts were coming, but the behemoths continued to hold a large portion of the American buying public. This was destined to continue into the 1990's.

The 1955 to 1960 period was as important to the automobile industry as the 1985 to 1990 era has now become. The first period brought forth product innovation and a degree of uncertainty about the size of future cars. The second period brings forth the same concerns about major progress in the manufacture of automobiles. Let it be said that the late 1950s was the era of the car itself. The late 1980s have become an era of the factory.

By 1955, the automotive pipeline to the American consumer had saturated the market. In 1956 automotive sales fell off, and, by 1958, the U.S. was experiencing a very serious recession. Recessions everywhere else in the nation become depressions in the automobile industry. When sales fall off, the easiest thing for the public officials, the media and the Wall Street financial analysts to do is to criticize the product.

Byron Nichols, vice president of sales at Chrysler Corporation, during that period said that when car sales are good people would say it was the triumph of the dealers, when perhaps it was the triumph of the engineers and of the cars themselves. "When car sales were bad," Byron said, "people would claim that it was because the product was so bad that the dealers could not sell it."

There was seldom a middle ground. The 1955-1960 period was one of product unrest. The Volkswagen Beetle was emerging as the new Model-T of the 1950s. It was Al Morris who told me how the GM annual report should be written. He said that it should be directed to all of the stockholders. He drew a large circle on a legal pad. Then he smiled at me and made a small dot in its center with his pencil. He said that one had to say something in the report that would be meaningful to the smallest stockholder; someone who might hold only five shares and might be concerned mainly about the condition of the front steps of his house. General Motors was the same as a house, only the front steps might be the factory in Flint. It had to be good and strong. Then Morris defined the dot in the center of the circle. "The dot," he said, "was Albert Bradley and Harlow Curtice. They were the ones who truly had to be pleased with the annual report for they were the ones who signed it." The circle, of course, represented the total number of individual stockholders.

In the 1958 annual GM report, which covered the 1957 period, Albert Bradley, chairman, had to make the decision whether to import one of the smaller General Motors cars from Europe to combat the VW. The decision needed to be made in time for the news to get into the annual report because there was unhappiness among the stockholders. General Motors was building cars that were too large, according to the critics, who included President Eisenhower.

Imports, especially VW, were taking an increasing share of the domestic market. Much of the criticism came from the East. It must be remembered that this period was not too far removed in time from Treblinka, Birkenau, Auschwitz and the Holocaust.   Resentment remained in many quarters against anything that had roots with Adolph Hitler. In that period, I recall seeing in our own neighborhood a five-year old boy spit on a Volkswagen. He said, simply, "Nazi car."

I had the freedom of the fourteenth floor, the executive stronghold of the GM building, for getting approvals for the various sections of the annual report. At one point, I found Albert Bradley in one of the sleeping rooms on the executive floor. These rooms were reserved primarily for the New York based GM officials who arrived late, or for others who may have worked late. They were sort of a hotel or motel substitute.

The paragraph concerning the importation of the Vauxhall had been written by William H. Trenn, who later became an expert on living conditions in all of the countries in which GM sent its domestic employees. My job simply was to learn Albert Bradley's opinion as to whether or not the Vauxhall paragraph should go into the annual report.

I have felt that the small car age began in the sleeping room on the fourteenth floor, as Albert Bradley put his right leg into his GM blue trousers. It was at that point he said, "Let us bring in the Vauxhall." As a GM lower echelon employee, I may have been the very first to hear that decision spoken out loud at a time when where there was great doubt among the members of the GM hierarchy whether GM should abandon the more profitable high end of the market and go after the VW. The decision was then made to go after the Volkswagen. The Vauxhall, was to be brought into the country to be sold by the Buick dealers as the first step into that market.

We hurriedly obtained a photograph of the Vauxhall car and published it in the annual report. Unfortunately, the photographer had made the vehicle look almost as big as a Cadillac because that was the GM thought process of that time. Bigger was better. Later, a stockholder wrote and criticized the photograph which made this small car look like those which George Romney, by then, was calling "gas guzzling monsters". I had to write the reply to the discerning stockholder. I assured the lady that the Vauxhall was indeed a small car, and that GM would support it in the marketplace. Soon General Motors brought forth the Corvair, Ford the Falcon, and Chrysler the Valiant.

Over the years, I became a bridge between the automotive industry and Wall Street and between Wall Street and the industry. Each land seemed foreign to the other. I cannot think of any more qualified mentor than someone who had crossed the automotive/financial bridge before me. He was Robert H. Savage.

Bob came from a Wall Street house to Chrysler Corporation. Earlier, he had been a reporter on the Wall Street Journal. In late 1957, Bob persuaded me to move from GM to the Chrysler Corporation. As a hired gun, I had drafted much of the 1957 annual report text to stockholders at General Motors under J.A. "Al" Morris who had been a confidante to

Alfred P. Sloan, Jr., and now was very close to retirement. I bridled a bit under the stern General Motors policy that employees could not talk to stockholders or to Wall Street officials. At that time, of course, there was no one at General Motors specifically tasked for such work, and, although I wrote reports and letters to and for stockholders and Wall Streeters, I was not permitted to talk to them.

GM, until 1986, de facto had a rule that the Corporation was not to have the close communications with Wall Street that were prevalent not only within Ford and Chrysler, but within almost all other industries. Until 1986, GM was the most introverted of all the companies in the Fortune 500. In April of 1986, General Motors, at last, opened its doors wide to financial analysts, a change which was too long in coming. Back in 1957, Chrysler Corporation actually employed a Wall Street analyst to represent the company and that man was Robert H. Savage, my mentor. I worked with him from late 1957 through 1962. Thus I first drafted the GM Annual Report, and then went to work for Chrysler where my first task was to draft the 1957 Chrysler Annual Report.

Robert Savage had a seemingly brash New York approach to communicating with the senior managers of Chrysler Corporation, and, after having experienced the disciplined and methodical GM pace, I was rather astonished to find, at Chrysler, rather harsh exchanges of viewpoints in staff meetings. Robert knew Wall Street, but he also came to know Chrysler quite well. Once, in the middle of a sentence in his office at 10:30 in the morning, he got up and walked out. He said simply, "I'll be back." All through the rest of that day and until noon of the next, I kept telling callers that Robert was out of the office and that he would soon be back. To this day, I do not know where he went or what he did. However, a day later he came back, smoking the same pipe, picked up in the middle of the same sentence and continued working.

In one of the staff Meetings, Robert said to L.L. (Tex) Colbert, the chairman and chief executive of that time, "You have $39 per share in your treasurer's cash register. The stock market is saying that you are worth at least $35 million, giving you no credit whatsoever for anything else at Chrysler. If you don't do something about raising the price of your stock, by showing good earnings for example, we'll all be outside walking the bricks, looking in." I have never encountered another executive who was so outspoken.

After I left Chrysler and moved into Wall Street at the beginning of 1963, Robert Savage soon also moved, to become a right-hand man to Harold Geneen, the chairman and chief executive at ITT. Harold Geneen always courted stockholders and, I believe, built ITT by seeing to it that the stock price was always at or above where it should have been. Robert Savage was a true pioneer in understanding Wall Street and the automotive industry. He was a financial and automotive genius, but needed someone with patience to hear what people had to say in many parts of the company. That became my task. I learned to differ with Robert as fully as he differed with others. This made us a good team, and I am thankful that I did not follow him to ITT. He wanted me there to work with the banks on a worldwide basis, but I preferred to stay in Wall Street.

President Eisenhower seemed to favor Chrysler Corporation cars. His personal car was a large Chrysler Saratoga. I also recall that, in 1958, when there was a recession and he was elected to his second term, President Eisenhower objected to the general aspects of the American automobile, saying that they were too big, too costly to buy and too costly to operate. He said that Detroit should consider moving toward the smaller European car. This was when Volkswagen was making major inroads into the U.S. market and automobile production was down to 4.2 million, only about sixty percent of normal production. Chrysler lost $72 million in 1958. The recession ended in 1959, and by that time President Eisenhower suggested that smaller cars had become a reality.

General Motors, Ford, and Chrysler, all within the same twenty-four hour period, announced their compact automobiles. Ford's became the Falcon. The deriders of it said that it was a "little brother." General Motors brought forth the Corvair. Later, a critic of the industry described it as "unsafe at any speed." Chrysler Corporation introduced the Valiant. Of the three, many felt that the Valiant was best designed. Remarkably, it had been totally designed in a fourteen-month period. Even by the late 1980s no automobile had beaten the Valiant timetable.

The 1955-1960 period brought great changes in the car and to some degree prepared the industry for the great Arab oil embargo of 1973 in much the same way the 1985-1990 period has been preparing the United States and Canada to compete effectively against Japan, Korea, Yugoslavia and other automotive exporting countries.

CHAPTER FOURTEEN
THE 1960-1964 ERA

Economic distress will teach men, if anything can,
That realities are less dangerous than fancies,
that fact-finding is more effective than fault-finding.
           - Carl Lotus Becker

The early 1960's carried forward the aura of flamboyance of the late 1950s, but this was soon to be tempered with reality and a modicum of practicality. During the 1960s, I became very well acquainted with Charles R. (Roy) Martin. People who knew him called him Roy. Others called him Charley. Everyone knew the members of the duPont families, but almost no one knew Roy. Yet, he was the principal adviser to the investment of the fortunes of the duPont family and, therefore, very important to them. I came to know him through my work as an analyst for Hayden, Stone and visited his offices in Wilmington, Delaware many times.

One did not ever schedule a mere half-hour visit with Roy Martin. Many analysts would not visit him at all because he was able to discern the total condition of people everywhere, and he wanted to discuss these matters. Roy said that the United States people were becoming lax, that they were becoming too wealthy. Business acquaintances who came from New York wanting to take him to a very expensive restaurant were amazed to find that the person who advised the duPont's on how to utilize their wealth would agree to be taken, not to a gourmet restaurant, but to the cafeteria of the duPont hotel. Roy had other unusual characteristics. He refused to take taxi cabs. Instead, he walked. In fact, he lived very frugally. He said that the duPonts spent the money; as an employee, his role in life was to save it.

Joe Consolmagno was one of the most imaginative public relations people that the automotive industry has produced. In 1960, Joe, two other Chrysler Corporation executives, and I chatted while waiting at the Grand Central Subway Terminal for the cross-town subway to take us to Times Square. Joe's face suddenly lit up, and he said, "Why don't we take the 1961 Plymouth to Cape Canaveral, box it, and send it off into orbit around the world, for all eternity? That," he said, "will make everyone think of Plymouth and buy Chrysler Corporation products." Lynn Townsend's Chrysler Corporation did not take Joe Consolmagno's advice in that instance.

The early 1960s were a period of weariness for the automotive industry. The stylists were trying very hard to come up with new acceptable concepts to put upon four wheels. William Mitchell of General Motors had again seized the styling leadership from Chrysler Corporation which had so badly mangled the GM psyche with the tailfins in the late 1950s.

During this period Alfred P. Sloan, Jr. continued work on a book entitled "My Years with General Motors" which even to this date remains as the most authentic history of GM. Alfred P. Sloan, Jr. shaped the automotive industry in three ways. He insisted on very careful financial controls and required a good return on investment. He insisted on good organization, giving his first-line managers the most practical authority to act. Finally, he instilled in General Motors a product strategy which has been used successfully ever since. Mr. Sloan – no one called him Alfred – used to say, "Never try to match your competition. Charge more and come out on top of him with something the customer would prefer."

Frank Misch was a no-nonsense financial officer at Chrysler Corporation in the late 1950s and on into the 1960s.

He was fond of saying at Chrysler Corporation executive staff meetings that Chrysler Corporation could always rise above General Motors, model for model. He felt that a public perception that Chrysler Corporation cars were well engineered had caused the public to expect more from the Chrysler products. He saw this as an opportunity to offset the larger shares of the market held by General Motors and Ford Motor Company. Frank Misch also succeeded, after several years, in removing the false spare tire concept from the deck lid of the compact Plymouth Valiant which was introduced in 1960. He insisted that it was beneath Chrysler dignity to indicate something where nothing existed. The false spare tire carrier was designed by Exner, and the car price was not lowered when the "toilet seat" was removed. Frank Misch, in my opinion, never received the proper credit as a straightforward individual.

In 1961, Chrysler introduced a new line of cars at the Americana Hotel in Gal Harbor, Florida. Since I was responsible for liaison with the financial community, I arranged for Frank to sit with the leading financial editor of that era, Dan Cordtz, who later became ABC's nationally-known network economist. Cordtz was a skilled questioner and elicited from Frank Misch words to the effect that Chrysler Corporation had lost money the previous fiscal quarter. Dan quickly excused himself to report this information to the network. The news of Chrysler Corporations' third quarter losses far overshadowed whatever impact the new cars may have had on the press and the public.

In the early 1960s, Chrysler Corporation, Studebaker and American Motors sales slumped badly. GM picked up those shares of the market and moved into the late 1960s with a solid fifty percent of the cars sold in the United States. Volkswagen's high water mark had been in the late 1950's, while the Japanese began their rise in the late 1960s, then taking about ten percent of the domestic market.

Throughout the 1950s, automobiles were getting bigger and bigger, actually requiring larger garages, larger parking spaces, and larger shares of traffic space. Engines were also getting larger in order to power the two-ton vehicles along the same, or even better, performance levels than their predecessors. Unfortunately, performance and engine size are inversely proportional to fuel economy, and big performing cars began to cost money, more money than the customers wanted to pay. What goes up must come down, and signals were being received by the American automotive producers.

The foreign imports were beginning to take a larger share of the market. It was becoming impossible to ignore the success of Volkswagen, Hillman, Renault or Morris. At first it was thought that the success these small imports enjoyed was due mainly to the trend toward multi-vehicle families. Soon it became clear that sales of small cars were increasing even more rapidly than was the number of multi-car families. Significantly, the AMC Rambler sold 80,000 units in 1955 and continued up to almost 500,000 units in 1960, while the imports accounted for an additional 700,000 units.

Clearly, the American public was now issuing a mandate. The Big Three American manufacturers finally decided to listen. There was no immediate outcry for import tariffs or quotas. On the contrary, the industry openly advocated the removal of all barriers to international trade. Restrictions were regarded as a two-edged sword. The Big Three at this point in history were also European producers and thus began importing such vehicles as the Taunus, Lancia, Simca and Opel.

In order to better recapture this part of the market, however, the domestic producers decided to go into the small car business on their own. The Europeans felt that as soon as their share of the American market reached ten percent, the big American companies would throw their hats into the ring. They were right. American Motors was already doing well with the Rambler. Studebaker entered the field with the Scotsman and the Lark in the late 1950s with only moderate success. Throughout the decade of the 1960s, compact American vehicles appeared and disappeared at a bewildering rate. The most prominent included Chrysler's Valiant and Dart, Ford's Falcon and Comet, and GM's Corvair, Tempest and Chevy II.

All of these models featured economy, simplicity and a smaller size. As soon as they appeared, however, it became obvious that the American public was still completely enamored with large cars and that compacts were only going to capture and maintain a small share of the market, and competition forced even these compacts to grow larger and more ornate each year, with larger and larger engines. When the need for compact cars became more crucial in the next decade, these earlier compacts were too large to capture this economy-minded segment of the market, and new "sub-compact" models were developed.

General Motors, with Frederic C. Donner as chairman and John F. Gordon as president, entered the early domestic small car sweepstakes with a vengeance. On October 2, 1959; Chevrolet introduced the Corvair which represented the most radical design departure of any domestic vehicle of that period. The Corvair boasted such innovations as a rear mounted, horizontally opposed, aluminum, air cooled, six-cylinder engine and four-wheel independent suspension. The location of the engine over the rear wheels made for excellent traction and nearly equalized braking power, front and rear. The Corvair came in several models, a two-door coupe, four-door sedan, convertible and even a station wagon and quickly gained public acceptance. It did, however, have one enemy: a consumer activist who wrote a book 'Unsafe at any Speed" which eventually killed the Corvair.

The engine used in the Corvair had an extremely low profile which enabled Chevrolet to also design a new van, in both passenger and cargo versions, and an extremely innovative pickup called the Rampside. The middle right hand section of the unitized pickup box was hinged at the bottom and could be opened to form a ramp aid in loading the truck. The engine was simply located under the cargo floor of all versions. The Corvairs, the Rampsides and the Corvans had several minor shortcomings. For example, air-cooled engines do not have a source of hot coolant to be used in the heaters. The first Corvairs were equipped with a gasoline heater. In later versions, the manifolds were jacketed and air circulating around the hot manifolds was ducted into the vehicle interior. This was an effective source of heat, but allowed even the slightest oil drip to smell up the passenger compartment.

Chevrolet continued to enlarge its extremely popular V-8 engine which was introduced in 1955 as a 265 cubic inch unit. The displacement was increased to 283 cubic inches in 1957 and up to 327 cubic inches in 1962. It became available in 250 and 300 horsepower versions. These engines still exist in the late 1980s as 5.0 liter and 5.7 liter units. In 1962, Chevrolet also introduced a second, and much larger engine, of 409 cubic inch displacement, which was installed in Bel Air and Impala models, the first "muscle cars." This 409 horsepower engine enabled Chevrolet to dominate drag and stock car races as much as Chrysler's 355 horsepower V-8 engine had when it was offered in 1956.

In 1962 Chevrolet introduced another line of compact vehicles named Chevy II. These were of conventional configuration but included two new engines, a 150 cubic inch four-cylinder unit and a 194 cubic inch six-cylinder version. The Pontiac Division also introduced an innovative compact car, the Tempest, which was equipped with a conventional, front-mounted water cooled four-cylinder engine. The

Tempest was innovative, however, in that the transmission was rear mounted along with the rear axle differential. The engine and transmission were joined by a forged, relatively thin propeller shaft which was forced into a continuously curved or sagging position by a center-mounted bearing. The curved prop shaft allowed a lower floor, smaller tunnel and maximum interior roominess. Later, Buick and Oldsmobile came out with their own interpretations of a compact car. The Buick Skylark and Oldsmobile F-85 shared the same basic body with still another Chevrolet downsized car, the Chevelle, which was introduced in 1964.

General Motors also devoted considerable attention to the truck market in this era. In the 1960s, GM produced a series of advanced design, turbine-powered trucks which served not only as showcases for the company, but also as test beds for turbine-engine design. One version, the Bison, utilized twin turbine engines, mounted in a pod behind the cab and at the same height as the trailer to provide aerodynamic continuity. The 300 horsepower unit was to be used for highway cruising. The other, a 700 horsepower power plant, was to be used for acceleration and hill climbing.

The second truck version, the Turbo Titan III, was more conventional in configuration. It utilized a 280 horsepower turbine engine which was about one-third as heavy as a diesel of comparable output. The Turbo Titan III featured such innovations as swing-out windows controlled by a key, a steering system which replaced the wheel with twin dials mounted on a pedestal and a full fiberglass reinforced plastic cab.

Turbine trucks suffered from the same lack of acceleration as did turbine cars. However, if the future holds any hope for the turbine engine, it is in trucks. The engine operates best at a constant speed and would thereby require an automatic transmission with an infinitely variable gear ratio with sufficient spread to provide good acceleration while fully loaded and with a satisfactory top speed.

General Motors, in 1960, also made an effort to improve the life of the highway truck driver by introducing independent front suspensions for all of the trucks, light, medium and heavy duty. All utilized torsion bars as the elastic members. Light-duty trucks retain this basic suspension design even into the late 1980s, but the torsion bars have been replaced by the old coil springs for most models.

The independent front suspension program for heavy-duty trucks was actually not worth the effort as it turned out, even though the idea and the design were sound. Truckers have a mind of their own. They are not about to allow manufacturers to force something upon them. By 1962, GM was offering the archaic I-beam and leaf spring suspension as an option, and by 1963 the heavy duty independent front suspension was gone. The stone-age I-beam and leaf spring suspensions continue on heavy duty trucks even into the late 1980's. If there ever are heavy trucks used on the moon, they will undoubtedly have I-beam and leaf spring suspensions.

The Ford Motor Company opened the 1960s with a brand new compact vehicle. It was a totally restyled big car line and a refined version of the four-seat Thunderbird. In 1958, the two-seat T-bird had given up its pursuit of the Corvette as a sports car and was now a sporty car.

On December 10, 1960, Henry Ford II summoned Lee Iacocca into his office and appointed him as general manager of the Ford Division. Lee would go on to become the driving force behind the Mustang, Ford's most successful product of the decade. Iacocca was a born salesman. He also spearheaded Ford's Total Performance campaign which injected interest into almost every Ford of the 1960s. Iacocca would eventually lose favor with Henry Ford II, but, at the beginning of the decade of the 1960's, he was the fair-haired boy.

The Ford Falcon arrived at the marketplace simultaneously with the Chevrolet Corvair and the Plymouth Valiant, but was not as innovative as the Corvair or as well engineered as the Valiant. In fact, it was dully conventional with a front mounted six-cylinder engine and rear drive. Nevertheless, the Falcon quickly established itself as the top-seller in its category.

Realistically, the Falcon was a modernized version of the old Model-A, a simple, reliable, no-nonsense car. It was eventually available as a two and four-door sedan, and as a two and four-door station wagon. Some regarded it as a throw-away car, to be purchased for as low as $1912, driven until it wore out and then discarded after a few years service.

With the arrival of the compacts, other vehicles, such as the Chevrolet Impala and the Ford Galaxie, needed a designation. Automotive writers quickly named them "full size." The full-size Fords for 1960 grew even larger with a lower, longer and wider silhouette. Overall length increased by 5.7 inches, and the width expanded to a huge 81.5 inches.

The Ford Thunderbird went into its third generation in 1961. Its new slogan described it as "Unique in All the World." Two clay mockups were in the running. One was by designer Elwood Engel; the other by Bill Boyer. Both worked for George Walker. Engel's angular, crisp styling was rejected by general manager Robert McNamara who decided the T-bird should look like a smaller version of the Lincoln Continental, and the 1961 Thunderbird was aircraft oriented, with big rocket type tail lights and an aerodynamic front.

The 1962 model year featured the introduction of the new mid-sized Fairlane, which was placed between the Falcon and the full-size Ford. At this point, Ford could do no wrong, and the 1962 Fairlane sold well at 297,000 units. The Fairlane was also equipped with Ford's new, small block, 221 cubic inch V-8. Its relatively light weight and low cost sent GM, Chrysler, and AMC engineers back to the drawing boards. In

1962, Ford also began merchandising the forward control Econovan. It immediately became a sales leader in its class and has remained there through the late 1980s. Lee Iacocca favored the half model year, so that special trim and other sales incentives could be added at mid-season to bolster interest in his products. Accordingly, in mid-1962 Ford added the 406 cubic inch V-8 to enter the high-performance arena. In mid-1963, Ford introduced a stylish hardtop version of the Falcon, as the new Sprint. A 164 horsepower, 260 cubic inch V-8 gave the Falcon plenty of performance.

Ford's greatest success of the decade occurred in the 1964 model year. One of the reasons was the April 1964 introduction of the 1965 Mustang. The early introduction was another of Lee Iacocca's merchandising ploys. Ford also introduced an all-new Thunderbird, a restyled Galaxie, and face-lifts for the Falcon and Fairlane. The new Thunderbirds emphasized quietness and refined luxury, with styling reminiscent of its predecessor. With almost total disregard for changes, Thunderbird owners just loved their cars, and Ford prospered.

In the Chrysler automotive arena, Tex Colbert in 1960 resigned the presidency in favor of William C. Newberg, but the reign of Newberg lasted only 64 days. It was discovered that he had personal financial interests in some of Chrysler's outside suppliers. He faced conflict of interest charges and quickly resigned. Colbert reassumed the presidency on July 12, 1960. The year 1961 saw the decline, and the fall of the Chrysler stylist Virgil Exner. Colbert was also losing popularity with the stockholders, and, on July 27, 1961, he was replaced as president by former administrative vice president, Lynn A. Townsend. George H. Love became chairman.

Chrysler's two most important engineering developments for 1960 were the introduction of the Plymouth Valiant and the adoption of unit construction for all models except the Imperial. This structural system was not new to the

American automotive manufacturers, having long been a feature of American Motors and its predecessors, Nash and Hudson.

Chrysler's approach was called "Unibody". It eliminated the need for a separate frame, while providing a one hundred percent improvement in rigidity and forty percent increase in beam strength. This method also resulted in weight reduction and in increased costs. Chrysler engineers made stress studies by using mathematical equations which could be checked by computers. These were then just coming into their own, mainly as electronic adding machines.

The Desoto carline lasted through 1960 and was discontinued in mid-1961. It had evolved to be an almost identical twin to the Chrysler, but was not as well respected. By this time, the Chryslers were selling for only $50-$100 more than the Desoto, and Desoto sales were falling steadily.

The 1960 model year also featured a major redesign for the full-size Dodge. However, the big news story for 1960 was the compact Plymouth Valiant, which joined the Corvair and the Falcon. The Valiant was labeled as "Nobody's Kid Brother", and was quickly recognized as the best-engineered but strangest-looking of the Big Three compacts. The Valiant was powered by a new Chrysler engine called the Slant Six because of its canted block. It had the appearance of having been a V-12, before some giant split it in two with a huge axe. It turned out to be a very reliable and durable power plant, continuing in production well over twenty years.

Chrysler Corporation stood generally unchanged for 1961. The Valiant was cloned and the result was called the Dodge Lancer. Both the Valiant and Lancer were now available in two-door hardtop and sedan versions', as well as four-door sedans and station wagons. The 1961 model year was significant for Chrysler. It marked the beginning of the end of the large tailfins on the Dodge and Plymouth models. Chrysler and DeSoto retained them, temporarily. All in all, the compact Lancer and Valiant were the best-looking vehicles in the Chrysler stable.

The 1962 model year was to include an all-new Chrysler model lineup. Virgil Exner was reluctant to give up the styling leadership to General Motors, so he designed an entire line of finless vehicles based on a central theme. The concept was approved by Bill Newberg – then president. However, when Newberg left in disgrace, Tex Colbert took back the presidency. He had second thoughts and ordered a redesign. As a result, the Chrysler design was carried over into the New Year, but without the fins, which made it the best-looking Chrysler of the generation.

The 1962 Dodge and Plymouth models were smaller than their 1961 counterparts. Sales fell disastrously. In fact, Plymouth fell to eighth place in model-year production, its lowest ranking in recent history. Dodge had a larger model mix and maintained ninth place, as in 1961. The Plymouth and Dodge were no match for Chevrolet's Impala and Ford's Galaxie. Furthermore, GM introduced the Chevy II, and Ford introduced the Fairlane. Both were roughly of the same size as the downsized Plymouth and Dodge.

It was during 1962 that Exner was dethroned as Chrysler's vice president in charge of styling. He was replaced by Elwood Engel who was lured away from Ford after his 1961 Thunderbird design was rejected by Robert McNamara. Engel was expected to lead Chrysler Corporation along a more conventional styling path. Exner continued as styling consultant through 1964 but was not permitted to exercise any originality or innovation. He left a legacy of vivid imagination and original styling concepts at Chrysler. After he left, it would be a long time before Chrysler cars would be as innovative and noticeable again. Exner was undoubtedly the greatest single influence in making Chrysler an automotive styling leader in the late 1950s and early 1960s.

When Lynn Townsend relieved Tex Colbert as president, he moved quickly to usher in a new and more aggressive leadership. He created an administrative committee to guide the firm. Among the members was administrative vice president Virgil Boyd who had been a vice president at American Motors since that company was formed from the remains of Nash and Hudson in 1954. Also a member of the administrative committee was "flamethrower" John Riccardo, whose nickname was built on his reputation as a tough, very aggressive administrator.

Riccardo came to Townsends's attention as an accountant. He came to Chrysler headquarters in Highland Park, Michigan in 1959 as financial staff executive for international operations. Later, he became Export-Import Division manager, a Chrysler Canada vice-president, manager of Dodge Sales, and manager of Chrysler-Plymouth and Corporate Marketing. John Riccardo was to succeed Boyd as president in 1970 and move up to chairman in 1975, a position he would relinquish to Ford's Lee Iacocca in 1979.

The big Chrysler news for 1963 was the "Engelbird," a Ghia-built turbine car designed to test customer reaction to that form of power. Chrysler contracted to have 50 units built in Italy. They were brought into the U.S. and loaned to chosen "consumer representatives". The test lasted three years and the consensus was that the vehicles were extremely attractive in styling and operated on a variety of fuels. On the downside, their fuel economy was less than satisfactory, and they all suffered from acceleration deficiencies, at least according to the standards of the 1960s. Considering the higher costs of turbine engines and the lack of any clear-cut advantages, the notion of a turbine car was shelved temporarily, or perhaps forever.

As part of a promotional event for the turbine car, Joe Consolmagno, asked me to do him a favor which I thought was not especially dignified. At that time, I was responsible for Chrysler Corporation's financial relations with Wall Street. Joe asked me to obtain a gallon of perfume from Arpege, at great expense to Chrysler, and to bring it to the turbine vehicle media event which was scheduled for the Idlewild Airport, today known as the Kennedy International. In full view of the press, I very obviously and ceremoniously poured the perfume into the empty fuel tank of one of the turbine cars. The vehicle was then started and ran quite well while emitting a very romantic aroma. The point of the demonstration was that the turbine engine could run on almost anything combustible. The writers were very much impressed with the engine, but I don't recall a single word written about Arpege being used as the fuel. I was fortunate not to have attended Joe Consolmagno's event at Portsmouth, Rhode Island, where he used whale oil to fuel the turbine car. I have no idea of what burnt whale oil might smell like. History has now recorded the turbine engine as a failure, in automotive usage, but perhaps not permanently. Slow acceleration characteristics and poor fuel economy put it to sleep, and not perfume or whale oil.

The beautiful Engel-designed, Ghia-built cars suffered a sad, lamentable fate. All but ten were cut up before the unemotional eyes of U.S. customs officials, because having been built abroad, Chrysler needed to pay import duty on the vehicles if they were to remain permanently in the United States. Chrysler did pay duty on ten of the fifty, and these were dispersed to various museums. Chrysler retained two for their files. The 1963 Chrysler was the first model over which Engel had any influence, and it was advertised as having the "Crisp, Clean, Custom Look". Others were to follow. Chrysler also sent the remainder of the industry into some turmoil by offering a revolutionary five-year/50,000 mile warranty on all power train components.

Dodge featured an all-new compact which replaced the Lancer and differed considerably from the restyled

Valiant. It borrowed the Dart name from the downsized 1962 line and was part of an industry trend toward larger, more luxurious and sportier compacts. The 1963 Plymouth Valiant also became larger but was not as stylish as the Dart.

Chrysler did quite well financially in 1963 and 1964. Corporate net earnings reached $161.6 million, with worldwide sales of $3.5 billion. Lynn Townsend credited the success to the "5/50" warranty program, an enlarged dealer organization and a broader market coverage. The Chrysler stock split four-fold and production exceeded one million units per year.

Chrysler also acquired controlling interest in Simca of France and began negotiations with Rootes of Great Britain. Cummins, a British diesel manufacturer, had been acquired in 1963. Chrysler was becoming a multi-national company on the order of General Motors and Ford. In 1963 and 1964, Chrysler also entered the compact truck market with the forward control pickup and van models. The 1964 model year was good for Chrysler. Chrysler car production was up and the Imperial saw a 65 percent gain over 1963. Plymouth regained its share of the market; Dodge was strong; and the compacts were doing well. Chrysler was again riding high.

CHAPTER FIFTEEN

THE 1965-1969 ERA

Get place and wealth, if possible with grace;
If not, by any means get wealth and place.
        - Alexander Pope

The latter half of the decade of the 1960s was very favorable to the automotive industry. The market had long before reverted back to the buyers' control, but the country was in the throes of an economic boom. Sales were relatively high for all manufacturers, though not for all of their lines or in every single model year. The era of tailfins and rocket styling had passed, but the cars, including compacts, were becoming longer, lower, wider and heavier.

Perhaps the outstanding aspect of this five-year period and a manifestation of the prevailing consumer philosophy of that era was the emergence of the muscle cars. These were usually mid-size vehicles equipped with some very large engines for a favorable power-to-weight ratio. They were not destined primarily for the drag strip or the race track, but rather for the customer who wanted a vehicle capable of outperforming most of the other vehicles on the highway or at the red light. These customers were actually buying potential rather than performance.

Examples of the muscle cars included the Pontiac GTO with a 389 cubic inch engine, the Chevrolet Impala equipped with a 409 cubic inch power plant, the Chevelle SS with 396 cubic inches, Oldsmobile 4-4-2 with 400 cubic inches, Plymouth Barracuda powered by a 383 V-8, and Ford Fairlane with 390 cubic inches.

Ironically, this was also the era which marked the U.S. government's entry into automotive design. This was done not as a partner in the endeavor, but rather as an autocratic entity demanding certain standards of performance in specific areas regardless of the costs to the manufacturers. In 1968, safety requirements were initiated, at first rather slowly. The initial changes were padded instrument panels, improved door latches and padded sun visors. These requirements multiplied rapidly until, in the mid-1980s, there are literally hundreds of specific safety standards that a vehicle designer must include in his product. This cost the customer hundreds of additional dollars in the sticker price of his automobile, but ultimately saved the public more money in reduced health care. Most importantly, the safety mandates saved lives.

But in the late 1980s, automotive safety, integrated into the, vehicle design, may have reached a point of diminishing returns. Automobiles are heavy machines, propelled at very high speeds. They are totally under individual control of persons of varying capabilities. Manufacturers build very safe vehicles, but individual drivers can refuse to buckle up their seat belts. They can drink alcohol before driving. They can ingest drugs before driving; they can refuse to maintain their vehicles, or they can even be psychologically unfit to drive at any one specific moment. Furthermore, much of the road system in the United States was not built for the requirements of the 1980s and beyond. An extreme example is a two-lane road, one lane in each direction, where there is no speed limit, as was the case in the 1950s and 1960s in some states. It is not too difficult to imagine the possible consequences involving two approaching vehicles with a closing speed of about 200 miles per hour, driven by drivers who may have been under the influence of alcohol or who have been temporarily blinded by each other's headlights. Just the idea of two vehicles routinely passing within three or four feet of each other at those speeds is mind-boggling. The point is that automotive manufacturers have been held responsible for a disproportionate share of vehicle safety. Extraneous forces may have to become involved before further real progress in safety can become a reality.

The U.S. government, at this time, also began establishing regulations with regard to the air pollutants being emitted by automotive engines. It began, understandably enough, in 1966 in California, where the Los Angeles area had problems with smog. Earlier automobiles of the 1960 time period were emitting, on an average, 10.6 grams per mile of hydrocarbons, 8.4 grams per mile of carbon monoxide, and 4.1 grams per mile of nitrous oxides. California requirements in 1966 called for maximums of 6.3 gpm of HC, 5.1 gpm of CO, and 4 gpm of NOx. Over the years, California has stayed at the forefront of emission requirements. The California standards of today became the federal requirements of tomorrow. Finally, in the mid-1980s, the emission requirements are ten times more stringent than they were in the original California law. Trucks enter into their own version of emission controls which also are becoming stricter every year. These laws lag behind the passenger car versions but are slowly becoming equivalent.

However, not all of the world's air pollution is caused by automobiles and trucks. In the process of living, animals exude tremendous amounts of air pollution. Plants and trees contribute huge amounts of hydrocarbons into the atmosphere. A measure of air pollution happens to be a by-product of industrialization. Most of the countries of the world are now involved in efforts to minimize air pollution caused by man, and tolerate that which nature provides.

For General Motors, and for the industry, the 1960s were years of refinement and growth. The major portion of the revolutionary changes took place early in the decade. The latter part of the 1960s was devoted to functionalism which translated into more sensible design. In 1965, James M. Roche replaced John F. Gordon as president of General Motors. On

November 1, 1967, Roche moved up to chairman of the board, replacing Frederic G. Donner. Edward N. Cole moved into the presidential office. This was the era of the engineers, and the products were to reflect that factor.

Edward N. Cole, president of General Motors, had been friendly with the O'Neils of the General Tire and Rubber Company. Jerry O'Neil and Ed Cole were particularly good friends. General Tire and Rubber, in addition to being the number five producer in the rubber industry, was also very advanced in plastics. The company was particularly experienced in the kinds of soft plastics that became necessary in the 1960's to pad instrument panels in compliance with federal safety requirements.

Ed Cole was in sales volume trouble with the Cadillac automobile when he was general manager of that division. I happened to be in Akron, Ohio when Ed Cole called Jerry O'Neil on the telephone. Cole simply asked if Jerry could deliver the foam plastic covers for the Cadillac instrument panels. Nothing at all was mentioned about costs. Jerry simply replied that he would do it as quickly as he possibly could.

I followed that transaction on my next trip around to Akron. During that particular period, in the late 1960s, it seemed that I beat a path from Goodyear to Firestone to Goodrich to General Tire. It turned out that, after Ed Cole and Jerry O'Neil made the deal, the accountants and the lawyers had a very difficult time putting the pieces together according to established bureaucratic procedures. My feeling is that GM got a better deal from General Tire than the tire company's accountants would have deemed prudent.

Oscar Lundeen was treasurer of General Motors when I came to know him. He was so influential and knowledgeable in the GM empire that Edmund Mennis, portfolio manager of Wellington Management Corporation, then in Philadelphia, always asked me to come and see him after each visit to Oscar. All that I was asked to report to Ed was whether Oscar was generally frowning or smiling. If he was smiling, things would go well for General Motors in the quarters ahead. If he was frowning or, at least, not smiling, according to the Mennis index of performance, General Motors would not be doing very well, which could have a "domino effect".

At any given moment in time, Oscar Lundeen indeed did know the health of General Motors from a financial viewpoint. The statistics he used to judge this health were right there in his office. Behind his work desk, he had a long wooden credenza which contained piles of reports. He kept these updated and in very good order and could always answer questions that came from those in GM high management who needed to know a particular statistical fact. Oscar was regarded in General Motors as a human facts book: an oracle. It was easier and more accurate to call Oscar than to call the library.

Investment brokers and portfolio managers rely, in part, on many intangibles to secure their financial knowledge. Involved are such factors as friendships in the areas of interest, unusual individual transactions, attitudes of investors and even rumors. Obviously nothing replaces an in-depth knowledge of the market.

Sam Duva was an aggressive securities salesman and market leader with Hayden, Stone. He headed the mid-west region, headquartered at the famed Merchandise Mart Building in Chicago, Illinois. Sam was so persuasive that many of his friends invested heavily in Hayden, Stone. This investment firm, however, was eventually forced to sell its assets, and many, including myself, suffered substantial financial loss.

Harold Geneen, as chairman of ITT, was one of the toughest taskmasters among all industrial leaders of his era. One of his officers later became my Wall Street supervisor. This was Burrell A. (Bill) Parkhurst who brought to Wall Street the first computer-driven financial research system. In

1965, an analyst named Eugene Quinn, worked many nights to put into an early model computer data from ten years' worth of balance sheets and earning statements. The computer was programmed to sort out the companies with the best records in eleven parameters and also to weigh a company's performance score against its Wall Street price-earning ratio valuation.

Bill Parkhurst could theoretically select the most underpriced stock, at a given moment, and also the most overvalued stock. His method was to simply sell the overpriced stock, buy the most underpriced and over a period of time maximize earnings. He found it wasn't that easy.

Lou Witt, another vice president of the old Hayden, Stone, headed the southeastern United States offices of the company. He became totally sold on Bill Parkhurst's analysis. Sadly, the computer selected stocks did not thrive any better in 1965 than they do in the late 1980s. Computers, at least on Wall Street, are simply overrated.

In 1966, the Lee Higginson Company, which went back to the time of formation of General Motors, became part of Hayden, Stone. We absorbed the Lee Higginson Company because, although it had run into financial problems in the expansion of the mid-1960s, it was a very well-known name.

I remember especially the career of Margretta Whidby. She migrated from Lee Higginson to Hayden, Stone offices, located on 25 Broad Street, very near to the back entrance of the New York Stock Exchange. She was one of the first women who rose to success on Wall Street. Margretta brought with a little black box which held hundreds of cards. These included the names and numbers of her contacts. She guarded the box very jealously, as if it contained diamonds. She was known to perhaps as few as seventy portfolio managers and corporate executives in the apparel industry. Her style was to come up first with new developments, and get the word on these new developments exclusively to her clients.

Hayden, Stone had a problem with this form of client protection. The rules of the New York Stock Exchange and the Securities Commission were then becoming stricter. It was necessary to provide the same kinds of information not only to the retail market but to the institutional market as well.

Hayden, Stone, at that time, had fourteen hundred registered representatives in ninety-four offices around the world. We never did quite resolve how to handle the type of information which Margretta Whidby provided to her institutional clients. How could we at the same time get this information to someone who might be interested in only fifty shares of one of the apparel companies stocks? There was absolutely no intent to withhold any information from the retail clientele. However, we, in research, had a difficult time in determining just what would be understood in the retail market. Neither the registered representatives of that period, nor their clients, had the time or interest to study the minor details of the changes in the apparel industry. The same kind of judgment which went into the apparel industry had to be used in determining the level of interest of retail customers in many other smaller sectors of the market. This contrasted with the sophisticated activity of the institutional portfolio managers and analysts.

In the latter half of the decade of the 1960s, General Motors, produced some very innovative automobiles, along with the normal and usual improvement of the species. The full-size Chevrolets were all new for 1965, and the Impala of that vintage was perhaps the most attractive car of the decade for Chevrolet. GM muscle cars could be found in all divisional offerings since large engines were available for most lines. However, those specifically labeled by automotive writers as such included the Buick Gran Sport, Oldsmobile 4-4-2, Chevrolet Chevelle SS 396, and the Pontiac GTO.

Station wagons introduced by Oldsmobile and Buick featured a sky-roof, which was actually a raised roof above the second and rear seats. This increased headroom to permit a forward facing third seat. The sky-roof included a short "windshield" and side windows, not unlike the observation decks found on some railroad cars.

In 1966, Oldsmobile introduced the front-wheel drive Toronado which was followed a year later by the front wheel drive Cadillac Eldorado. Both cars were the domestic forerunners of the wave of the 1980s where almost all domestic and import vehicles have front-wheel drive. However, the vehicles of the 1980s are equipped with transversely mounted engines while the Toronado and Eldorado both had longitudinally located power plants.

Two very popular GM cars were first introduced in 1967 -- the Chevrolet Camaro and Pontiac Firebird. These were both intended as competition for the Mustang, but have outlived that equine breed by a number of years. These were low-slung, sporty vehicles with a long hood and a short rear deck and were known as the "steel" Corvettes. In the 1980s, these vehicles are into their third generation and still retain the front engine, rear drive chassis configuration. Their popularity with younger buyers remains.

The Chevrolet Corvette was totally redesigned in 1968. In addition to the convertible and hardtop version, a third model offered lift-off roof panels. Soon other models would emulate this body style. The largest engine available was a 435 horsepower, 427 cubic inch V-8. The driver could easily surpass the speed limit in first gear, with almost nothing to do with the remaining three.

Chevrolet, in 1969, introduced the Chevrolet Blazer which was intended to compete with the Willys Jeep, the Ford Bronco and the International Scout. The Blazer was based primarily on the half-ton smooth side pickup and, as such, was larger than any of its competitors. The larger size seemed to be the reason for its popularity. Chevrolet projected sales of

7000 units for the first model year. Instead, some 45,000 units were produced and sold.

The Blazer, along with the Jeep, Bronco and Scout, helped to create a new demand for four-wheel drive vehicles. In the 1980s both Chevrolet and Ford continue with two versions of the Blazer and Bronco, respectively, one small and one large. GMC's versions of the Blazers are named Jimmys. In 1984 and 1985, the U.S. military placed a large order for Chevrolet diesel-powered, light-duty vehicles, a large percentage of which were Blazers.

Sadly, 1969 was the last year for Chevrolet's Corvair. It was killed by an automotive critic who had never even driven the car. He had developed an aversion to the Corvair, and had access to the nation's news media. In the two-generation, nine-year production period, 1.7 million Corvair passenger cars and 79,000 pickups and vans were produced. In the mid-1980s Corvair clubs existed all over the country. Owners attended various meets to bargain for parts and to exchange Corvair stories, as well as to show off their cars. The Corvair was truly a unique product.

With the imminence of safety regulations, GM tried to anticipate safety features which would eventually be mandated. Thus, in 1966, before the law became effective, GM equipped its vehicles with instrument panel pads, safety glass, padded sun visors, improved door latches, and standard seat belts. For 1967, GM continued with a dual-circuit brake system, energy absorbing steering wheel and column, energy absorbing instrument panel and low profile control knobs. In reality, GM and the other manufacturers have been safety testing their vehicles for the entire duration of their existence but not to the degree now required by the government.

In the 1960s, and specifically in 1965, Ford added still another name to a memorable list of classic vehicles which included the Model-T, the Model-A and the Thunderbird. This name was the Mustang and was Lee Iacocca's creation. It was actually introduced April 17, 1964 as a 1965 model. It was sporty, long-hooded and the first of a line of Ford pony cars. American buyers went wild over this vehicle. Ford originally projected first year sales of 100,000 units, but by December 1965 an astounding 680,989 Mustangs were sold, and a legend had been created.

The Mustang was a youth-oriented car, offering a variety of options, with a chassis based principally on the Falcon design. In 1965, Ford also introduced an all-new full-size Ford, including another future favorite, the LTD.   The 1966 model year was Ford's greatest time for total performance. The Fairlane and Falcon were all new and included versions which would join the muscle car group. The Mustang continued to do well since the Camaro and Firebird were still a year away and the Corvair was dying. Mario Andretti won the 1967 Daytona 500 stock car race driving a Ford Fairlane.

A completely new Thunderbird was introduced in 1967. The car included a four-door sedan which Lee Iacocca had fallen in love with. Ford suffered from a decline in sales for full-size and mid-size cars, but the Mustang continued to do well, especially after the introduction of a fastback model.

The "Ford has a better idea" slogan, complete with a light bulb, arrived in 1968. This "better idea" was actually a collection of little ideas, the biggest of which was a brand-new line of intermediate vehicles. Many of the Ford better ideas came at the request of the government with regard to safety. Safety improvements included such features as shock-absorbing steering column, front and rear side marker lights, anti-glare interiors and low-profile handles. The intermediate-size Torino was actually approaching full size and substantiated the theory that Americans prefer big cars; they always did and, likely, always will. Horsepower also continued to escalate.

The Mustang then started falling out of favor, faced with competition from GM's Camaro and Firebird, as well as from AMC's handsome Javelin. In addition to its other faults, the U.S. car buying public has traditionally been extremely fickle, and one year's sweetheart car can become the next year's wallflower, even though, or perhaps because, it may have changed very little.

In early 1968, Semon E. "Bunkie" Knudsen resigned as a General Motors executive vice president after his corporate presidential train apparently became derailed. Soon thereafter Henry Ford II appointed him to the Ford presidency, a move that was to send shock waves throughout the industry. The last shift of this magnitude came a half-century earlier when Bunkie's father, William S. Knudsen, left Ford after an argument with Henry Ford I and went to Chevrolet. Turnabout, apparently, is fair play.

In 1969, Lee Iacocca was promoted to executive vice president of Ford which made him third on the totem pole, under Knudsen and Henry Ford II. Knudsen quickly raided GM's personnel arena and hired Larry Shinoda, who was responsible for many of the General Motors show vehicles. Soon his effect would be felt by Ford automobiles.

On April 17, 1969, another pony car, the Maverick, was introduced as a 1970 model. The Mustang was also all-new for 1969 but did not meet the success of its predecessor.

Late in 1969, Henry Ford II dismissed Bunkie Knudsen and in 1969, Lee Iacocca became the overall Ford president to lead Ford into the decade of the 1970s. In another arena of the 1960s, the son of a Ford Motor Company dealer emerged as one of the most brilliant professional pension fund and overall money managers of that period. The son was Dr. Robert Blixt.

Bob became very important to Hayden, Stone and especially to me. He was extremely interested in automobiles and always wanted to know what was happening in the industry and especially at the Ford Motor Company. He followed other industries as well because he was the generalist who also managed $3.2 billion of pension money in St. Paul, Minnesota, for the Minnesota State Board of Investment.

It was Bob Blixt who first identified for me, and tried to communicate to municipal and state fund managers all over the country, the necessity of having enough pension money available to fund the very generous labor offers and contracts which were being written in that period. It was not until the late 1970s and early 1980s that the possibility of trouble would surface and it became apparent to everyone that unfunded pension fund liabilities could greatly reduce the earnings of automobile companies and others who did not have sufficient return from their investment portfolios to pay the pensioners. Many cities also found that they had been too generous to their retiring policemen, firemen and other public servants. This failure of funding affected even the United States Social Security System.

In the automobile industry, analysts began looking carefully at various companies such as Uniroyal, which was the old U.S. Tire and Rubber Company, and Chrysler Corporation. These two had heavy unfunded pension fund liabilities which had been, in the case of the Chrysler Corporation, written into the contracts with the United Auto Workers. These generous agreements were made to appease U.A.W. labor union negotiators in three-year cycles, not only at Chrysler but throughout the automotive industry. Later, these contracts caused grave financial difficulty and eventually led to increased prices. In the case of municipalities and government agencies, these agreements, obviously, had to increase taxation. In the case of Uniroyal, these contracts reduced the company credit rating and caused an increase in paid out interest rates on money borrowed.

The lesson that Dr. Robert Blixt tried to convey to all from St. Paul was that fiscal responsibility had to be exercised at the time of the contract or investment and that this responsibility included consideration of consequences for as many as thirty or forty years in the future.

The period of the 1960s was also a period of administrative change for the Chrysler Corporation. Chairman George H. Love was replaced by Lynn A. Townsend on January 1, 1967. Lynn Townsend, who had been president from 1961, was replaced by Virgil E. Boyd at the same time. K.T. Keller, the Chrysler legend, died in January 1966 of a coronary, just short of his 85th birthday. In 1958, he had predicted that the era of tailfins, gingerbread and increasing car size had to eventually end. He claimed that cars must be good, dependable, utilitarian products. Time eventually proved him correct, but it took some thirty years for his prediction to become reality.

Chrysler vehicle sales were very good in the latter half of the 1960s, even though the products may not have fully merited the vote of confidence. Chrysler brand cars were, in fact, outselling Cadillac. However, the intermediates were the best sellers. In 1966, Chrysler's share of the market rose to a very respectable 16.6 percent. This was the year for the resurgence of the Dodge vehicles. Several new models were responsible for the best sales in the vehicles' history. However, the Plymouth volume was down with sales going to Dodge and Pontiac. The Chrysler line, and especially the Engel restyled Imperial, took up the slack.

At the 1967 time frame, Chrysler Corporation was building about a quarter million Chrysler units annually. However, this was also an era of economic decline and labor discontent, so the volumes kept gradually decreasing toward the end of the decade. Chrysler-Plymouth kept on building muscle-cars; and 1967 was probably the peak period. The Plymouth Barracuda was probably the best of its class: sleek, clean, gracefully curved, and powered by a 383 cubic inch, 280 horsepower V-8.

In 1967, Chrysler Corporation bought the controlling interest in the British Rootes group for $56 million. The Rootes products included Hillman, Humber, Singer, Sunbeam and Commer truck. This was Chrysler's effort at internationalization. However, the amalgamation was in trouble even at the time of purchase; and Chrysler's several efforts at selling these imports in the United States were all unsuccessful. Finally Chrysler established ties with Mitsubishi of Japan, and these have endured into the late 1980s.

In 1968, Dodge introduced a new Charger which was probably the nicest Dodge of the decade. Plymouth designed and built a budget muscle car which was called the Road Runner. It even had a horn which mimicked the cartoon character's "beep-beep" sound.

In 1969, Chrysler Corporation established Chrysler Realty which was to conduct all of the Corporation's real estate transactions. All in all, Chrysler was entering the 1970's in far better shape than it did in the 1960s. Plymouth was now perennially in fourth place behind Chevrolet, Ford and Pontiac. Dodge was the hot car of Chrysler Corporation, and Chrysler vehicles themselves were running neck and neck with Cadillac.

The automotive executives have always had a love-hate relationship with the Wall Street Journal. In the 1960s, American Motors had some very profitable "George Romney" years. George Romney was in the throes of his famous infatuation with the Rambler, and the four inch, one-column Rambler advertisements in Time magazine had, I believe, more clout than the double-page spreads which General Motors could afford.

Many in American Motors benefited, at last, from their stock options. Richard Purdy was one. He was the controller. One morning he came to work and found that someone had placed a Wall Street Journal on his desk, opened to an article which indicated that he had sold American Motors stock. This 'rankled' Richard because he had indeed sold stock in order to exercise an option to buy other stock, an option which would have otherwise expired. He had borrowed from the bank on the original stock, and the note was coming due. The Wall Street Journal, in this instance, reported on Richard's sale of stock as an implication of his lack of confidence in the future of the company. Such activity was rather common, especially in the 1960s and 1970s. There was some thought on Wall Street that if an insider sold his stock, there was bad news ahead for that particular company. The reality was that high-ranking officials in the automotive industry often had to manage their own personal affairs as people who started from humble origins. They had to borrow money in order to exercise their stock options, and later they would have to sell stock to pay the bank. Dick Purdy was especially unhappy about the treatment that he had received because his motives were totally misinterpreted.

Wall Street has always been fascinated with the automotive industry. However, Wall Street was also interested in Washington. As head of research at Hayden, Stone, I assembled at the Bankers Club of America a handful of economists who, by reputation, were the leading authorities on the subject. These were the individuals who traveled to Washington, often at the bidding of the President or of various governmental agencies, to testify or advise on some aspect of the economy.

My favorite among them was Orson Hart. He was vice president and chief economist of New York Life Insurance Company. Orson brought to these meetings such luminaries as Martin Gainsbrugh, who headed the economic staff of the conference board, William Butler, vice president and chief economist of Chase Manhatten Bank, Jack Noyes and James O'Leary. I was not a trained economist, but I always enjoyed the role of asking questions and letting these intellectual giants discuss where things were going and how.

Each of the attendees was a leader in their own right, and collectively they tried to forecast interest rates, the direction of the stock market, the national budget, inflation rates, employment and unemployment. They even got into the strength of the dollar and anticipated automotive sales volumes. Small wonder that Washington was interested in what Wall Street economists had to say, and vice versa. Whenever we would gather on the fortieth floor of 120 Broadway, in the President's Room of the Bankers Club of America, the floor would be given to the person who had been the most recent visitor to Washington. Meanwhile, the automotive industry eavesdropped.

Automotive suppliers are a power in their own right. William Ylvisaker was one of the most dynamic executives who surfaced in the late 1960s. Bill had been a junior analyst in Wall Street and later became an official at GATX in Chicago, Illinois. He was very imaginative, a very sound financial thinker and had the capability to dramatize just about every situation into which he entered. In 1968, Bill was chosen by Gould National Batteries of St. Paul, Minnesota to revitalize the company and to expand it into the electronic giant, which it has become in the 1980s.

The combination of Wall Street, the automotive industry, and Washington is good for many stories, in all eras of its history. Many more stories will, unfortunately, never again be told because they are buried with the story teller, and this will ever be so as generations come and go.

CHAPTER SIXTEEN
THE 1970-1974 ERA

The ever-whirling wheel of change;
the which all mortal things doth sway.
- Edmund Spenser

The fall of 1973 marked the end of a generally euphoric period for the automobile and the automobile industry. Up to and including 1973, the automobile industry had developed its product to a very high level of perfection. Unfortunately, the product it had developed was dependent on readily available, low cost fuel, and OPEC's oil embargo made fuel both more costly and less readily available.

In 1973, OPEC became part of our language. So also did petro-dollars. The literal meaning of OPEC is the Organization of Petroleum Exporting Countries. Key among them are Saudi Arabia, Iran, Iraq, Kuwait, Indonesia and many smaller others. The Middle East countries, especially, had become important petroleum producers by this time. While before World War II, Arabian crude at the wellhead cost 25 cents, spot prices of petroleum reached a record high of approximately $45.00 per barrel during the height of the OPEC strength.

Until the mid-1960s, leaders of the automobile industry had managed to establish their own norms for cars and trucks, but, by 1971, Washington had imposed a strong regulatory pall over Detroit, and leaders of the industry were very disillusioned. George Huebner, chief stylist for Chrysler Corporation and a relative of Zeder, who was a member of the famed trio which built Chrysler engineering's long-lasting fame, lamented, in 1971, that when all of the costs of government regulation were assessed, by 1975, the total bill would amount to $500.00 per car in additional costs. Huebner felt that Senator Edmund Muskie ought to bear some popular ire and it should become known that he was a prime Washington force in adding to the governmental regulation of Detroit, particularly as he had presidential aspirations at this time.   And if Washington was difficult for Detroit, OPEC proved virtually impossible to contend with.

In the 1950s, George Romney, then chief executive officer of American Motors, had coined the term, "gas guzzling monsters" when promoting the very popular American Motors Rambler compact car, a nomenclature which, while perhaps accurate, was of little importance when gasoline cost less than bottled water.

But by 1973, the average fuel consumption per car had deteriorated to a mere 13.3 miles per gallon. The truth of Mr. Romney's analysis of the mainline Detroit product became suddenly even more important than he had reckoned. I remember well the moment when the Arab oil embargo was announced. As I mentioned earlier, Dennis Enright, a railroad analyst, saw the news on the tickertape and told me that Detroit and the auto industry would now soon be dead.

Until the embargo, automobile sales in this period rose from 9.3 million to 10 million in both 1971 and 1972. 1973 brought a record of 11.4 million new U.S. cars. The 1974 year, understandably, brought with it a sharp decline to 8.8 million. Curiously, the share of market for import cars held quite close in 1974 to the 15.2 percent of 1973. It was not until 1975 that the import share rose sharply to 18.2 percent of a total market of 8.6 million. Import share continued to rise through 1980. Wall Street went into a tailspin in 1970. I had become the head of Research at Hayden, Stone on May 1, 1969. The stock market turned sharply downward in the middle of May. Our research department found it impossible to recommend stocks which were to go upwards.   Our vice president, Stewart Clement, put it well when he said, "How can you find elevators that are going up when all of them are going down and staying in the basement?" It was a troubled time for high volume Hayden, Stone and its 1400 brokers in 96 worldwide offices.

George Murray was a brilliant marketer. He reminded me of Alfred P. Sloan, Jr., not because of any special marketing similarities but because each had a bad back. George came to us from Merrill, Lynch, Pierce, Fenner and Smith. Our chairman Alfred (Buddy) Coyle told us at a research seminar that George could look at a brokerage office for one minute and predict the volume of commission generation from that office within five percent of the total. He had been involved in the building of the Merrill-Lynch retail empire and knew full well the standards which were present in Merrill-Lynch. He transferred some of these standards to Hayden, Stone. Years later, I learned that it was Donald Regan who was a main architect of the Merrill-Lynch retail empire. Our George was one of his avid disciples.

George rocked in his rocker while he talked, as had Alfred P. Sloan, Jr., when I last visited him. "Up your gross," George would say over and over. To George this was the secret of success for a brokerage house. Each registered representative had to up, or increase, his or her gross. Sadly, there simply was not enough undervalued merchandise to give to a hungered retail labor force. As an officer and director, I sensed quickly that Hayden, Stone was in trouble as a firm. On my own, I contacted George H. Love who was recognized as one of the strongest coal industry executives. He headed Continental Coal Company which was part of the Hanna Mining interests. In the late 1950s, Continental Coal began buying Chrysler Corporation stock. This allowed George Love to become chairman of the Chrysler board in September of 1961, a position he held through 1966. When he returned to the coal industry and to his private investments, he retained an interest in the Chrysler Corporation. I kept in touch with George until well into the 1980s.

When Hayden, Stone began to flounder, it was natural that I should go to George Love. I told him that I was acting as a single member of the board and I felt that a consortium of automotive executives could be put together to raise as much as $35 million to restructure and save Hayden, Stone.

In early September of 1970, I had received a telephone call at our Scarsdale home from the United Press. The question was: "Would Hayden, Stone be able to open their doors that day?" I answered accurately that we would, but shortly thereafter there was, indeed, no more Hayden, Stone on Wall Street. My furtive effort with George Love never really got off the ground. I was also not encouraged by any of the senior officers of Hayden, Stone.

One superb moment remains. I had approached Dayco Corporation's Richard and Robert Jacob. They had sold their Cadillac Plastics Company into the old Dayton Tire and Rubber Company. When the acquiring firm suffered business reverses, the brothers Jacob came to the rescue and by the late 1960s were in charge. It was a golden moment when Dick Jacob called me with a firm oral commitment to take a $2 million participation in the $35 million needed to save Hayden, Stone. He called and said simply, "Arvid, put us down for two."

But George Love never became persuaded that Hayden, Stone could reverse its earnings losses. He did, however, remain in close touch until the firm was purchased by a partnership of four of the most entrepreneurial Wall Streeters of the 1970s. They had begun operations in 1965 and by 1970 had amassed enough positive cash to be able to deliver an offer of $9 million for the purchase of the assets of Hayden, Stone. The four young executives, Cogan, Berlind, Weill, and Levitt, took over the assets of Hayden, Stone ten minutes before the bell sounded for opening of the exchange on September 10, 1970.

I had a true professional love affair with Hayden, Stone. I was saddened when the only founding family member, David Stone, left the firm in 1969. In retrospect, this signaled the end of Hayden, Stone. I continued to chide him for leaving what his grandfather had built so well.

The automobile industry and Wall Street both had problems in the early 1970s. These were my two great business passions. When Dennis Enright, the railroad analyst, chortled that Detroit was dying, I immediately took the opposite views. I committed myself to the proposition that Detroit not only could handle the oil embargo but would also move onward and upward into the twenty-first century. Not to do so would have been to disenfranchise seventy years of blood and guts progress by American industrialists, managers and laborers who survived two world wars and the Great Depression, intact. I didn't base my commitment so much on trends, fuel costs, or computerized calculations as on people, many of whose lives I've touched upon in this book. To me, if all the experiences that these people went through were valid, real experiences, then the American automobile industry would also have to be a valid force, at least as long as automobiles are produced. Imagining an automobile industry without American autos was, and is, to me like imagining the American League, in baseball, without the New York Yankees. In fact, when the oil embargo came, General Motors, the New York Yankees of the American auto industry, went into a crash planning phase. GM knew that the industry could no longer continue to make gas guzzling monsters. The time had come to create energy efficient automobiles.

The 1975 Energy Act decreed that miles per gallon figures would simply have to go up. The period from 1975 through 1983 marked an engineering product revolution. Never before had an industry so fully met the national dictates of conservation as did the auto industry in that era. Meanwhile, Wall Street became very negative about not only the auto industry but about industrial companies generally. It was not until 1985 that professional investors, by and large, could see a future for the domestic auto industry, and even then there existed immense doubts for valid reasons.

A significant meeting took place in New York in 1985 which had its roots in this 1970-1974-period when a new international business climate was being established. During that period Japan's yen moved up sharply over the dollar, making it very easy for the Japanese to export vehicles into the high-profit North American market. American consumers rejoiced in the perceived quality and excellence of Japanese cars and heaped criticism onto the Detroit products, some of which was deserved.

It was impossible for the industry to communicate to the public that it was going through the extremely difficult phase of having to downsize its products while at the same time, competing with a Japanese product which was manufactured in an environment where manufacturing costs were substantially less than they were in the United States. Many in Wall Street saw the end of Detroit. Would Dennis Enright be right?

Mayday, 1975, had been much heralded in Wall Street as the end of the golden age of the securities industry. It was on May 1, 1975, that the commission rates charged to both retail and institutional customers would be fully deregulated.

In 1973 I had the opportunity to defend a rate structure in Wall Street which assured some money for research. One of the strongest advocates for deregulation was Donald Regan, then on the rise toward Wall Street's most powerful and prestigious position, as president of Merrill-Lynch, Pierce, Fenner, and Smith.

My voice on the witness stand in Washington, before the Securities and Exchange Commission, was entirely out of phase with the mainstream. I was aware that we at Hayden, Stone had spent 1.2 cents of each commission dollar for research, and that Merrill-Lynch had spent five-eighths of a cent of each dollar received on research. Many firms, the so called institutional houses, spent as much as fifteen percent of the commission dollar. I foresaw a time when the big Wall Street firms would continue to amalgamate and when only a few houses could afford research budgets in the two percent, and larger, area. It was in that kind of climate that the "boutique", a small specialty shop, was created. Walter B. Delafield, the father of the boutique, also formed Alliance I, a group of superstar analysts who were able to command large commissions from institutions. It turned out that there were too many superstars. They could not work together. At one point, Walter returned from field travel to find that he had no boutique and no job. Walter immediately formed Delafield Childs, Incorporated; and it was to that firm that I was drawn in 1971.

In my Wall Street experience, I came to know a young officer of the United States Trust Company in New York, John F. Gordon, Jr., who came regularly to my bank-automotive analyst seminars. These were luncheon meetings usually held at the Bankers Club of America. Wall Street loves to talk about the auto industry when it can get its eyes off the ticker tape or, more recently, off the digital readout. At one point, John Gordon, Jr. and I talked of the early days of the auto industry. John's father had left the U.S. Navy as a commissioned officer, joined GM in 1923, became an engineering giant, and later became GM's president. John F. Gordon, Sr., was a man among men.

One of John, Jr.s' fondest memories was of sitting at the side table in the Gordon home as a 5-year-old during the 1936 sit-down strikes at GM, resting his feet on a plaster of paris mold. He recalled, during my leisurely visit to his elegant offices on Wall Street, that his father had brought the plaster mold to the house to protect it from the vandalism which had developed in many GM plants. The plaster mold was of the GM's newest future engine, the ninety-degree V-8, which later became a corporation standard. Indeed, when six-cylinder engines came back into vogue in the late 1970s even these were built along the configurations of the original V-8 on which John F. Gordon, Jr.'s, feet had rested forty years earlier.

John Gordon, Sr. was part of an engineering team that had, in my view, far greater influence on the automobile industry than had Ford's Whiz Kids after World War II. He was also an engineer's engineer. When I knew him, in his role as one the advisers to the General Motors Engineering Journal, he loved to discuss engineering principles and engineering personages. It was his son, in later visits, who used again the very same names that I had heard in his father's offices.

There was Fred Arnold, chief engineer, who once told me that he did his best engineering work at the kitchen table of his home, in his stocking feet, wiggling his toes. There was Carl Rassmussen, a young engineer just coming along who became chief engineer of Cadillac in the late 1960s. It is difficult now to underestimate the influence of a Swede, Ernest Seaholm, who was an early Cadillac chief engineer and a mentor of John F. Gordon, Sr. right after he'd taken off his Navy uniform and donned the blue of General Motors.

There also were many others, including Peter Drucker, Roger Kyes, Edward N. Cole, Harry Barr, M.S. Rosenberger, David Crockett, Victor Olson, and William Carnegie. Many of these names were later to be found on the lists of GM hierarchy. This team of engineers not only designed the V-8 engine to a far more advanced stage than had Henry Ford engineers, but also joined it to an automatic transmission. Out of that core of engineers in the John F. Gordon, Sr. design section came both the V-8 engine and the famed Hydra-Matic automatic transmission. Victor Olson and Bill Carnegie left Cadillac to form the engineering brainpower of the Hydra-Matic Division. Victor was actually the father of the famed Hydra-Matic.

By the time John F. Gordon, Jr. put his child feet on the plaster cast of the V-8 engine, the project had been underway for more than seven years, but the plaster mold was the only authentic design record of the engine up to that time. The John Gordon design group functioned out of the Detroit Clark Street plant of Cadillac, and since the main thrust of the United Auto Workers sit-down strike was in Flint, there was not a great danger of problems at the Cadillac plant. Nevertheless, even the unionized workers who were involved with the Cadillac engine were in accord with the chief designer's precautionary decision to take the plaster mold to his home in Rosedale Park for the duration of the strike.

The decade of the 1970s was one of product transition, a transition still not fully accepted by the buying public even into the late 1980s. The period began with performance and ended with fuel economy. No greater change was conceivable. At General Motors, the 1970-1974 period began with James M. Roche continuing as chairman of the board until January I, 1972, when he was replaced by Richard C. Gerstenberg. Edward N. Cole continued as president until late into 1974.

The muscle car reached the pinnacle of its popularity in 1970. With the exception of Cadillac, each GM division offered big-block engines with ultra-high performance by mid-size automobiles. However, by 1971, the federal government was becoming increasing concerned about automotive exhaust emissions and safety; also, insurance companies were becoming more reluctant to offer policies on high performance cars. As a result, the horsepower figures began to drop dramatically. Advertising began placing less and less emphasis on the power figures until, in the late 1980s, no one knows or cares about the output of an engine except the pure aficionado. Engine capability is now measured in terms of its displacement rather than its horsepower.

Another factor reducing the output of GM's engines was their decision to utilize catalytic converters as the principal means by which exhaust emissions were to be controlled. These catalytic converters were standard on all GM cars by 1975. To prepare for the advent of the converters, it was decided that all 1971 GM engines would operate on unleaded gasoline since leaded gasoline contaminates the converter and makes it totally ineffective. The use of unleaded gasoline led to a reduction in engine compression ratios, a loss of efficiency and a reduction in horsepower. Nonetheless, General Motors produced 4.8 million cars in 1971, with Chevrolet alone, led by its all-new full-size vehicle which featured a long hood, plush exteriors and luxurious interiors, selling 2.3 million units.

However, the one GM car which was to be the harbinger of the 1970's and even of the 1980s, was the 1971 Chevrolet Vega. Totally new from the ground up, the Chevrolet Vega was designed to compete with the growing threat of foreign imports and to test the market for a small fuel-efficient car. The Vega was the first American car whose manufacturing process made extensive use of computerized robots to perform tedious, repetitive tasks such as spot welding. The Vega was also designed to be maintained by owners, with a detailed repair manual explaining most basic repairs. Unfortunately, the Vega is not fondly remembered by former owners. The body and sheet metal attracted inordinate amounts of corrosion; furthermore, the overhead cam, aluminum 4-cylinder engine was beset by various problems which led GM away from aluminum block design for the future.

In 1972, the GMC Truck and Coach Division introduced an all new motor home. This was also new from the ground up and perhaps the most comfortable, efficiently shaped, and totally integrated motor home ever produced. It slept six people, included an air suspension at the rear and was powered by a 6.7 liter GMC engine. However it quickly became an unfortunate victim of the times. The 1974, oil embargo killed the recreational vehicle market, and the GMC motor home went with it.

During this period, GM performed extensive testing on the Wankel rotary engine, believing that it had potential as a replacement for the reciprocating engine. The engine, throughout its existence, had two basic problems, emissions and sealing. Neither problem was solved by GM. All efforts were abandoned in 1974.

The cold, snowy winter of 1973-1974 was made even more miserable by the Arab OPEC nations' embargo which severely reduced the petroleum availability in the United States. The U.S. is currently the world's third largest national producer of crude oil, behind Russia and Saudi Arabia. We produce 16 percent of the world's volume or 8.76 million barrels of crude oil per day. However, we also have the greatest thirst. Our output has to be supplemented by more than 5 million barrels per day, about half of which comes from OPEC nations.

The embargo created immediate problems. Gasoline stations were swamped with customers who waited for hours in lines of cars which extended for blocks. To expedite matters, the station operators usually had the line of vehicles parade past the same side of the fuel pump. Car owners whose fuel-filler provisions were on the side of the vehicle away from the pump were in trouble. However, necessity breeds invention and many would get in line backwards, then back-up for blocks until they reached the pumps for a fill-up.

After the effects of the OPEC embargo were fully realized, the federal government set machinery in motion to minimize the effects of another such embargo. First, the nation's petroleum storage capacity was increased to provide the equivalent of at least a 90-day supply of import oil. More importantly, the government created the Energy Tax Act of 1978. Under the law, standards were established wherein automobile manufacturers had to meet a certain fuel economy average for the entire model year production, an average which continued to rise annually. This Energy Act literally and completely changed automotive design.

Ford entered the 1970s with a new compact car, heavily restyled intermediates and a new president. After operating with a trio of presidents following the dismissal of Bunkie Knudsen in 1969, the company appointed Ford division general manager Lee Iacocca as the overall president.

In 1971, Ford brought out its competitor to the Chevrolet Vega, also classified as a sub-compact. This new entry was the Pinto, a chunky-looking two-door sedan. Both the Vega and Pinto were designed to combat the fifteen percent share of the U.S. market owned by the VW Beetle in 1970. While the Vega sported more sophisticated engineering designs, the Pinto was an honest, straightforward vehicle. The Pinto would go on to have a long ten-year production run, remaining a consistent best seller despite an early fuel tank which was publicly reported unsafe. Throughout the competition, the Pinto consistently outsold the Vega and managed to get Ford through some difficult years.

The 1972 model year saw Ford bring out the brand new mid-size Torino, and the new Ford Thunderbird. The latter was now a very large car, sharing the same body structure as the Continental Mark IV. The Pinto line now also gained a station wagon model.

The 1973 and 1974 years were fairly quiet for Ford. As was true of all manufacturers, Ford spent much effort on redesigning bumpers to meet safety standards. The oil embargo also brought about a reduced demand for full-size cars. However, such smaller Ford vehicles as the all-new Mustang II and the Maverick benefited from the fuel shortage.

Chrysler Corporation's journey through the perilous and demanding 1970s was a rocky one. The firm had more difficulty meeting safety, emission and fuel economy requirements than did the competition. It seemed somehow less prepared with fewer cakes in the oven. The Chrysler 1970 model year program included a good number of muscle cars which were expensive to build and were built in low volumes. Its 1971 fleet brimmed with full-size heavyweights powered by thirsty V-8 engines. Chrysler, then, had nothing to field against the Pinto and the Vega.

Chrysler Corporation in the 1970s fell into the same treadmill that eventually killed Studebaker and periodically threatened American Motors. Declining sales led to reduced or nonexistent profits which prevented expenditures to develop new products or improve existing ones. This led to further reductions in sales, then to greater losses and finally financial disaster.

The 1971 sales year was totally underwhelming, and if Chrysler did not have bad luck it would not have had any luck at all. Some Dodge dealers attempted to build up interest in the Dodge Challenger by agreeing to supply Challengers for the Indy 500. Accordingly, fifty orange convertibles were prepared to be used for pre-race festivities. Two were to be especially outfitted to be used as the pace car and backup. The pace car, loaded with dignitaries, went into a skid as it was leaving the track, following the warm-up lap, and plowed into a press box. Several reporters were injured and, naturally, lawsuits ensued. The promotion turned into a nightmare.

Chrysler Corporation had acquired a fifteen percent interest in Mitsubishi Motors Corporation of Japan in 1971 and further acquisitions of ten percent per year were scheduled for 1972 and 1973. This investment paid well, giving Chrysler a significant presence in the sub-compact field with the Dodge Colt, as these vehicles were called.

As with other manufacturers, Chrysler was forced to lower compression ratios on its 1972 engines to permit the use of unleaded fuel; and its muscle cars now became sheep in wolves' clothing. The 1973-1974 OPEC Oil Embargo hit Chrysler below the belt. Corporate decisions had already been made, based on Chrysler's earlier periods of success, and now it would take a long time to change direction. However 1973 was still a fairly decent year for Chrysler Corporation with some 1.8 million vehicles sold.

For 1974 Chrysler Corporation came out with a completely redesigned line of full-size automobiles, right into the teeth of the oil embargo. In defense of Chrysler, the embargo came without warning, and the gestation period for new automobiles is about four years.

However, a decade or so before the oil embargo, the clean air and safety mandates came along. It is a small wonder that there was an immense shouting match between Washington and Detroit in the 1960s and 1970s. It was not until the oil embargo in 1973 that Washington and Detroit began acting somewhat in concert. The 1975 Energy Act enabled the automotive industry to downsize its cars systematically, with no manufacturer being able to avoid the law.

There were dynamic forces underway in the 1970s. As noted, the main one was fuel economy, followed closely by clean air and safety. Very possibly, changes were made at costs which the consumer would have found unacceptable, but the consumer didn't fully understand the cause of rising automobile prices, and the manufacturers had no choice but to implement government mandated changes in their product.

The 1974 model year closed on a gloomy note for all domestic manufacturers. The buying public was clamoring for smaller cars and all too frequently went to foreign imports to find what they were looking for. All U.S. producers were now going back to the drawing boards to design and produce the type of car that was required in the marketplace. That, however, would take time and money.

CHAPTER SEVENTEEN

THE 1975-1979 ERA

Double, double toil and trouble;
Fire burn and cauldron bubble.

-William Shakespeare

The term "rebate" originated in financial circles in the railroad industry. Railroads gave rebates or some money back to large shippers and these were eventually declared to be unfair and in restraint of fair trade. Lynn A Townsend, Chairman of Chrysler Corporation, also used the term "rebate" for a marketing plan which began in mid-January of 1975. It quickly became a marketing tool which has endured since that time.

Throughout this entire century, the automobile has played a most important part in this country's growth and development. The major-prophets had been such giants as Henry Ford I, R.E. Olds, Walter P. Chrysler, Alfred P. Sloan, Jr., William F. Kettering, Henry Ford II, George Romney, Roy Chapin and Ernest Breech. A group of minor-prophets also held sway until Roger B. Smith and Lee Iacocca emerged as the major prophets of the 1980s. Important among the minor-prophets was Lynn A. Townsend, an extraordinarily talented financial official who had cut his money spurs as paymaster on the aircraft carrier U.S.S. Hornet during World War II and later as partner of the respected certified public accounting firm of Touche, Ross.

Lynn Townsend, in his time, was more praised and derided than any other official holding office in the automotive industry. However, when he restored Chrysler Corporation to nearly five percent net on sales in the early 1960s, he was the darling of Wall Street. He was the official whose name analysts liked to drop into their closed door research meetings which have shaped stock market values for decades. Lynn Townsend was in the doghouse of these same analysts by the end of 1974. In fact, the entire industry was in a shocking tailspin which many felt could not be reversed.

The year 1975 brought rebates and the United States Energy Act. Earlier, Lynn Townsend's home had suffered a furnace failure in mid-winter. This inopportune breakdown of a necessary manufactured product influenced Lynn to implement the first 50,000 mile or 5-year auto warranty.

In one of my meetings with Lynn, he said that anyone can handle the routine maintenance of a house. However, when one loses a major item such as a furnace, one appreciates the guarantee of a replacement by the manufacturer, if such guarantee exists. He said, "That is why we warrant our engines and transmissions for 50,000 miles or 5 years, whichever comes first."

That kind of warranty from Chrysler led to a flurry of quality seeking from automotive suppliers. Incidentally, in almost all of the automobile company annual reports I have ever read, there appears the claim that, "This year our quality level is the highest ever", but manufacturing claims, in many cases, were subjective; and critics such as Ralph Nader declared the industry quality as being simply sloppy. At a Kiwanis meeting in Scarsdale, New York, a Pontiac dealer came by to describe all the automobiles of the second half of the century as "do it yourself kits". Lynn Townsend, being an accountant, wanted to quantify Chrysler Corporation's claims.

In early January of 1975, the industry was still moving downward in sales. Chrysler Corporation then announced a historic $500.00 rebate which would go directly to the customer and, for the first time in automotive history, actually bypass the dealers.

Chrysler's rebates spread to General Motors, Ford, American Motors and into retailing, generally. Automobile sales had bottomed out in December of 1974 and then started on an upward spiral up to and including March of 1979. During that 51 month period, 45 million automobiles were sold. It required the Iranian Khomeni crisis and a resultant embargo of eight percent of the world's oil supply to stop the sales rise and cause another crisis. A panic over fuel supplies began in April of 1979 and did not really end until June of 1982. In that 39 month precipitous decline of automobile sales, not even rebates could hold off the skid. It was the worst decline in Detroit peacetime history, surpassing even the fall-off which began in 1929 and extended through the Great Depression.

The period from 1975 through 1979 was one where the design initiative moved entirely from Detroit to Washington. The 1975 Energy Act caused a sharp downsizing of passenger cars. The average curb weight in 1973 was 4500 pounds. When the results of the 1975 Energy Act were fully implemented, the average curb weight had come down to 2800 pounds, with some vehicles offered which weighed in at below 2000 pounds. The best way to meet the ratcheting demands of the government was to eliminate weight, which permitted the use of smaller engines, although many other modifications were tried by both the manufacturers and by the customers on an after-market basis. Included were higher axle ratios, aerodynamic rearview mirrors, higher tire pressures and other mouse milk remedies.

One of General Motors' earliest economists was Andrew Quart. In the 1940's, he tried to lead General Motors into lightweight metals. He did not foresee an energy crisis, but he argued, rather unsuccessfully in the GM councils, that it was GM's oligopolistic responsibility to create maximum fuel economy by using abundant and light metals.

Cars of the late 1970s, as noted, were designed in Washington. The engineers vied with each other to minimize weight, for that was the easiest way available at the time to increase fuel efficiency. In every possible way, the engineers sought to reduce mass, by the ounce, pound, kilogram and more. Aluminum came to the fore as an automotive material. The steel industry fought back with high strength, low-alloy steels. The plastics industry made great gains but eventually lost out because petroleum, from which plastics originate, kept on climbing in price. One of the major advancements in the plastics field was the reaction injection molding procedure.

Once I visited Coleman Hogan at the plastics works of Davison Rubber Company which had, by then, become a part of McCord Corporation and which, in turn, in the 1980's, became a part of Ex-Cello Corporation. Coleman, whom everyone called Colie, moved to Detroit and became head of McCord Corporation. Paul Casey came along and also became an executive of McCord, and later it was Paul Casey who headed Ex-Cello Corporation. So Ex-Cello acquired McCord, which had acquired Davison. The latter, interestingly enough, was developed by Coleman Hogan's mother. Davison had many of the marks of a matriarchy.

On this particular day, Colie introduced me to a young lady who was making instrument panels using the reaction injection molding technique, an operation which required only 50 pounds per square inch of pressure contrasted to many tons of pressure required to stamp out a similar component from heavy gauge sheet metal. Colie spoke with great admiration of a young engineer from Pontiac Motors whom he credited with bringing forth the reaction injection molding process, a Pontiac engineer named John Z. DeLorean.

The 1975-1979-period was characterized by the longest uninterrupted sales rise in American automotive history, the greatest product change forced by the 1975 Energy Act, and a very limited stylist influence on automotive design. The available money had to be used to downsize and there was little left for cosmetics. Indeed, during this period, cars became boxes. A favorite phrase in Wall Street was, "Oh, Detroit makes nothing pretty, only econo-boxes." The early 1980s continued this trend. A significant financial development raised the Japanese import opportunities. Acting on the findings of a study which began in 1975 and ended in 1977, Volkswagen Works of Wolfsburg of West Germany brought forth in 1978 the first of the "hybrid" automobile plants to be built in North America. VW made its major commitment by buying a plant at Westmoreland, Pennsylvania. Chrysler Corporation had intended to complete this facility east of Pittsburgh in the late 1960s, but instead left it with its steel work whistling in the wind for almost two decades.

Lynn Townsend's economist, Dr. George Elgass, had foreseen a great shortage of automobiles into the 1970s. Chrysler Corporation, heartened by Townsend's successes, wanted to expand but that expansion proved uneconomic, and the Westmoreland plant was never used for Chrysler manufacturing.

The Westmoreland plant also proved to be less than successful for Volkswagen. No sooner had VW made its commitment in the U.S. than the deutsche mark began to strengthen against the U.S. dollar. Changes in international currency valuations have always affected the automotive industry. In the case of Volkswagen, the 1978 investment found itself competing in the United States on an uphill plane. Many of the components used in the U.S. plant were made in Germany and were, thereby, becoming more and more expensive as the mark went up in value. Thus, Volkswagen, both imported and made in U.S.A., was destined to decline in sales as the mark strengthened against the dollar.

The last half of the decade of the 1970s was indeed a formative time for the U.S. automotive industry. It was impossible to make a quick turnaround from huge stone-boats to small flivvers, and this opened up the gates to foreign competition who had long been producing smaller, more fuel-efficient vehicles. This was especially true of the Japanese.

General Motors started the last half of the decade with a new chairman of the board, Thomas Murphy, who on December 1, 1974 replaced Richard Gerstenberg. GM also installed a new president, Elliot M. (Pete) Estes, who succeeded Edward N. Cole on October 1, 1974. These two executives were at the forefront of a difficult period for General Motors, which extended even into the late 1980's.

The fuel crisis in 1974 precipitated a new emphasis on fuel economy. The first response was the 1976 Chevrolet Chevette which at that time became the most fuel efficient American-built car in the country. It was powered by a 1.4 liter, 4-cylinder engine. In 1977 a 1.6 liter unit became optional. The fuel efficiency emphasis spread to the large GM cars as well. Cadillac introduced its first "small" car in 1976, the Seville. The Seville was nearly one thousand pounds lighter than the 1975 Coupe de Ville yet maintained the same traditional levels of luxury, comfort and performance. Also, on April 21, 1976, Cadillac built the last American convertible of the 1970s. All other manufacturers had previously abandoned this once very popular model. It had become incompatible with requirements of safety, and customers had begun to choose the closed air-conditioned comfort over the wind-blown effect. Cadillac built 200 "last" white convertibles, keeping the actual last car for its collection. Cadillac was inundated with orders for this milestone model, with customers believing that the era of the convertible was gone forever. In reality, it only became dormant. Public tastes would demand their return, in small numbers, in the 1980s.

GM's other lines also shed several hundred pounds in weight but sacrificed little in comfort. While Pontiac celebrated its 50th anniversary in 1976, Oldsmobile went on to break sales records and took over Pontiac's third place sales slot. Extensive downsizing of Chevrolet's full-size Impala and Caprice models led to an overall weight reduction of more than 600 pounds. With the six-cylinder engine, these vehicles were rated at 22 miles per gallon, highway, and 17 miles per gallon, city. New in 1978 was GMC's RTS (Rapid Transit Series) bus which represented a new generation in bus design, a bus for the 1980s. The RTS featured a self-contained climate conditioning system and a new, fuel efficient, turbocharged diesel engine. Chevrolet's Corvette was completely restyled for 1977. In 1979 Buick introduced its fifth generation Riviera. For the first time, Buick joined the Olds Toronado and

Cadillac Eldorado with front wheel drive. The 1979 Olds Toronado and Cadillac Eldorado were both reduced in weight by some 900 pounds. They became 20 inches shorter and 8 inches narrower than the 1978 version.

Closing out the decade of the 1970s was the GM X-car's front-wheel drive development program. The X-car was a new compact design, offering the traction and packaging advantages of front-wheel drive. The car had outstanding roominess for five adults and provided fuel economy of over 20 miles per gallon in city driving. Taking a page from Lee Iacocca's book, the X-car was introduced in early 1979 as a 1980 model. It was offered under various names by all of GM's divisions except Cadillac.

By the end of the decade, high fuel costs were changing the buying habits of the American public. Small import vehicles were increasing in popularity. Government mandated fuel economy standards were becoming more stringent. The entire marketplace was changing drastically. Starting in 1979, GM began introducing a new generation of automobiles which would carry over into the next decade.

Ford Motor Company began the second half of the decade of the 1970s with the same problems and shortcomings as existed with General Motors. Fuel costs were rising, as were the economy requirements, and the consumers were vacillating between their love of big cars and the practical aspects of the small ones. Buyers were also showing an increasing preference for better equipped, more luxurious smaller cars. The embargo accelerated that trend. The model year 1975 marked the twentieth anniversary of the Ford Thunderbird. However, the 1975 sales sank to 43,000 units, about 16,000 less than in the previous year.

The all-new Granada was designed to replace the Maverick and was touted as the "car designed for the times." Maverick sales held up and the Granada became an addition to the line, taking its place between the Maverick and Ford's mid-size cars. Granada struggled with European styling, but never made it. It did not look American, but the U.S. buyers purchased 303,000 of them the first year, and it outdistanced the Maverick by a ratio of two to one.

Meanwhile, special MPG or fuel-economy versions of the Pinto and Mustang II were introduced. These now featured catalytic converters which then allowed the engine to be tuned for greater efficiency and economy.

The model year 1976 was quite unspectacular for Ford, with most of the models carried over with only minor facelifts. The 1977 Thunderbird was all-new, dramatically downsized, reduced in weight, and reduced in price. It became an immediate success.

In 1978 Ford, along with other manufacturers, had to meet the government-directed fuel economy figures for the first time. Automobiles had to average at least 18 miles per gallon, highway, on a "sales weighted" basis. The target figure was then scheduled to rise progressively until it reached 27.5 miles per gallon fleet average in 1985. The penalty for non-compliance was $5.00 for each one-tenth mile per gallon below the standard, for each vehicle sold. However, credit could be banked for three years at the same rate as the penalty if the standard was exceeded. Conversely, a shortfall could be carried as a liability for three years on the premise that the shortage would be made up in the intervening time period.

Manufacturers scrambled to respond to the law by introducing diesel engines, and, of course, by building smaller cars. Ford's partial response was the "Ford in your future", the Fairmont. It was to become the true foundation for a whole new generation of Fords.

The Fairmont was designed with the aid of computers and featured relatively low weight for a vehicle its size, aerodynamic styling and a roomy interior. Computer-aided design saved tremendous amounts of time, effort, and money in that it allowed engineers to pinpoint areas which required increased strength without the need to build any hardware. All future Fords would be so designed.   The Fairmont made extensive use of lightweight materials such as aluminum, high-strength steel and reinforced plastics and was greeted with almost unqualified praise; some automotive writers even calling it the American Volvo. It also became a sales success, scoring over 312,000 sales during its first year.

The other Ford lines were relatively unchanged for 1978. The Mustang II was now in the last year of its existence. A new generation Mustang and a downsized, redesigned, full-size Ford LTD were the second biggest news for 1979 by a long shot. Shortly after the models were introduced, a major shake-up took place at the "Glass House" which was Ford's world headquarters in Dearborn, Michigan. In a surprise move, Chairman Henry Ford II abruptly fired President Lee Iacocca, right on Iacocca's 54th birthday, October 15, 1978. Clash of personalities was given as the official reason. Iacocca was succeeded by Philip Caldwell.

The new Mustang, with computer-aided design, lightweight materials and aerodynamic efficiency, followed in the footsteps of the Fairmont. It offered a drag coefficient of .44 which was then considered low, but which is not low by late 1980s standards when designers strive for .35 coefficients. The new breed of Mustangs found buyer favor and became Ford's second best seller, after Fairmont.

Ford's downsized LTD was less successful even though it was a match for GM's smaller full-size cars. It fell far behind Chevrolet's Impala/Caprice series. Pinto received its final facelift. Fairmont was basically unchanged. Granada, now advertised as "An American Classic", featured only minor revisions. The same was true of the Thunderbird. However, all manufacturers would suffer in the spring of 1979 with rising inflation, higher gasoline prices and a sudden general downturn in the national economy.

Chrysler Corporation's fortunes took a turn for the worse again in 1975. Initial 1975 model sales dropped to 1970 levels, and a two-month inventory piled up. Chairman Lynn Townsend refused to slash prices. Instead, he slashed production. By November 1974, Chrysler sales were down almost thirty-five percent. In all fairness, GM was down forty-three percent, but Chrysler was in worse shape since its fixed costs were spread over a smaller volume.

Chrysler was then forced to lay off 18,000 employees in an effort to cut $120 million from fixed costs. Chrysler blamed Washington politicians for its problems, claiming that the Ford administration had failed to stimulate the economy. Washington claimed that the automakers made their own bed by raising prices. In early 1975, Lynn Townsend inexplicably raised prices again and the backlog grew to 300,000 units.

Clearly something had to be done to save Chrysler and this was the cash rebate program. For the first time in history an automaker would pay people, in part, to buy its product. Others had to follow and did.

In the meantime, Townsend took steps to restructure his company to survive on long-term total industry sales of 6 million vehicles annually, instead of the typical 9 and 10 million. Such drastic structural revisions reflected upon the new products as well. The first change brought out the "small" Chrysler which was called a Cordoba. It was only two and a half inches longer than the very first 1924 Chrysler. Hollywood actor Ricardo Montalbon was asked to extol its virtues in numerous magazine advertisements and on television. The Cordoba became a genuine success, with 150,105 deliveries in its first year. Except for higher prices, the rest of the Chrysler line was little changed for 1975. The Imperial line retired in mid-1975.

On October 1, 1975, Lynn Townsend retired as Chrysler Corporation chairman in favor of President John Riccardo. Moving up to the presidency was Eugene A. Cafiero who came out of a strong production background at Dodge. Lynn Townsend retired at age 56, nine years before it would be mandatory, but insisted that he was under absolutely no pressure to do so. He said, "The automotive industry is entering a new era. There are going to have to be new methods. Even if I were to stay on to age 65, I would not be here to see the culmination of many decisions made at the present time." He was much more of a prophet than he realized.

In 1976 the Dodge Aspen and Plymouth Volare were brought out in mid-season to replace the Dodge Dart and Plymouth Valiant. Both new vehicles were reasonable market performers with a good balance of looks, economy, and performance. However, they did become the most recalled cars until the advent of GM's X-cars.

At the end of 1975, Riccardo and Cafiero arrived at a decision to drop the full-size Plymouth and Dodge by 1978. They were both of the opinion that the big car was doomed. New model developments at Chrysler Corporation for 1977 concentrated on a compact-size for two larger cars. These were the Chrysler LeBaron and Dodge Diplomat. There seemed to be a growing market for luxurious smaller cars.

Chrysler Corporation was often accused of standing by helplessly during the turmoil of the 1970s, but that was not the case. The entire industry had its design initiatives taken over by the government. Meeting safety, emission, and fuel economy standards was unbelievably expensive. Customers were jumping feverishly from large to small cars and back again. Gasoline prices were totally unpredictable, and inflation rates were skyrocketing. In the face of these problems, American Motors would not exist today if they had not been rescued in the early 1980s by Renault of France. Similarly, Chrysler would not exist today if it were not for assistance from the federal government.

Chrysler Corporation had historically brought out the right product at the wrong time, and vice versa, but in 1978, with planning and a modicum of luck, Chrysler finally introduced a product for the times. The federal CAFE, or corporate average fuel economy requirements were met head on with the Dodge Omni and Plymouth Horizon. These were the first domestically produced front-wheel drive small cars.

They employed a small power package with a Volkswagen engine mounted transversely under the hood. They were not spectacular performers or candidates for road racing but did offer fuel economy, reasonable interior roominess and a comfortable ride. They appealed to Americans to the tune of 82,000 Omnis and 107,000 Horizons the first year.

After 1978, Chrysler Corporation deserted the big car market entirely.   John Riccardo and Gene Cafiero were moving rapidly to dispose of losers, be they automobiles or other assets. They sold an unfinished assembly plant in Pennsylvania to Volkswagen. Airtemp was sold to Fedders. The Big Sky recreation facility in Montana was sold on the open market. Rebates were used wherever necessary, except for the well-selling Omni and Horizon. In late 1978, Chrysler arranged to sell all of its European subsidiaries to Peugeot of France. In 1979 Chrysler sold a solid money maker, Chrysler Realty.

In August of 1979, the firm's Supplemental Unemployment Fund ran dry, exhausted by the 27,600 laid-off workers. Chrysler lost $205 million for 1978. In 1979 the loss was a staggering $1.1 billion. Inflation was pushing interest rates beyond the reach of many customers, yet Chrysler was the only member of the Big Three to lose money in 1979. Their share of the market by this time stood at an anemic ten percent.

Riccardo hoped to convert all of the company products to front-wheel drive by 1985-86, but designers and engineers could not afford to experiment because waste was absolutely intolerable. The relentless government regulations were requiring Chrysler to spend hundreds of millions to meet fixed deadlines for safety, emissions. Riccardo, in 1979, decided that Chrysler had no choice but to seek temporary assistance. He claimed that the company needed $1 billion in advance tax credits and an immediate injection of $750 million in operating capital.

U.S. President Jimmy Carter had a simple solution to Chrysler's problems. He said, in effect, "Automaker, heal thyself." Earlier, Secretary of Transportation, Brock Adams, had blithely told the stricken industry to "reinvent the automobile." President Carter was suggesting that Chrysler's troubles were self-inflicted and that its management had to be restructured or even replaced to build more fuel-efficient cars. Yet, by government measures, Chrysler had the best corporate average fuel economy of any of the Big Three in 1979.

On November 2, 1978, Chrysler announced third quarter losses of $160 million. That was also the day that Lee Iacocca joined Chrysler as president, with John Riccardo remaining as chairman. Iacocca was to replace Riccardo on January 1, 1980, but, as it turned out, Riccardo resigned in September, 1979. Iacocca assumed the top position earlier than anticipated. As soon as he came aboard, Iacocca began the belt tightening process. He claimed that there were 35 vice presidents, each with their own turf which they guarded jealously. Over a three-year period, he fired 33 of those 35 vice presidents, or almost one a month.

Iacocca also decided that a government "bailout" was the only possible solution. He personally appeared in Washington to present Chrysler's automotive plans for the future. He absorbed varying degrees of abuse from the government officials; and yet, just before Christmas of 1979, he won.

As ironed out between House and Senate conferees, the Chrysler survival package provided $3.5 billion in aid, including $1.5 billion in federal loan guarantees. However, it required $475 million in wage concessions from the UAW and $125 million in salary concessions from management. In addition, Chrysler was to issue $150 million in new stock, under a new employee stock ownership plan, and had to raise an additional $2 billion from the private sector in order to qualify for the federal loan backing. The bill passed both the House and the Senate by a substantial margin. The lawmakers must have listened to Iacocca when he told them that a bankruptcy would eliminate the jobs of 140,000 Chrysler employees, as well as some 600,000 jobs in related industries. A ratio of five related jobs to each one directly involved in automotive manufacture holds true even in the late 1980's.

Nevertheless, just about everyone was against a Chrysler bailout, on principle, including GM chairman Thomas A. Murphy and most of the financial community. Lee Iacocca wrote that, "For most of them, federal help for Chrysler constituted a sacrilege, a heresy, a repudiation of the religion of corporate America; and other assorted bullshit." However, the financial help to Chrysler was not without precedent. The government previously had made loan guarantees to Lockheed, five major steel companies, and the cities of New York and Washington, totaling some $409 billion. When the loan guarantee was granted and borrowing began, the Chrysler 1980 line was already in the marketplace and Chrysler went on to lose $1.7 billion that year. The loan guarantee was not an immediate salvation but only a reprieve which Lee Iacocca, eventually, would put to spectacular use.

Very often personal success depends not so much on talent or preparation but upon perspiration or the capricious Lady Luck. One person's failure can often provide a glorious opportunity for someone waiting in the wings. Many minds are filled with memories and recriminations of "what might have been".

This is very often true in the automotive industry at all levels of endeavor, including the very top. The two most prominent examples of this harsh reality are Lee Iacocca and John Z. DeLorean. Now, where to proceed with this essay? Perhaps I should zero in on Lee Iacocca, for his is a leader's role in the half generation just behind us. Lee Iacocca's is a name known throughout the world. However, he had to be discharged, or fired, by Henry Ford II, to become as visible as he now is.

Henry Ford II released Lee Iacocca quite suddenly, unexpectedly, and apparently without reason. However, I'll not criticize Henry, knowing that there are at least two versions of any argument. It is noteworthy that in the new generations since we graduated into a Horatio Alger world, the common thought is to emphasize the dark sides of the moons, to the point of forgetting the existence of the bright sides.

In his period of travail, I very much wanted to see Lee Iacocca to offer whatever help I could. Dorothy Carr, Lee's executive secretary, finally arranged a visit for me. I knew a good bit about Dorothy from my niece Diane Jouppi Yagerlenner, a legal secretary also at Ford Motor for a time. Dorothy Carr was a devout Christian, and a kind lady.

Lee had been fired, but not yet relegated to the warehouse, where he was to wind up his Ford affairs. Although Lee and I had appeared together on a Canadian film and TV documentary entitled "Henry Ford's America" in 1976, I really did not know him well. Moreover, I don't regularly go into such presidential offices. I saw Lee's office and expressed only polite admiration. After Lee's Statue of Liberty time, I can now more properly place his decor choices into four centuries of cultural perspective. Lee has expressed his admiration of Christopher Columbus, and it was in the 1400's that Italian baroque architecture came into vogue. In the time of Columbus, baroque was beautiful. Now, baroque has come to mean something so extravagantly ornamented as to border on less than the best taste. Lee's office, to me, had a touch of the baroque. I remember it well because I had expected smooth, clean lines, as found in the executive offices of Ford's mid-town antagonist, General Motors. Lee's office had both color and ornamentation. The center, to me, was a work space behind Lee's big, big chair. There, as at his Chrysler Corporation work table later, were portraits of his wife, Mary, and of the girls.

Lee's office goes down as the second most striking I've seen in my career. The most elegant belonged to a former Fort Worth baseball player named William Grace. After he could no longer knock balls into the nearby Hobbs Trailer Company lot, he went there and got a job. Later, he found himself part of a company formed by a blacksmith named August Fruehauf, on Shoemaker Street, in Detroit, Michigan. The by-now-aged baseball player became head of Fruehauf Corporation and, among other things, built himself the most beautiful office I have ever seen. He also coined a phrase which he engraved into plates he gave to visitors: Stick and Stay and Make It Pay. Yet, this tale is not about offices.

Now, in Lee's office in 1978, I found little to remind me that here was the father of the great Ford Mustang, an administrator whose leadership was so powerful that it could not possibly mesh with the management of a proud Ford dynasty. I sensed the root reasons why Iacocca and Ford did not get along well at the end. I also sensed why Henry Ford II had recognized in Lee Iacocca a great talent which was not to come to full force until after Henry let Lee leave Ford Motor Company.

I asked for a half hour and offered to leave promptly, but our conversation lasted close to an hour. We expressed mutual admiration for Jack McDougall. Jack was a young Scotsman who left the old sod as a young man. He entered Ford Trade School and later came to be, in my view, the most gifted factory builder and manufacturing genius of the 1960s and 1970s. Lee said, in our visit, that Jack was the only man he knew who could one day look at a green field and then, three years later, have high quality cars coming off from an efficient production line. Indeed, Lee felt that Jack could very ably succeed him as Ford president. Then Lee let out with the only slightly negative comment about Henry Ford II of that visit.

Lee said, and I believe the quote is accurate, though from memory, "Jack would make an excellent interim president for the next two or three years, until things get settled down a little." Lee paused, and then continued, "But with Henry, no one campaigns anyone for an office, not even for sheriff."

We talked about his opinion of a "world car". He talked about the possibility of writing a book, and commented that he had tapes at home of most of his public utterances over a period of years. Walter Murphy, a public relations official assigned to help with most of Lee's Ford Motor Company activities put these together. I urged Lee to think in terms of a car that would be as affordable, for a new billion people, as was the Model-T in the time of Henry Ford I. I also expressed, with a certainty founded only on faith, that his greatest contribution to his time was up ahead somewhere.

My visit with Lee Iacocca, in his office, was now over, by common consent. Lee's left hand was on the door knob of that very nice office. As men will, we looked at each other, not knowing exactly what to say. Lee must have read some of my concern, either in how I looked, or in what I might have already said. At that moment I felt, regardless of the conditions present, the industrial world needed Lee, but that there might never again be anything so lofty for him as being president of Ford Motor Company. I believed then and believe now that the greatest worldwide company on earth is Ford Motor Company, and Lee had helped to build it.

Now I will quote, as best as I can remember, what Lee said as I exited, "Arvid, don't worry about me. When I was at Lehigh, I was not the greatest of engineers. At about that time, Robert MacNamara and a gentleman named Beacham came into my life. They had a hand in my coming to Ford from Princeton Graduate School of Business." Then Lee voiced the most significant thought which he has, in my opinion, expressed in print or orally, in private or publicly, "The Lord had His hand on me then. He has had His hand on me since then, and now. And He will have His hand on me in the future." We shook hands and I left.

I thanked his secretary Dorothy Carr for making possible a very fine visit. I left in an almost agonizingly sad but beautiful delight. Here, I felt, was a man of history. I did not know whether his contribution to history had ended, but I suspected not. I'm sure I was the last Wall Street financial analyst to visit there, and perhaps I was even the last visitor to his great office. When I left, waiting to enter was a decorating consultant, burdened with fabric samples, color chips and sketches. I presumed she was to do her thing for the next occupant.

Later, I mentioned Lee's endorsement of him to Jack McDougall, who remained a true-blue Henry Ford II loyalist to the end. I sensed, without Jack's saying so, that he was very pleased to have such an endorsement, even coming from the depths of Lee's agony, as it must have. I once heard Henry Ford II say something about Iacocca, after Lee had revitalized Chrysler. Henry said, on Late Night America, in answer to a Dennis Wholley question: "I don't want to talk about him, but I will say that no one likes to be called a bastard in public". Lee had done so on a spectacular NBC documentary which showed an "unvarnished" Iacocca.

At this point, I want to emphasize that I publicly applauded Lee's move to Chrysler, but I also had a great deal of respect for Henry Ford II. Indeed, when John DeLorean was making his mid-1970s moves to get his gull-winged car off the launching pad, I made an overture to Henry Ford II to consider taking on John into the Ford organization. I wrote to Henry, at John DeLorean's suggestion, recommending him, but making it, as would be understood in such delicate matters, appear to be my own idea. I went to Henry through good friend Theodore (Ted) Mecke, a Ford vice-president. I called Ted "the vice-president in charge of Henry". Actually, Ted was a skilled and disciplined administrator and quiet Ford Motor Company public policy maker.

Henry Ford II found himself in the University of Michigan hospital in Ann Arbor during that time. Lee then took charge of Ford Motor Company in that dark period and did a mighty fine job of it, as the results proved. I did not expect to ever hear from Henry about my thoughts in regard to John DeLorean. But lo, word did come back, through Ted Mecke. Henry thanked me for the suggestion but indicated that he was fully satisfied with his senior management – and that included Lee, of course. I have never before set this thought down in print. Perhaps, in some way it will help to heal a wound in a business friendship which turned into a publicized feud between Lee Iacocca and Henry Ford II.

I gave the news to John DeLorean and he went on to try for a top position as American Motors. That failed also. I stayed in touch with John until two weeks before the great cocaine "bust". I immediately sent him a few dollars for a defense fund with a note stating that I hate the sin but love the sinner. I have not heard from John since, but have followed his trial and problems, and now his expressions of sublime experiences.

Greatness has a way of re-emerging, often time and time again. The last time I saw Lee Iacocca close enough to have a word with him was at a New York meeting to which Chrysler Corporation had invited us Wall Street research types. I was on the outer fringe of a cluster of people who were complimenting him on a talk and asking questions. Lee's and my glances touched for just an instant. In that instant, Lee did not appear to recognize me, nor acknowledge that he did. I sensed, however, that I was to him more than a stranger in the crowd.

In December of 1983, I was among several hundred guests of Chrysler, and Lee was the main speaker. Ordinarily, I sit in the back rows. This time, Stanley S. Kresge, who died recently, having overseen the giving away of some $300 million to all manner of good causes, did not come and his chair was vacant. Someone from Chrysler asked me to sit there. In the question period most people asked about current "this year" things. I'd been waiting for my opportunity to ask what I felt was the most important question anyone of us could ask. Earlier that year, I had asked Henry Ford II who would build the next "world" car, and he referred me to the Company. There David McCammon virtually said, "Not Ford Motor." I, therefore, posed the same query to Lee, "With the automotive industry outside of North America growing twice as fast as it is here, who will finally build a car for the world's masses, something like the Model-T Ford, that will do the job and be affordable?" Lee was silent for a time, and then answered with one word, "Korea."

Since then Korea has emerged as a new automobile-making nation, and Chrysler Corporation is committed in Korea. By the year 2000 A.D., there will be 6 billion people on earth, needing at least 600 million cars and trucks for transportation and just to get food moved around from the fields to their mouths. We now have 4.7 billion people and about 470 million cars and trucks in use on our terra firma. I do believe Lee Iacocca will be heard from in the matter of a true Model-T type vehicle for the world.

Lee Iacocca is perhaps the most successful businessman of this generation, perhaps even of the century. He is being given complete credit for saving Chrysler from bankruptcy. His autobiography "Iacocca" for a time was outsold only by the Bible. He was ostensibly the driving force behind the restoration of the Statue of Liberty and for that, also, he was given full credit. He is, in the mid-1980s, one of the most admired men in America and one of the most successful, if financial rewards are a measure of success. Various organizations are expanding efforts to convince Lee Iacocca to seek the Democratic presidential nomination for the highest office in this country and perhaps the world. Should they fail to convince him to seek the office willingly, a draft is even being considered. Lee Iacocca, seemingly, can do no wrong.

John Z. DeLorean, on the other hand, in the mid-1980s was on the opposite side of the spectrum from Iacocca.

DeLorean was, seemingly, an automotive business failure. He quit General Motors as group vice president, to go into business for himself, producing very advanced and innovative automobiles in Ireland, for sale mostly to the U.S. His efforts to build his own automotive empire quickly ran into difficulty. However, in my own personal experience with both men, things could have been very different for each. The degree of difference must be left to speculation. John Z. DeLorean resigned from General Motors when Lee Iacocca was still employed by the Ford Motor Company. I talked to John soon after his resignation and told him that I thought his move was unwise. I said, "John, if you have ambitions in the automotive industry, at the highest levels, you need a power base to operate from. There is no power base in this country stronger than the one you just voluntarily left, as group vice president of General Motors." We talked a while longer and I left for my car. John followed me out to the parking lot to ask my advice as to what he should now do, and where he could now go. I told John that I would talk to John Riccardo at Chrysler to see if there was any interest in John Z. DeLorean. On that note our meeting ended.

I did contact John Riccardo and told him about my now self-employed friend. Riccardo seemed genuinely interested in DeLorean, and a meeting was arranged for the following Monday which would include the three of us. I relayed that information to DeLorean and he seemed pleased. However, on the weekend immediately preceding our meeting an article appeared in one of the newspapers in which DeLorean laid some heavy and bitter criticism on the automotive industry in general, and on Chrysler Corporation in particular. Riccardo immediately called me to cancel the meeting, saying that at that point he had no interest in DeLorean.

Subsequently, Iacocca was fired by Henry Ford II and hired by Riccardo at Chrysler. It is interesting to speculate the alternatives. Perhaps if DeLorean had not vented his spleen in a newspaper article he would, today, be in Iacocca's shoes. Instead, after rejections at Chrysler and Ford, DeLorean continued to form his own company.

John began with the vehicle design, about which he had some definite ideas. Soon his undertaking required a location for his assembly plant, a plant itself, and heavy financial backing. Various cities, including Detroit, expressed an interest, as did several countries. John DeLorean was finally offered a multi-million dollar subsidy and a manufacturing plant in Ireland. The British government had hoped that an endeavor of this nature would, perhaps, help heal the wounds of the violent and bloody struggle between the Irish Protestants and Catholics which was breaking out sporadically at that time. John DeLorean designed the car, built the plant, hired the workers and even began some production. Yet, he seemed to be in constant financial difficulty.

I had been in touch with John at the beginning of 1973 which was when he began his struggle, already owning a well publicized prototype model, but in great need of money. Several others and I tried to do whatever we could to help him. We even contacted more than a hundred existing dealers to seek their opinion of the car. They all thought the car to be excellent, and very saleable.

Meanwhile, John was also meeting Ray Dirks, an innovative, highly talented financial person. At one of these meetings, I transmitted the opinions of the dealers to Ray Dirks and John DeLorean. They both seemed encouraged by the information. Ray Dirks finally arrived at a four stage plan for John to raise money to support John's established four year four-year business model. Ray suggested raising money through a stock offering at $1 per share. The initial offering would have attached three classes of warrants, each providing additional stock in successive years.

The first warrant required John to give up a large ownership share if he had not achieved target performance in the first year. The second and third warrants still required him to give up more and more of his company to the investors if he continued failing to meet the planned targets. John DeLorean considered the plan to be satisfactory and exhibited confidence in his ability to meet deadlines.

However, John's other financial advisers persuaded him to have a conventional stock offering at $10 per share and not to be involved with warrants. Ray Dirks said that the plan would not fly, but DeLorean went ahead, regardless.

John continued to talk with me. Actually, my earliest effort to raise money in his behalf was even before the Ray Dirks period. I telephoned a bank in Indonesia to suggest a $25 million commitment for John's project which was then moving from Detroit, to Puerto Rico, to Northern Ireland, and back to Detroit, depending on the latest news report. Indonesia was interested only if John DeLorean or a personally appointed representative would come there to discuss the matter.

However, at that time, John was interested in the failing International Harvester Scout which was being built in Fort Wayne, Indiana. He thought about buying the tools, moving them to Indonesia and manufacturing the Scout there, with cheap labor, for export to the United States. Nothing came of that notion.

On another occasion, John asked me to work out a rental plan whereby DeLorean cars would be available at various airports on a premium basis. While I was pursuing that idea, he called to ask if I could possibly raise $5 million among the Detroit automotive executives. He felt that he could use that $5 million as leverage to borrow $100 million. He even suggested that I act as chairman of his company.

I telephoned just one executive who could have put up a large share of the money. He told me that I should avoid working with John and added that this was his easiest financial decision. The answer was simply and quickly, "No." I did not contact anyone else in Detroit, knowing full well that all of the answers to this same suggestion would have been outright refusals. I called John to tell him of my failure, and to pass on the suggested chairmanship.

Not too much later, I received a telephone call from a writer for the Los Angeles Times, telling me of John DeLorean's indictment on a charge of trafficking in drugs. I told the caller that I could not believe that this could be true. He assured me that it was. I replied that if, indeed, John DeLorean was so charged, my position was clear. I loved the sinner, but hated the sin. He was eventually acquitted on the drug charges, but his automotive endeavor failed completely. However, I'm sure that John will never lose the dream of some day having his own successful car company.

CHAPTER EIGHTEEN

THE ERA OF THE 1980'S

All the world's a stage, and all the men
And women merely players
- William Shakespeare

As the American automobile industry reaches the hundredth anniversary of its development in the mid-1980s and enters its second century, it should now be a mature entity. Yet the market uncertainties, the design confusion, and the economic roller coasters are as much in existence now as they were almost one hundred years ago. Major changes continue, and the early 1980s, perhaps more than any other period, have contributed to the American automotive structure of the future.

Until the relatively recent past, the design and engineering of a vehicle were the primary motivating force. The manufacturing and assembly plants, at times, had to turn cartwheels to carry out the designer's precise instructions. This was followed by a period when pressure from Washington was so strong that neither the customer nor the manufacturer had much to say about what the automobiles should be.

Now, however, the manufacturers have learned how to meet the government-mandated requirements; and creativity and innovation can again be utilized. However now, if the American manufacturers are to meet the threat of a very aggressive and capable foreign competition, a new way of making cars has to be developed. This has to be the era when the manufacturing facilities have to be king. Maximized productivity, even if it requires design compromises, has to be the unwavering goal. How well the U.S. automotive manufacturers accomplish this will dictate the degree of success or failure of the future.

It is entirely within the realm of possibility that the American manufacturers will not be able to meet the threat of foreign competition within the limits of their resources and that the U.S. industry will begin a slow process of decay, degenerating to a level of specialty manufacturers of trucks, tractors, buses and a few restricted automobiles. In the interim, this country's love for automobiles will not diminish. It will just be that many more people will be driving foreign-made cars. The ratio in the mid-1980s was about thirty percent foreign made, and slowly climbing. That climb may never stop.

However, regardless of who produces cars and trucks, the need for them, on a worldwide basis, is as important as ever. Cars and trucks are hunger-fighters, especially in the third-world countries. As mentioned previously, food production is not the biggest problem. Getting the food out of the fields, to the markets and into people's mouths is the primary concern. And once hunger is defeated, the cars and trucks will be needed to speed the process of industrialization in those same third-world areas.

Finally, the people of the third-world countries are yet to experience the joys of the automobile as a source of pleasure, recreation and transportation. Historically, those joys are unending and never diminishing. The people of the United States have had access to the automobile for almost a hundred years, yet the love affair shows no evidence of subsiding.

The automobile and the truck have a bright future based on want and necessity. At this point in history, however, it is difficult to predict just where and by whom the cars and trucks of the world will be produced. If the American automotive industry is doomed, it fails to recognize the symptoms of fatality, even into the end of the decade of the

1980s. Huge amounts of money are being spent on new programs and on new more efficient plants in an effort to become more competitive with the foreign imports.

The decade of the 1970s ended with the American vehicles striving to become smaller and more fuel efficient. This same effort continued into the 1980's. However, in 1970, a war began in the automotive industry. That was the year when GM's Lordstown, Ohio plant was opened. Lordstown was run by the General Motors Assembly Division and the formation of this division opened the way for change to the Alfred P. Sloan, Jr. organization, a reorganization which was finally completed in the 1980s.

The Lordstown plant was so automated that even the vehicle "OK" sticker was put on by a robot arm. I toured this plant in 1971, under the auspices of the Financial Analyst Society of Chicago. The tour was arranged by Andre Archambault, a brilliant auto analyst who, at that time, worked for Continental Bank of Illinois. Later at the luncheon table sat Jules Hoffman, who had seen the 1913 Ford Motor plant in Highland Park, and was still active with Capitol Research of Los Angeles. He commented to the group that this plant would open up a new era, as progressive and as valuable as was the first moving production line of Ford Motor Company in 1913. All the analysts around the table, including me, agreed that this was indeed the situation. Lordstown was a place where cars could be built at a rate of 100 per hour; Lordstown was a place where robots could reach and weld in places where human beings found it most difficult; Lordstown was the plant that could have the advantages of high technology and, at the same time, have relatively easy work assignments for the employees.

The GM Assembly Division officials of that time, however, had forgotten one important feature. They were miles ahead with robots, but they neglected to consider the opinions of the workers. This was a period when the blue collar blues were very high and actually took the top fifteen cars per hour from the plant capacity. Lordstown became an 85 rather than a 100 vehicle per hour plant and was, thereby, a great failure. It set the whole idea of a high technology plant back by about twenty years. While we of the financial community toured the plant and were enamored with it, some union workers of that time simply opposed the operation and it never really succeeded.

There were also other visitors, and they were from Japan. They saw the robots at work. They saw the high technology facility. They went back to Japan. Not having the problem of work rules, restrictions, and high numbers of job classifications as was then the case at Lordstown, and which continued into the 1990s in the United States, they were able to move forward with a rather quantum leap into high technology by emulating Lordstown. Japan was able to move forward to greater progress. General Motors, in the meantime, had to back off on high technology and automation since these were unacceptable by the labor unions. GM built the Ste. Therese plant in Quebec, an old-style plant which used proven technology and labor systems. It did well, but it was not a spectacular plant.

About this time, F. Joseph Lamb Company was emerging as a giant in factory automation. This company developed, for the first time, a commercial system by which a plant could continue operation even if one part of the plant was shut down. If trouble developed in one section of a production line, the other segments would continue to operate from storage silos which had been put into place along the line, and which contained extra parts. When one part of the line was shut down, spare parts would be fed into storage. These silos, which I saw in operation, were a bit like rest stations on a mountain which give the mountain climbers time to stop and rest. They made the plant more valuable.

One of the senior officers of F. Joseph Lamb Company gave me a remarkable insight. He said that the plants of the 1970s would not use the silo principle because it had not been proven. The compensation system within the automobile industry at that time, and continuing into the late 1980s, required that one get a good return on the investment without taking very many risks. Some executive, one notch removed from making it as a vice president, would want to play it safe and not make a major mistake. Therefore, when he had the responsibility to give the approval for the design of a new plant, he would lean heavily toward proven technology knowing that the methods which had worked in the past would probably work in the future.

This mentality provided continuity of technical progress, but eliminated the possibility of making quantum leaps such as were being made, even in that period, in such areas as calculators and uses of the microchip. The auto industry had become known as a laggard industry, one which did not take chances.

On the other side of the Pacific Ocean, the Japanese were not inhibited in this fashion because, for one thing, they did not have three or four generations of automobile plants. Their plants were new. They started many factories with a green field and were thus able to introduce advanced technology without the necessity of anyone losing face if there were failures along the way because some failures were expected.

Japan was ideally equipped to experiment with advanced technology. Their plants were well ahead of the U.S. versions and, since they were highly automated and therefore not as subject to human error, human weariness, human absence on Monday mornings, and early exit on Friday afternoons, the quality of the Japanese automobile came to the forefront. This quality image actually lasted into the late 1980s and early 1990s, even though, by this time, the United States producers had caught up to Japan in quality. Japan emerged as the perceived quality leader during the last one-third of the century.

It was really Cadillac, however, that had established the quality aura for the U.S. automobile industry.   It   was John F. Gordon, Jr., the son of the former president of GM, who said that Henry Leland was the real founder of the U.S. auto industry, and the creator of excellence standards. Henry Martyn Leland was actually as much of a father to the automobile as had been Henry Ford I. He took the automobile from the stage of an eight horsepower toy and made it into a full-fledged machine so that high-powered engines were feasible, as were such exhibitions of automotive excellence as the Indianapolis 500 race. Without Leland, the automobile would have remained a plaything and it would not have been practical to establish a moving production line for only a toy. Leland comes through as one of the great heroes of the automobile industry.

I recall once driving around Clark Street of Detroit where the Cadillac plant was located. There was a sign which many had forgotten, a sign which said "Craftsmanship a creed, accuracy a law." Actually, this was that kind of bond which had built the U.S. automobile industry. It was this bond, plus the dedication of people such as the six Fisher brothers who would destroy automotive patterns if they contained the slightest flaw, even though craftsmen may have invested six months in their development. The Fisher brothers worked toward absolute accuracy, and this is what made the high-volume, high quality automotive industry possible.

It was at Lordstown that this accuracy was brought to a very high level in the early 1970s. Yet, once the industry was established, there was also this great fear that if one tried to reach too far into the future, to use untested methodology, untested equipment, and untested human equations, the risk of failure was indeed great, and that the industry could destroy itself. This also was shown at Lordstown. On January 1, 1981, Roger B. Smith replaced Thomas A. Murphy as chairman of the board at General Motors. A month later, on February 1, 1981, F. James McDonald replaced Elliott M. (Pete) Estes as GM's president.

Both then inherited a situation wherein General Motors was a highly regarded organization that was now being challenged by the Japanese. They inherited an organization that had been built by Alfred P. Sloan, Jr. He perfected the organization which extended through the 1920s, through the Depression, through World War II, through the great changes that took place after 1952 when controls of materials were discontinued by the government and through the relatively unstable period of the 1970s. By 1980, the Sloan method of dividing an organization into pieces, into separate smaller organizations left to compete among themselves, had ended. The Sloan system had been extremely successful for General Motors, but GM had developed an inability to communicate internally between its divisions. General Motors, because of the Sloan approach, had taken on the same kind of attitude that Henry Ford II had brought into Ford Motor Company. Henry Ford let each of the arms of the company, such as engineering, manufacturing, marketing, and finance, develop independently of each other and he was unable to unite them. That became the task for Philip Caldwell who managed to do it very well after Henry Ford II stepped down.

The General Motors state of affairs was slightly different from the Ford's situation. At GM, the separation was imbedded into the very culture of the organization. Pontiac, Buick, Oldsmobile, Cadillac and Chevrolet people seldom exchanged views. They regarded themselves as competitors. Indeed, at GM, sometimes the competition between two divisions was greater than the competition between General Motors and Ford or Chrysler, and this was the type of organization that Roger Smith inherited. He also inherited an organization that no longer was consistently able to establish a good profit margin. Therefore, his first determination was to somehow restore the profitability.

Roger Smith, by 1984, had begun to break down the old Sloan walls. The divisions of the organization finally were able to talk with each other; and it was a bit like the formation of the United States, where states rights advocates had to succumb to Federalists. The divisions were pooled together under the direction of group vice presidents Lloyd Reuss and Robert Stempel. Reuss had distinguished himself at the Buick Division as an outstanding engineering-type manager. In 1986, he found himself meeting with 150 financial analysts, myself included, having to answer financial questions. The straight engineering approach to his answers engendered considerable unhappiness among his financial analyst audience.

Not so Robert Stempel. Bob Stempel, at this same meeting, was able to field all questions which came along, and did it with seeming ease. He was able to respond almost intuitively to the types of needs which the analysts had. That was General Motors' very first display of its senior management attitudes to the financial community, and the GM stars turned out to be Robert Stempel and Alex Mair, another group vice president. It was Alex Mair who enlivened the financial community with his candor and with his complete honesty in answering questions, without giving away any GM secrets.

If Lloyd Reuss appeared somewhat unprepared to speak before 150 financial analysts, be it said that he received the assignment on the night before, GM had to juggle its speakers because Roger Smith was still in South Africa where he had been considering the problems of apartheid with the senior managers there. He was unable to return to the U.S. on schedule. This was the time when the U.S. armed forces bombed Tripoli, Libya. Roger's GM advisors would not permit him to land in Europe, where terrorism was a threat. Thus, the military operation forced General Motors to come up with a makeshift speaking team for our analysts' meeting.

Also coming on strong at the meeting was executive financial vice president Alan Smith who was, of course, speaking to his kind of people. General Motors president F. James MacDonald, the dinner speaker substituting for Roger Smith, was also somewhat in the same position as was Lloyd Reuss, a last minute replacement.

After the dinner and the talk, Jim MacDonald found himself having to field unfriendly financial questions. He appeared shocked by the boldness of critics. Some analysts wondered when General Motors would take the steps needed to allow the stock market to increase the value of General Motors' stock. The emphasis of present day Wall Streeters and present day GM is clearly different. Jim tried to explain how General Motors was looking into the future and spending major amounts of money to assure future success. But, many in the audience had purchased GM stock and thereby had a selfish interest in the value of GM on the market. At the time, GM was the stock market laggard among the Big Three. The "Street" simply was reluctant to pay anything for earnings which might be realized in the 1990s, and the fund managers and analysts wanted General Motors to have stronger earnings now. The stock market was, and is, a cruel taskmaster. Though I personally disagreed, even as a Wall Streeter, many felt that General Motors overstepped good judgment in moving so swiftly with its long term Saturn project. As a person who had been in both the automotive industry and in Wall Street, I felt the presence of both the General Motors ethic and the Wall Street ethic, but I could not, in that instance, be a bridge person to span the differences.

Changing the boxes in an organization chart does not create unity. Certainly there has always been competition within General Motors, and changing the names associated with the jobs was not going to change the viewpoints of the various divisions. For decades, the profit-making leader of GM was Chevrolet. If Chevrolet were to be excluded, GM would not have been able to amass the financial resources to be the leader which it became.

When the consolidation came, immense competition remained among the divisions as to who was going to be the most important of the disciples who were going to shake the world, and this competition caused some concern. However, the secret weapon of that particular era in the mid-1980s was EDS, Electronic Data Systems, which GM had purchased for $2.5 billion. It became the arm of General Motors which was to open all the communication blockages that were used by the divisions in talking to each other by giving them a common computer and communication set-up. EDS, well into 1986, was despised within General Motors because they came in generally with very young people who started telling the older GM personnel how to run the corporation. The EDS youngsters were unschooled in diplomacy, and many simply came in and began lording it over the people who had actually built up the assets of the corporation.

GM insiders were, for a time, calling EDS "Ever Declining Services" and joking about its presence. Some of the jokes were, "Why did California get AIDS and Michigan get EDS? California had first choice." Another, "How many EDS people does it take to screw in a light bulb? They don't know yet. They're still hiring more people." EDS personnel were accused of always traveling in groups of three. One does the work, one talks about it, and another observes. EDS, however, is making a huge impact on General Motors. Its payroll, in 1985, grew from 14,000 to 43,000 employees, and, in that year, its bill for services to GM was $2.42 billion, almost the size of its original cost. It immediately became GM's largest supplier, surpassing even the steel industry which is remarkable since automobiles and trucks are made of steel and not of computers.

The automotive industry always had great flexibility in its ways and means. It could move easily across all of the technologies from a blacksmith hammering out a shape on an anvil to the computers, robots and microchips of the 1980s. Enter H. Ross Perot and his Electronic Data Systems into the General Motors organization. GM chairman, Roger B. Smith, had for several years been promising the automotive and financial world a "lulu". He now claims that "lulu came home" with the Hughes Aircraft Division purchase in June of 1985. Actually, in my opinion, "lulu" came home earlier when Roger reached out for H. Ross Perot and EDS.

H. Ross Perot is now considered to be an industrial genius. However, in 1970, he made a brief foray into Wall Street to reorganize F.I. duPont, Lor Forgan and Company. Perot did not succeed in spite of a reported $23 million investment and in spite of his own personal TV commercials, selling his cause, long before Lee Iacocca did his for Chrysler. Perot returned to Dallas, Texas and his Wall Street adventure was deeply submerged under his electronic curriculum. Nobody's perfect.

There were times when it appeared certain that GM would fail in its reorganization. Wall Street observed some of these problems, and actually began to view Ford Motor Company and Chrysler Corporation more favorably. General Motors actually became second-rate. It was not until the entire idea of Roger Smith leadership jelled into a good, composite GM plan in the late 1980s that the Smith era proved to be not a destructive period, but rather a preparatory period necessary for the 1990s and the 21st century.

One specific appearance of Roger B. Smith before the Detroit Economic Club was, to a large degree, derided in Wall Street and also in the auto industry. A concept he put forth was that General Motors and other successful corporations of the next century will be paperless organizations. The wags in General Motors said that one could try for a paperless operation, but it would take more paper to instruct and explain it than it would take to do the job in the first place. However, I believe the concept Roger Smith spoke of will eventually become a reality, even in the homes of the future. I already see the beginning of this process on Wall Street, where today one has difficulty providing enough ammunition for a traditional tickertape parade, and trash must be used in a pinch.

Group vice president Alex Mair, to all intents and purposes, was the chief engineer of Saturn, at least at its inception. He was the one who said that the industry should start with a clean sheet of paper, that GM should come up with a program that did not use the old machines, the old methods, the old materials, the old labor agreements, the old plants, or anything that had been proved as fitting together. Alex recognized that Lordstown could have succeeded, yet did not. He and others at GM recognized that the Japanese had succeeded where the U.S. had failed. They recognized that the future of not only General Motors but of the entire North American industrial complex lay in establishing, for the next century, industrial might, industrial capability, industrial equipment and factories which can match anything in the whole wide world. There were those at General Motors, especially in the GM financial offices, who thought that Japan was going to take over the world. Personally, I felt that Japan would not take over because I can remember the depths from which the U.S. emerged against that country in World War II, after Pearl Harbor and about the time of Guadalcanal. Victory for Japan seemed imminent, beyond the shadow of any doubt. Yet the U.S. recognized its problems, pulled itself up by its bootstraps, and went on to eventual triumph.

Saturn

Most of my Wall Street associates and competitors felt that Saturn was an automobile, but it was perceived as an automobile only because when Roger B. Smith announced it, a mockup of the car was ready and was shown publicly. Actually, at that time, the factory which was to manufacture the Saturn was far from being built. There has been criticism from the financial community about the car, and General Motors has had extreme difficulty in persuading the news media, the public and the financial and automotive analysts that Saturn is a new way of making automobiles, not the automobile itself, although there eventually will be an automobile named Saturn.

The key to the new factory which the Saturn concept brought forth is flexibility. In 1986, when Lloyd Reuss, GM executive vice president- in charge of American car groups, was named as successor to the original director of the Saturn project, he stressed that the new GM-10 program should not only be viewed as a new kind of car but also as a new kind of factory. The GM-10 family of automobiles precedes the Saturn and is intended to serve as a prototype for many of the Saturn concepts.

David Smith, as editor of Ward's Automotive World, was one of the deans in the media when the GM-I0 program was announced. The March 1986 issue of WAW brought forth, for the first time, major details of the GM-10 program. Cliff Merriott, director of GM media relations at that time was the man who was closest to Roger Smith whenever Roger was making public appearances. I always likened Cliff's relationship to Roger Smith as I likened Jim Brady's relationship to President Reagan.

Concerning the GM-10, Cliff told Jeffrey Shu, an associate from another financial service company and me, that the GM-10 program would be like a tree, with Saturn a bush in comparison. The factory changes contemplated for Saturn were advanced in the GM-10 program. The mid-size car would be made in GM-10 factories. One of the major keys was a Swedish-development called the A.G.V., Automatic Guided Vehicle. When GM's William Hoaglund introduced the president of Volvo at a December 1985 meeting of the Detroit Economic Club, he praised Volvo not only for its automobile but more importantly for the advanced factory methods which Volvo had developed and introduced in Sweden.

A key to the new factory is a new kind of robot, a guided vehicle which goes down the assembly line and can also be programmed to move away, as needed, to pick up and deliver components to the workers on the line. In the teens of the century, the overhead conveyor made its mark in the factories of the time. It remained at the heart of automotive assembly from Henry Ford's Highland Park, Michigan, plant all the way through the mid-1980s. The Automatic Guided Vehicle, the A.G.V., has eliminated the need for much of the overhead conveyor and also permitted a new kind of labor.

As the Saturn plant emerged, there were those in 1986, including the Wall Street Journal, who said that it had failed. The reasoning was that there was no way in which GM use experimental automatic guided trolleys, controlled by untested computer boxes, in conjunction with unproven robots to build world-quality vehicles. Even the very name of "automatic guided vehicles" for those trolleys was uncertain. Was it automatic "guided" or "guidance" vehicle? The name had then not become stabilized. However, General Motors had committed itself to a $3.5 billion investment in Spring Hill, Tennessee, and that was the situation in the late 1980's. There were those, in 1986, who felt that the wave of the future was definitely in favor of the Japanese. The Europeans, including iron curtain countries, Brazil, and Korea showed more promise as well. Many thought that there was no way by which the United States could emerge from this situation with any degree of industrial competence.

Be it said for the GM board of directors, and for Roger Smith, that there was then no relaxation of effort or rise of an attitude of futility. The planners for Saturn were not forced to pull back just because they were being pressured by the media. Saturn and Spring Hill were also receiving pressure from the financial community where the idea was brought forth that cars could not be produced fast enough and profitably enough for the facility to pay for itself. Nevertheless, through this entire period, Roger Smith steadfastly stayed on course. It was not until 1986, that researchers from the Wall Street Journal discovered the major setbacks the Saturn concept was encountering. In May of that year these difficulties were published in a major article.

My convictions about Saturn throughout that period were positive, as they had been through the Chrysler period of difficulty and as they were through the difficult Lordstown period until some progress and peace finally arrived on the scene. It is my conviction that, with its superb educational facilities, the United States has not only the ability but the indomitable will to come back from setbacks.

Wall Street

From a Wall Street viewpoint, one of my real heroes was Gerald Martin Loeb whom I considered to be one of the fathers of the financial research business. It was Gerald who became interested in the Chrysler Corporation in the 1920s when Walter P. Chrysler worked with his sleeves rolled up at his desk. It was Gerald Loeb who discovered a company called Haloid which became eventually Xerox. He also discovered Land, the Polaroid Camera Company. It was also Loeb who first boosted Charles Bludorn who eventually built the great Gulf and Western conglomerate.

I've frequently told people that if they could only read two books on how to make money in the stock market, they should be the only two books that Gerald Martin Loeb ever wrote, "Battle for Investment Profits" and "Battle for Investment Survival".

Another Wall Street hero was Bernard Baruch. I never knew him personally, but I admired his work. He was said to have often been seen sitting on a park bench I passed often. He was a great investor who had two secrets. First, he felt that when the public wanted to sell, he would buy. Secondly, he felt that when the public wanted to buy, he would sell what he had previously bought, at a profit; simple rules.

Bernard Baruch was very well known, but according to him the real heroes in America were not the people who were well known, such as the people who may have been discussed in this book. According to Bernard Baruch, the real heroes were the people who cleaned the streets, picked up the garbage, and did the countless menial tasks necessary to a society day after day, and week after week. He said this in a small paragraph in one of his writings.

I brought this up at a Kiwanis Club meeting in Scarsdale, New York, where I was a member. I suggested that we adopt the Bernard Baruch award for the Scarsdale Kiwanis Club, and that we present it every month. The suggestion was adopted and we did that for a period of time, singling out people who would otherwise go through life totally unrecognized. This even included my next-door neighbor, a fireman who did nothing more spectacular or long lasting than to enter a burning building and bring out a person who would have otherwise perished. These were the kinds of people who Bernard Baruch felt were America's real heroes. These were also the people who won World War II and who will make the necessary changes in the factories to make them competitive on a world-wide basis. These are the people who took out of their vocabulary the very costly expression, "That's not my job." This idea of "not my job" created all kinds of extra job classifications. These had to be diminished in number in order to let people work harmoniously together in an interested, helpful fashion, caring for themselves, for their unions, for the owners of the business and also for the customers.

Gerald Martin Loeb was adept at identifying future success at an early stage. Bernard Baruck simply had the great gift of discerning human nature. He took advantage of that, from a financial viewpoint, by buying when others sell, and selling when others buy. He won by going against the stream, but he also had the great ability to see, among all the human frailties, the human strengths that keep the streets clean. For these special abilities, such men will always remain my heroes.

Labor Relations

Recently I took a group of financial analysts to visit Donald Ephlin, U.A.W. vice president in charge of the GM Division and he told us then that the U.A.W. would work with management to continue to bring forth the most advanced kinds of technology and manufacturing equipment. Don reminded us that Walter Reuther had built the union on the basis that the automotive manufacturers and suppliers could use whatever advanced technology was available. This was true, but at the same time, Walter Reuther insisted on good wages and benefits, and these good wages and benefits have succeeded in making General Motors into an industrial worker aristocracy. In Japan, the workers have received the same advanced equipment but have worked for much smaller wages, and that formed the basis for Japan's movement toward upsetting the American and Canadian automotive industries. This manifested itself in considerably lower prices for vehicles of equivalent perceived value. The differences could amount to a Japanese price advantage of as much as $2000 per unit.

Japan made efforts to forestall the possibility of tariff or quota imposition on the import of its products by the establishment of its own assembly plants within the U.S. and Canada. This was accomplished through outright purchase or the entry into partnerships with domestic manufacturers. Actually, Japan's movement into the U.S. and Canada was slowed by the reluctance of the U.A.W. and the C.A.W. to accept the transfer of Japan's working culture to the domestic production lines. U.S. production lines brought forth Automatic Guided Vehicles; and GM, along with Ford and Chrysler, the latter two were fast followers, were destined to save the automobile industry for North America and indeed to save the entire industrial complex.

World Financial Exchange

James Baker III, Secretary of Treasury, had at the New York meeting of the Group of Five in September of 1985. These men were the five leading industrial nations' senior financial officials. James Baker, having recently traded jobs with Donald Regan, used gentle persuasion to present the United States viewpoint at this meeting, and the group reached a majority opinion that a re-evaluation of world currency was necessary. By January of 1986, when the Group of Five met again in London, the moves to realign currencies were already well along. Within six months of that historic September meeting, the yen had moved from above 240 to below 180 to the dollar, making the competition between American and Japanese cars in the American marketplace much more equitable.

In Savannah, Georgia, in February 1986, Lee 1acocca, appearing before financial analysts, brought to view the Gulfstream Aerospace Company and gave credit to Secretary Baker for doing what governmental people had said earlier was impossible, which was to go and say the right things to cause the Japanese currency to move from 243 yen to the dollar in September, 1985, to the low of 180 yen in early 1986.

CHAPTER NINETEEN

AUTOMOBILES OF THE 1980 ERA

Dese are de conditions dat prevail.
- Jimmy Durante

Historically, the 1980s began with General Motors continuing its efforts to reduce the size of its automobiles and engines to meet the requirements of greater fuel efficiency. However, the stabilization of fuel supply and prices would invariably trigger renewed interest in full-size cars and higher output engines. Conversely, any hint of trouble in the fuel supply would bring about a desire for smaller cars. The direction of the marketplace was, and is, difficult to predict.

The GM full-size vehicles were trimmed by about 900 pounds in 1977. However, GM continued development of a new generation of front-wheel drive cars. This form of chassis configuration concentrates all of the drive components under the hood, maximizing interior space with the smallest exterior dimensions. Front-wheel drive vehicles also seem capable of negotiating snowy, slippery conditions for the normal driver better than their rear-wheel drive counterparts. The weight of the engine rests over the front driving wheels, optimizing traction. Some claim the fact that the front wheels pull the vehicle, rather than being pushed by the rear wheels, also provides stability. On the opposite side of the coin, stock car racers completely avoid front-engine, front-drive cars because of the relative complexity of the power train, because of the smaller engine sizes, and because of the fact that front-wheel drive vehicles handle differently, especially at very high speeds.

GM's first series of compact front-drive cars was the X-body, introduced in 1979 as 1980 models, and available in four lines, the Chevrolet Citation, Olds Omega, Pontiac Phoenix and Buick Skylark. These vehicles were available with either a 2.5 liter 4-cylinder or 2.8 liter V-6 engine. The transverse-engined front-wheel drive configuration preserved a roomy five passenger interior, with ample luggage space but with substantially smaller size and weight than the models they replaced. These X-cars were attacked by consumer groups as having unsafe braking characteristics, and the vehicles were discontinued at the end of 1985.

In 1980, GM embarked on a massive, wide-reaching, multi-billion dollar investment program. Its vehicles were to be rebuilt as smaller, high-tech, more fuel-efficient units, new assembly plants were to be built to take advantage of state-of-the-art technology for optimum efficiency, and existing plants were to be modernized and expanded.

The first products to emerge from this totally dedicated effort and commitment were the subcompacts, the front-engine, front-drive Chevrolet Cavalier, Pontiac J2000 and Cadillac Cimarron. These were offered initially in 1981, and were designed from the ground up to meet import competition head-on. At one point in its existence, the Cavalier became the best selling car in the United States. The new vehicles emulated the X-body with spacious interior and compact exterior dimensions and were available in a variety of models.

For 1982, 30 percent of GM's car lines were completely new. Leading the parade were the mid-size front-wheel Chevrolet Celebrity, Pontiac 6000, Oldsmobile Ciera and Buick Century. Pleasing to the eye, aerodynamic and economical, these vehicles attracted buyers of full-size cars because of their efficiency and ample interior room, if not because of their performance.

Debuting in 1982 were the totally redesigned Pontiac Firebird and Chevrolet Camaro. Both were striking in design, wedge shaped and aerodynamic, and both were an instant hit with the young and young at heart. They were available with four, six, or eight-cylinder engines with varying degrees of performance. These were front-engine, rear-wheel drive vehicles and remained so until the late 1980's.

Automobiles were not the only vehicles in need of diets. Light-duty trucks were also the subject to fuel economy restrictions, emissions and safety. Moreover, Japan had been making huge inroads into the small truck market. GM countered by importing and merchandizing the Isuzu LUV pickup. However, as an import, it could not be counted in the fuel economy fleet averages. Therefore, GM decided to bring out domestically produced smaller commercial vehicles.

In 1982, the S-series of pickups was introduced by both Chevrolet and GMC. In 1983 the lineup was expanded to include a four-passenger utility model, an extended cab unit and a new generation of four-wheel drive chassis which included independent front suspension for good ride and low overall height. In 1985, GM introduced a high-quality smaller van which was labeled Astro by Chevrolet and Safari by GMC.

On October 1, 1982, GM officially opened its World of Motion exhibit in the Epcot Center of Walt Disney World near Orlando, Florida. The exhibit takes a lighthearted view of the history of transportation and some of the trials and travails associated with its progress.

With economic recovery underway by mid-1983, sales began to rebound as customers were attracted by vehicles which combined state-of-the-art engineering, aerodynamic technology and attractive styling. Leading the way in that regard were the sophisticated 1984 Chevrolet Corvette and the Pontiac Fiero. The latter, GM's first mid-engined car, was a two-passenger vehicle with a fiberglass skin over a steel substructure. The Fiero became a "poor-man's" Corvette but apparently only had a limited market because sales went soft in 1986.

One of the effects of emission and fuel economy regulation was the eventual inclusion of on-board computers for all GM cars by the mid-1980s. The system, called Computer Command Control, was first introduced in California in 1978 and became standard on all GM gasoline automotive engines in the 1981 model year. The computer continuously monitored and adjusted fuel-air ratios, spark timing, and exhaust to control emissions and to improve fuel economy.

With the onset of computers, the conventional carburetors disappeared to be replaced by a throttle body injection system. When all systems worked well, the vehicles provided amazing performance, hot or cold, and good reliability. However, any engine failure was a "walk-away" failure. It was fruitless for the driver to open the hood and search for a cause. One might as well just walk home. It took a diagnostic computer plugged into the vehicle's on-board computer to determine cause of failure and method of repair. The back-alley mechanics were relegated to lawn mower and garden tractor repair.

Throughout the 1970s and early 1980s, the American marketplace remained as unpredictable as the weather. The last American convertible ever, a Cadillac Eldorado in April, 1976, was driven off the assembly line straight to a museum. However, consumers of the early 1980s were eager for ragtops once again and automotive manufacturers, existing as profit-making organizations, could do nothing less than respond. Buick was the first GM division to respond to this new demand, offering a convertible version of the 1983 Riviera. Chevrolet followed quickly with its Cavalier convertible and Pontiac with the 2000 Sunbird.

GM in the 1980s remained a strong force in the medium and heavy-duty truck business. In 1983, GMC introduced the Aero Astro highway tractor. Standard features included a special aerodynamic grille, special front bumper and air dam. The air dam was an adjustable drag-foiler atop the cab roof which permitted smooth air flow from the cab contours to the trailer and filler panels between the tractor and trailer. The Aero Astro was one of the first highway tractors capable of attaining over 7 miles per gallon, fully loaded, in highway operation.

Even in this area, however, foreign competition was making inroads with quality products. Mercedes-Benz and Isuzu began exporting diesel powered, medium-duty trucks which featured quality, innovation and low price.

In 1985 and 1986, General Motors made another effort at merchandising an electric vehicle. GM's subsidiary in England, Bedford, had been successfully marketing, domestically, an electric van which had a 50-mile per hour top speed and a 50-mile range. With encouragement from electric power companies, efforts were made to introduce this vehicle into the United States. Each electric vehicle uses the energy equivalent to that of a single household while in use. Electric vehicles would normally be recharged at night when the power companies had a surplus of generating capacity. However, the high dollar value versus the British pound made the selling price of an electric van unattractively high.

In 1988 and 1989, GM is introducing an all new line of light-duty full-size truck models which represent about a$3 billion investment in tools and facilities. A world van is scheduled for 1990, or soon thereafter, which is intended to satisfy both the American and European markets.

During this era of the 1980s Ford Motor Company encountered the same problems as did General Motors and arrived at similar solutions. It also faced the future with the same uncertainty and trepidation. With the beginning of the 1980s, Ford, along with the other domestic manufacturers, had two basic problems. The first was the Corporate Average Fuel Economy requirements. The second was the rising tide of foreign imports.

The 1980 CAFE target was 20 miles per gallon, up from 19 in 1979, and this was going up to 22 miles per gallon in 1961 and progressively higher in successive years. The government was trying to reduce the dependence on foreign oil. Failure to comply could mean millions of dollars in penalties.

The imports were a problem of even greater significance since the foreign advantage was seemingly insurmountable, even into the late 1980s. In 1974, the imports accounted for some 1.4 million sales in a market of about 8.7 million vehicles, or a little over 16 percent. By 1979, the numbers had increased to over 2.3 million foreign imports in an almost identical domestic market. The ratio has now grown to 26 percent in 1986.

These conditions prompted Ford to plan a model-realignment for 1980 and for the near-term future. The company's product plans were labeled the "Fox" program. It started out fairly slowly. The pride of the 1980 fleet was the all-new Thunderbird which was nearly 16 inches shorter, 4 inches narrower and 700 pounds lighter than its predecessor. However, the vehicle failed to make the hoped-for impression on the buying public, and its sales volumes were down 40 percent. A number of refinements marked Ford's other 1980 models, but nothing spectacular.

The 1981 year was more memorable for Ford. The major reason was the introduction of the Escort, an all-new replacement for the Pinto and proclaimed as a true "world car". The vehicle, as it appeared in the American marketplace, comprised front-wheel drive, all independent suspension, a transversely mounted overhead cam 4-cylinder engine, and a truly international package size. This was Ford's great hope to challenge the imports, especially those from Japan. Its sales were to be an indication of how well the U.S. could compete with the imports.

The Escort was introduced when Ford appeared to be in a modicum of trouble. The recession was suppressing vehicle sales. Inflation was pushing vehicle prices upward and, at the same time, interest rates on loans were also climbing. By the end of 1980, Ford Motor Company's share of the market was reduced to 16.5 percent. Furthermore, Ford had committed billions to new vehicle projects. Some pessimists were of the opinion that Ford would not see its hundredth birthday.

The Escort was developed under the code name "Erika." The project began as far back as 1972 within the Engineering and Research Staff at Dearborn, Michigan. Simultaneously, Ford of Europe had plans for a new front-wheel drive car to replace the British and German rear-wheel drive units. The new European model was called the Fiesta and was introduced in 1976. Some were even sold in the U.S. Then, Ford's European executives decided to offer a larger version. This idea coincided with U.S. plans for a smaller vehicle to replace the Pinto, and the "world car" Escort was born. Over 60,000 units were sold from October through December 1980. Total for the model year was 320,000, making it second in popularity only to the Chevrolet Chevette.

The new Escort was accompanied by a Granada which had lost some 350-400 pounds in weight. In 1982, the Escort rose to the top of U.S. sales, besting Chevrolet's Chevette by 75,000 units.

For 1983, Ford presented its most exciting lineup in many years. This was an indication that, by going into the teeth of the wind of the recession, Ford, if not the rest industry, would survive. Some critics were saying that considering the events of the previous several years, the industry would never be the same again. They were correct, but in 1983, it appeared that the Ford Motor Company was on the threshold of a rebirth. The Ford model lineup for 1983 included an all-new Thunderbird which was the forerunner of the "jelly bean" aerodynamic design which was to distinguish most Ford vehicles of the future. The Ford Mustang was extensively restyled, including the addition of a new convertible model.

In early 1983, Ford announced the introduction of its new 1984 model, the Tempo, as a replacement for the Fairmont. Tempo carried the jelly bean styling and a drag coefficient of only .36. In future years, Ford was to continue its emphasis on aerodynamics as a legitimate means of improving fuel economy.

However, a wedge shape is not always the most slippery to the wind. Many smaller changes can produce excellent improvements. For 1986, Ford introduced perhaps the most striking models in a new generation of vehicles. These are the Ford Taurus and Mercury Sable. These, too, carry the rounded theme but are sharply sloped at the front, with a high rise rear. However, the most unusual feature of these newest models is the flush-mounted side window glass. Many vehicles utilize flush glass which is stationary. However, Ford has developed a system of channeling which permits this flush glass to be installed in the front and rear side doors, and to be effectively raised and lowered as with the recessed variety.

For Chrysler, the 1980 model year was one of retrenchment. Lee Iacocca was in full control and busy reducing expenses, including the work force, both white and blue collar. The federally guaranteed loan was in place and beginning to be used productively. The biggest product news was a smaller, second generation Cordoba. All the other vehicle lines were basically carried over with minor face-lifts.

The much heralded K-cars appeared in dealer showrooms as 1981 models. Details of the models were the industry's worst kept secret and, for a year before announcement details, the cars appeared in newspapers and magazines. Furthermore, Iacocca had to divulge future plans to the congressional committee to obtain the loan guarantee. The media found Chrysler's problems extremely newsworthy, and Chrysler was betting its entire mortgage on the success of the K-cars.

The K-cars arrived with appropriate names. The Plymouth version was Reliant, and the Dodge, Aries. These got off to a poor start, stumbled briefly, and then took off, which was exactly what the doctor ordered for Chrysler's ills. Reliant sold nearly 230,000 units and Dodge over 180,000 for the first year. The K-cars were front-drive compacts with a transversely mounted engine and very good interior room. The vehicles were not innovative but were well engineered and offered a good ride. With most of Chrysler's available resources directed toward the K-cars, the other lines had to accept hand-me-downs for 1981 and sported only minor face-lifts. Chrysler continued its quest for stability and profits with a reorganized lineup for 1982, led by luxury versions of the new K-cars. Emphasis was also placed on replacing older models with smaller, front-drive units.

A new Chrysler LeBaron was essentially a plushier, restyled K-car. In mid-1982, the LeBaron was offered as a convertible which marked Chrysler's re-entry into the ragtop market. With some interesting minor changes in existing models, Chrysler was beginning to look, and act, like a survivor. Thanks to the K-car's success, and Iacocca's belt tightening, the company cut its 1981 losses to $475 million, and in 1982 actually turned a profit of $170 million. This profit was achieved with great difficulty, however. Iacocca had decided to sell its lucrative Chrysler military tank making operation to General Dynamics. Chrysler was now very lean.

In 1983, Chrysler was able to raise its share of the market to a still low ten percent level, but, at the end of that year, Lee Iacocca announced a bona fide profit of $925 million, the highest in the corporation's history. To emphasize the fact that Chrysler's salvation was complete, Iacocca decided that he would pay back its major creditors by mid-1983, seven years ahead of schedule. The payback was announced on July 18, 1983, five years to the day since Henry Ford II had fired Lee Iacocca. Iacocca was quoted, "Don't get mad, get even."

With a true sense of showmanship, Iacocca announced the payback by paraphrasing a popular investment house commercial. He said, "We at Chrysler borrow money the old fashioned way. We pay it back." This was his moment in the sun, but extremely well-earned.

Chrysler's advertising agency also prevailed upon Iacocca to begin personally appearing in many of his own commercials. He balked at first, thinking it too egotistical, but later allowed himself to be convinced that it was for the good of Chrysler, and this proved to be the case. The advertisements were very well received, and Iacocca went on to become a nationally recognized celebrity. This was not entirely to Iacocca's liking. In his autobiography, he wrote, "The ads wrecked my privacy. It was fun for a week. After that it's a pain in the ass." He said he couldn't have dinner in a restaurant without some guy coming over to talk about his 1965 Mustang that is still running, or perhaps not running.

The major Chrysler product story for 1983 was the E-car which was a stretched derivative of the K-car. These arrived as the Chrysler E-class and Dodge 600. The E-car featured an Electronic Voice Alert which talked to the drivers and informed them if a door was ajar or their seat belt unfastened. Many owners hated this talk feature and cut the system's vocal cords. Chrysler and Dodge retailed more than 80,000 E-cars in the first model year.

By 1984, it was certain that Chrysler Corporation had managed to perform the miracle which had seemed so impossible only four years earlier. The company survived, paid off its debts, and began to prosper, an achievement which would have been remarkable even in good economic times. Astonishingly, the recovery took place during a period of unprecedented inflation, record interest rates, high fuel costs, strong foreign competition, and a horrible sales performance by the U.S. auto industry.

Chrysler entered the 1984 model year with a group of cars which were totally different from those they offered at the beginning of the decade. By now, Chrysler could boast about a reputation of having the industry's highest corporate average fuel economy, with more fuel efficient models than GM as a percentage of total production, and of a big lead over Ford in front-wheel drive development. Furthermore, Chrysler, traditionally a strong engineering organization, now claimed the industry lead in robotics and computer-aided design and manufacturing (CADAM.)

Several high-performance coupes were introduced for 1984. These were the Chrysler Laser and Dodge Daytona, both combining front-wheel drive with transversely mounted, turbocharged engines. Both models were winners in the market place. Even more amazing was the other line of new models, the Dodge Caravan and Plymouth Voyager. Both were front-wheel drive vans which found instant appeal among customers who were finding the passenger car station wagons too small for their purposes and yet considered the large vans too high, long and unwieldy. The Caravan and Voyager were more car than truck yet could carry up to eight passengers. These, too, became instant successes, and their superiority continued into the late 1980s with neither Ford nor General Motors capable of fielding reasonable competition.

Into the late 1980s, Chrysler has many innovative new models on its drawing boards, or, more accurately, its computer terminals, and its future success appears a certainty, assuming there is a future for the American automotive industry. Foreign competition is becoming increasingly strong and competent, and U.S. manufacturers are finding it difficult to offer to customers comparable value. I believe some solution will be found and it will have to be based on technology, which in the late 1980's has yet to be developed. Automobiles and trucks will always exist, because, not only do they expand personal scopes of pleasure and entertainment, but they also are genuine and useful tools. As emerging nations become industrialized, the automotive market will have no limits for decades to come.

EPILOGUE

GM's Saturn manufacturing and assembly complex is located in Spring Hill, Tennessee, yet, the corporate headquarters are located in Troy, Michigan, some 600 miles away. Both were located where they are by choice rather than for reasons of necessity. On the surface, the lack of proximity appears impractical except for the modern miracle of communications. Teleconferencing, utilizing both audio and video systems, makes meetings between distant parties a practical reality. Computer-aided design and computer-aided manufacturing systems can be relayed at great distances by telephone. Paper and mylar blueprints are quickly becoming extinct. Electronics are king.

We have survived and maybe even won the industrial revolution. Now, in 1986, we are in the throes of a high-tech revolution. How well we fare in that arena is still highly speculative. There exists one certainty at this point in time. Sitting in our kayaks, we are rushing along the torrent of high technology. There is absolutely no turning back. Our choices are possibly only in direction. We do need to paddle, or else we may land where we would rather not. The eventual destination is still too far away to clearly see. What is visible is obscured by fog. Furthermore, our river has many tributaries which we can inadvertently get swept into or perhaps even choose of our own volition.

One of the principal reasons for the apparent lack of firm, long-range objectives within the high-tech evolution is that new trails are continuously being blazed. Firm direction is difficult to perceive, and even more difficult to predict.

Even the management goals for high technology, in the late 1980s, seem to lack planning and specific objectives. As an example, on June 27, 1984, General Motors purchased the Electronic Data Systems to help guide the corporation through the electronic wilderness, paying $2.5 billion to H. Ross Perot, the founder, for full ownership. Perot was retained as the chief operating officer and, in fact, was also made a full-fledged member of the GM board of directors. Chairman Roger Smith had extremely high praise for both EDS and H. Ross Perot.

Yet, on December 2, 1986, General Motors paid $700 million to Perot for all of his GM stock. He was also apparently forced to resign from the GM board, and as chairman of EDS. The amount paid him was almost twice the market value of the shares of stock. GM paid an additional $50 million total to three other top EDS officers who also agreed to leave. GM immediately appointed Lester M. Alberthal, Jr., an EDS employee, as president.

H. Ross Perot had become increasingly and publicly critical of the GM way of doing business. The real reason for his departure is veiled in mystery. The popular opinion holds that he displeased Roger Smith who convinced the GM board to buy Perot out and thereby silence him through one of the terms of the agreement.

The less popular opinion is that Perot, himself, made the decision to leave GM. EDS had failed to achieve fixed-price contracts with GM as the customer. His salary was, therefore, not a constant since it was to be a percentage of the profits. This minority opinion claims that, for these reasons, Perot precipitated the showdown with Roger Smith and walked away with most of GM's cash.

At any rate, EDS was originally intended to be an autonomous organization, with GM as the owner. With the departure of Perot, EDS is now just another "division" within General Motors and must toe the marks established by the GM bureaucracy. Whether this development will establish GM as the leader in electronic technology and all of its ramifications remain for the future to decide.

The Saturn project has been characterized as a completely new way of producing an automobile. It was to be a quantum leap from the high technology plants of the mid-1980s. Computers, robotics and electronics were to be the dominant entities utilized in the creation of the Saturn automobile. Along with quality and consistency, the prime objective of the Saturn system was to reduce the costs of producing an automobile. The GM Saturn, Chrysler Liberty and Ford Alpha were to be the salvation of the U.S. automotive industry from the onslaughts of foreign competition and its unfair price advantages.

However, in the late 1980s it appears uncertain whether the industry is capable of a quantum leap from the present into the future. Historically, for the last hundred years, the auto industry has progressed through the process of evolution, not only in the design of the vehicles, but also in the system of manufacture. Probably the biggest leap forward was Henry Ford's assembly line in Highland Park, Michigan, in 1913. However, that involved mainly human beings, who are flexible and forgiving. Robots and electronic controls are not. Robotics used in the installation of the windshields, for example, must enjoy optimum, accurate conditions. The tiniest fraction of an inch in irregularity will result in breakage.

Saturn, Liberty and Alpha are wonderful concepts. However, the technology does not yet exist which would make these viable projects.

The Saturn, Liberty and Alpha programs were considered as the saviors of the American automotive industry. However, now in the light of at least postponement, if not partial failure, the future of the industry can evolve into at least two scenarios.

The first is that the U.S. automotive industry will now never be capable of competing with the foreign imports. It is a decaying industry which will eventually reduce itself to the manufacture of specialized vehicles such as highway trucks, off-road vehicles and a few passenger cars. With the eventual loss of manufacturing capacity, the United States armament production and defense potential will be severely handicapped.

However, there is at least one other scenario which is much more optimistic. It has to do with the very nature of the American people. Americans have always been able to stand up to the problems at hand, regardless of the magnitude. A nation that is capable of landing a human being on the moon and bringing him back is not too shabby in technology. Similar encouragement can be gleaned from some of the wars in which the U.S. was embroiled, not of its own volition and which seemed impossible to win.

After World War II, the United States taught Japan everything it now knows. In the process, we made it one of the industrial giants of the world in the mid-1980s. Until then, Japanese products were considered junk, with an attached stigma. In America, to buy Japanese "anything" was to buy the lowest quality "anything". After the U.S. defeat of Japan, we brought representative delegations to this country. We taught them about quality manufacturing. We showed them how to build high-technology manufacturing plants and even helped to finance their efforts. Now the student is apparently teaching the teacher. It does not need to remain so. The United States has to again find the drive and initiative to become the leader. We have not grown old and senile, just contented and complacent. We need to stoke our fires.

At this point in history, the United States is ahead of the world in quality technology and especially electronics. All other things being equal, there is absolutely no reason why the United States could not out-produce and undersell any other country in the world. Unfortunately, all other things are not equal, especially labor costs. Several trends seem to be developing which may diminish the advantages that the foreign manufacturers are holding over the U.S. producers.

First of all, the domestic car makers are asking for, and receiving, wage concessions from the unionized employees.

To their credit, the labor unions are recognizing the dangers of allowing the imports to gain too large of a foothold in the market. Tariffs and import quotas are not a solution since they are, in the main, a two-way street. Manufacturers are, further, reducing the size of the white collar labor force, adopting centralized design procedures, rebuilding old plants, building new ones for greater efficiency and finding new ways of cutting piece costs from the fabrication of an automobile.

Conversely, the foreign manufacturers have not yet reached the U.S. level of industrialization and therefore materialism. Currently, their products are new and contemporary, but the work standards lag behind. Even in a country as proud and patriotic as Japan, greed is rearing its ugly head; and workers are demanding greater rewards for their efforts. The inflation of the yen against the dollar will help in that it makes domestic products more competitive, both at home and as exports to Japan. These same conditions will eventually exist in the other countries which produce automobiles in volume and export them to the United States. For one thing, it is not natural for workers to be building a product as desirable as an automobile without being able to afford one themselves. Eventually, they will demand the wherewithal to own a vehicle.

The United States manufacturers are also now pursuing a prudent design philosophy of building vehicles for the world market. Heretofore, American cars were too large and too expensive for high-volume export. Events of recent years, however, have forced carmakers to start all-new design programs with enough built-in flexibility to permit the tailoring of the same basic vehicle to several markets. This is a highly commendable direction since it will permit the exploration of various other markets and maintain the higher sales volumes so necessary for efficient production.

More importantly, however, this direction will eventually result in vehicles which will be attainable, available, and useful to the third world and other emerging nations in their fight against hunger. As was often brought out in this writing, the growing of the food is not the basic problem. The problem is delivering the food from the fields and distributing it to those in need. The domestic and foreign automotive industry will eventually fully recognize the problems and adopt a means of affecting a solution. In the interim, the struggle continues on many fronts.

AN AFTERWORD FROM THE EDITOR

David C. Strubler, Ph.D.

Automotive Heads and Tales is the story of the U.S. automotive industry from its inception to the end of the 1980s as recounted by one of its most passionate advocates, analyst Arvid Jouppi. According to Jouppi, "Imagining an automobile industry without American autos was, and is, to me like imagining the American League, in baseball, without the New York Yankees" (p. 296). This automotive biography is replete with Jouppi's intimate encounters with industry giants, e.g., a 2 ½ hour meeting with visionary Charles "Boss" Kettering, his friendship with Mario Andretti, and Jouppi's role as a personal sounding board to Lee Iacocca during his pugnacious clash with Henry Ford, to name a few. He takes us on a personal tour through the giant edifice of the automotive industry into a General Motors conference room with Roger Smith, down the legislative hallways of Congress for the bailout of Chrysler Corporation, and out into a dangerous and competitive but exciting global landscape. Like a wise professor, he integrates scenes from old movies, employs eloquent word pictures, and tells tantalizing tales. Beginning with a self-effacing prologue, Jouppi leads his readers through nineteen chapters of automotive history and insights. He closes with a realistic but simultaneously, reassuring epilogue - - hope for a rapidly changing global industry on the edge of the information age revolution. Still, he assures us of one constant - - that people will always replace their old automobiles with new, technologically-advanced transportation. All of this will continue, in spite of the cyclical nature of the industry and the fluctuating economies that influence the industry's success. In fact, according to Jouppi, the automotive industry has a moral obligation to produce vehicles "for the good of mankind."

According to John Holusha, New York Times (June 27, 1995), Arvid Jouppi was "a longtime and much-quoted automobile industry analyst" whose "views and comments were eagerly sought by journalists because of his long experience with the auto industry and his interest in matters that went beyond strict financial analysis. He would regale reporters with stories of how Chrysler Corporation's near-collapse in the early 1980's could be traced to big bank loans it took out in the 1950's." Jouppi was not only a graduate of the U.S. Marine Corp Electronics Intelligence Service and Michigan State University, he is one of the most eloquent and knowledgeable alumni of "The Greatest Generation." Jouppi commenced his career as a news editor in the Associated Press bureau in Detroit. Developing an interest in automobiles, he worked for an automotive supplier and, five years later, joined General Motors communications staff. By 1957, he was head of Chrysler Corporation's eastern division of public and investor relations. In 1963, he entered the world of Wall Street as an analyst with Hayden, Stone, Inc. As a Senior Vice President of Keane Securities, he launched Arvid Jouppi and Associates in 1975, a Detroit-based automotive research services company which he lead until his death at age 77 in 1995. His book, "Automotive Heads and Tales" was completed, but not published, in 1986.

ACKNOWLEDGMENTS

The Jouppi Family acknowledges Slim Litwin, who assisted Arvid Jouppi in the telling of this automotive tale. He is a retired writer from General Motors.

Written in 1986, this manuscript was discovered by Arvid Jouppi's son, Jim, in the 1990's. Recently, Arvid's son, Bill, and his daughter, Mary, approached me about publishing these memoirs which are a tribute both to their father and the American automotive industry that he loved.

It is the hope of the Jouppi Family and this editor that Automotive Heads and Tales will provide a longer term perspective on the peaks and valleys of one of the world's most important industries with an eye toward a bright and thriving future.

Many thanks to Michael Strubler for his many hours and expertise in copy editing. We also appreciate the help of Rochester Media for helping get this document to print.